D1388148

OPINION WRITING

OPINION WRITING

Inns of Court School of Law

BLACKSTONE
PRESS LIMITED

First published in Great Britain 1996 by Blackstone Press Limited,
Aldine Place, London W12 8AA. Telephone (020) 8740 2277
www.blackstonepress.com

© Inns of Court School of Law, 1996

First edition 1996
Second edition 1997
Third edition 1998
Fourth edition 1999

ISBN: 1 85431 955 8 ✓

British Library Cataloguing in Publication Data
A CIP catalogue record for this book is available from the British Library.

Typeset by Style Photosetting Ltd, Mayfield, East Sussex
Printed by Ashford Colour Press, Gosport, Hampshire

FOREWORD

These manuals are designed primarily to support training on the Bar Vocational Course, though they are also intended to provide a useful resource for legal practitioners and for anyone undertaking training in legal skills.

The Bar Vocational Course was designed by staff at the Inns of Court School of Law, where it was introduced in 1989. This course is intended to equip students with the practical skills and the procedural and evidential knowledge that they will need to start their legal professional careers. These manuals are written by staff at the Inns of Court School of Law who have helped to develop the course, and by a range of legal practitioners and others involved in legal skills training. The authors of the manuals are very well aware of the practical and professional approach that is central to the Bar Vocational Course.

The range and coverage of the manuals have grown steadily. All the manuals are updated annually, and regular reviews and revisions of the manuals are carried out to ensure that developments in legal skills training and the experience of our staff are fully reflected in them.

This updating and revision is a constant process and we very much value the comments of practitioners, staff and students. Legal vocational training is advancing rapidly, and it is important that all those concerned work together to achieve and maintain high standards. Please address any comments to the Bar Vocational Course Director at the Inns of Court School of Law.

With the validation of other providers for the Bar Vocational Course it is very much our intention that these manuals will be of equal value to all students wherever they take the course, and we would very much value comments from tutors and students at other validated institutions.

The enthusiasm of the staff at Blackstone Press Ltd and their efficiency in arranging production and publication of the manuals is much appreciated.

The Hon. Mr Justice Elias
Chairman of the Board of Governors
Inns of Court School of Law
September 1999

CONTENTS

CONTENTS

ONE

INTRODUCTION

1.1 Written Word Skills

Before we start work on opinion writing and drafting skills specifically, we shall explore certain aspects of written word skills which are common to all the writing skills of a barrister, though particularly opinion writing and drafting. We call this first stage simply 'Written Word Skills'.

Although it is inevitable that anyone embarking on training for the Bar already has considerable skill in the use of the written word, nevertheless barristers do use words in particular ways that you will not have come across before and for purposes which are new to you. This part of the course is therefore intended to act as a bridge from the word skills you have already acquired to those that are specific to the barrister.

1.2 Objectives

By the end of this part of the course you should:

(a) appreciate the importance to a barrister of words and the way they are used;

(b) be able to identify weaknesses in your own written word skills and see how you might work to improve them;

(c) have begun to think more deeply about the precise meaning of the words you use;

(d) have started to use words in a way that will be useful in opinion writing;

(e) have started to use words in a way that will be useful in drafting;

(f) appreciate the need for clarity and the value of plain English at all times.

1.3 Words and the Barrister

1.3.1 TOOLS OF THE TRADE

For the barrister, arguably more than for any other profession, words are the dominant tool of the trade. A barrister can do nothing of consequence without using words. Surgeons, architects, surveyors, accountants, soldiers and police officers can all carry out their professional functions to a greater or lesser extent without the use of words. But virtually everything a barrister does involves speaking or writing. A barrister's performance will be judged almost exclusively on how well he or she speaks or writes.

1.3.2 SPEAKING AND WRITING

Speaking and writing are two ways of communicating. Communication is the only purpose of either activity. Whenever we speak or write, either in everyday life, or professionally, we are trying to communicate some inner content: thought, idea, feeling, information or message. That inner content is largely expressed in words. The better we express ourselves, the better we choose our words, the better we put them together, the more effectively we communicate.

1.3.3 COMMUNICATION

A barrister must communicate well; so a barrister must use words well. To explain something to your client, you must put it in such a way as to be sure your client understands. To make a point to a judge or jury effectively, not only must they understand it, you must express it in the most telling way. To get what you want from a witness, you must frame the question in exactly the right way. All this involves skill in the choice of words, the order in which they are put and in the structure of sentences, paragraphs and speeches. In the ideal world, a barrister's every word would be chosen, and every sentence composed, with great care.

1.3.4 THE SPOKEN WORD AND THE WRITTEN WORD

There is no difference in essence between spoken word skills and written word skills: only the context changes. You may use different words in writing than you would orally, and your sentence structure may change, but you should still choose your words with care, putting them into the best order and composing the whole piece of writing or speech with a view to achieving perfection. The need to communicate effectively, to be clear in what you say, to be precise in what you mean is unchanged. In drafting, particularly, there is a need for precision and unambiguity in what you write that exceeds what is required in any other context.

1.3.5 STANDARDS

A barrister is a specialist lawyer. No matter what kind of practice you have, you will be presumed a specialist in advocacy, in the provision of written advice and in drafting. All these skills are dependent on your word skills. A barrister is supposed to be an *expert* in the use of words and the use of language. You must not just speak and write well — by the standards of everyday life you must speak and write *exceptionally* well. You will be offering your services and charging a fee for which you undertake to speak and write better than those paying you could have spoken or written.

It follows that the standards of clarity, precision, grammar, punctuation and stylistic elegance that you need to set yourself throughout your professional career are almost certainly higher than the standards you have regarded as satisfactory up until now. And you need to set your standards even higher when you are writing than when you are speaking. In speech, the advocate is largely extemporising, having to compose sentences and thoughts even while speaking. Errors and stumbles can and do creep in. You don't always manage to think of just the right word. You don't always express something as accurately as you would like. But when you are writing, you have the opportunity to revise, correct and improve. There can be no excuse for errors and inaccuracies.

You should make up your mind that you will strive to reach these very high standards. With practice, you can attain them.

TWO

QUALITIES OF GOOD WRITING

2.1 The Qualities

To write a chapter on the qualities of good writing takes some courage. There is a danger of being controversial, hypocritical and idealistic. Controversial because good writing is impossible to define, and so there will always be different views as to what constitutes good writing. Hypocritical, because one can only too often find in one's own writing the very faults one is criticising in other people's. Idealistic, because it is very rare to find a piece of writing with all the qualities described below in full measure. Nevertheless, some guidance as to what constitutes good writing is desirable, so that you can take steps towards improving your writing.

Rather than attempting to describe good writing it seems simpler to list some of its qualities. It goes without saying that the qualities described are those required of barristers, but doubtless many of these qualities are desirable in many other contexts too.

2.2 Making Choices

Everything that appears in the final version of what you are writing should be there because you intend it to be. Nothing should have crept in by accident, or thoughtlessness; nothing should have been left out by oversight. What you end up with should be exactly what you want. Every word you have used should be there because you have chosen to use that word as opposed to any other. The words should appear in the order you have decided upon. The sentences and paragraphs should be composed as you have designed them.

In other words, you have choices. You can only write well by making choices. Those choices may be conscious, where you have weighed up two alternative words or phrases and chosen one rather than the other; or they may be subconscious, where a word or phrase has come into your mind and you have put it down because it is clearly right. But where a word or phrase comes to you intuitively, you still have a choice: whether to keep it, or to discard it and search for something better. Never, if you can avoid it, simply write down the first thing that comes into your head without examining it critically and *deciding* that it is just right.

When we speak, we frequently say things we do not mean to say, or we do not say them in the best possible way, or we forget to say things. This is the natural result of extemporising. A barrister must of course learn to minimise 'accidents' when speaking, but you will never eliminate them entirely. When writing, however, you have an opportunity you do not have when speaking: to go back over what you have written and improve it. Do not waste this opportunity. At every stage you have a choice: to leave what you have written or to improve upon it. Make that choice.

2.3 The English Language

The English language is both your resource and your vehicle. Good writing involves drawing upon it and using it well. You should understand the language and the way it works, you should understand its vocabulary, so that you can make the language work for you rather than find it to be a hindrance or an obstacle that gets in the way of what you are trying to say.

Plain English is important: it has the qualities listed here. Try to write in plain English wherever possible. This means avoiding inappropriate jargon, archaic language, unnecessary verbiage, pedantic superfluities and antiquated sentence structures. 'Legalese' gives lawyers a bad name, creates barriers between you and your client and can narrow rather than broaden your thinking.

Nevertheless you are a lawyer and what you are writing may serve a specialised legal purpose rather than a general one. Plain English involves using the simplest and clearest language possible in the circumstances, not the simplest and clearest language available. A lawyer cannot sacrifice precision for simplicity, or clarity for the sake of shorter words. It is more important that what you are writing should fulfil its function than that it should make sense to someone who has no need to understand it.

There are times, therefore, when technical terms are preferable to lay terms; when uncommon words carry precisely the meaning you want while commonplace ones do not; when a long complex sentence gives the right emphasis while a short simple one does not. The rule is to use everyday language wherever possible but not at all costs.

2.4 Clarity

Good writing has total clarity. The meaning springs instantly from the words, which do not need to be pondered, reread or analysed. If you ever feel that a sentence you are writing is not expressing the idea behind it clearly, stop, and start writing it again.

The whole purpose of much of what a barrister writes is to clarify what would otherwise be unclear. An opinion may try to explain a complex situation so that it can be understood. A statement of case tries to define issues and bring them into the open. It follows that there is a great need for clarity in what a barrister writes. If it cannot be understood by those reading it, or if it is open to different interpretations, not only is it poorly written, but it has failed to serve the very purpose for which it was written.

Clarity of expression can never be achieved without clarity of thought behind it. In other words if you are not clear in your mind about what you think or what you want to say, you haven't the slightest chance of being any clearer in writing. So a barrister never, except in cases of extreme urgency, writes anything without long and careful thought first. Everything you set out to write must be planned and thought through.

Thereafter clarity will best be achieved through correct grammar, punctuation, precision, non-ambiguity, conciseness, completeness and elegance, which are dealt with below.

2.5 Grammar

A barrister's writing should be free from grammatical error. The rules of grammar dictate word forms, word order and sentence structure. If a verb is in the wrong tense, an adverb in the wrong place, or a sentence improperly composed, the only possible result is obscurity of meaning. You cannot write clearly if your writing is not grammatical.

Grammar is particularly important where you are using long sentences. If the structure of a sentence is not abundantly clear at first reading, almost certainly it suffers from being too long. Any grammatical inconsistency is therefore likely to destroy the value of the long sentence.

Good grammar is the grammar of clear usage, rather than the grammar of pedants. Beware of absolute rules of grammar, such as 'Never split an infinitive', 'Never put a comma before "and"'. In the end the best grammar is the grammar that makes the meaning clearest.

2.6 Punctuation

Good writing must be properly punctuated. This is often essential for clarity in all forms of writing. It can be crucial to the meaning of a legal document. Take care to use commas, semicolons and colons properly and in the right places. The sense of a sentence can be destroyed by a comma in the wrong place or the lack of a comma where one is needed. The structure of a sentence can become immediately unclear when a comma is used instead of a semicolon. Do not open a bracket and then fail to close it. Do not start a subordinate clause with a dash and end it with a comma. None of these common errors belongs to good writing.

Barristers need to take particular care over punctuation when drafting. Drafting can occasionally involve complex grammatical structures, long sentences and numbered subclauses. The wrong punctuation can easily destroy the whole relationship between various parts of the sentence, or detach a subclause from the main clause to which it belongs. The choice of punctuation marks is just as much a part of drafting as the choice of words.

2.7 Precision

Barristers need to write with precision. Everything you write should ideally say exactly what you want to say, neither more nor less. This is an essential part of clarity and is inevitably something you have always attempted to achieve whenever you have written anything. But there are degrees of precision. Whenever we communicate either orally or in writing, we always manage to say more or less what we mean, otherwise we would fail to communicate altogether. We are usually inclined to be rather more precise when we write than when we speak, because we have the opportunity to be (see **2.2**). But even then, we frequently express our thoughts and feelings in a vague or generalised way. Only occasionally do we attempt to write with exactitude.

As a lawyer you will need to write with a greater degree of precision than you would probably use in everyday life. This is true generally, particularly true of opinions and advices and quite fundamental in drafting. In statements of case there can be no room for anything less than absolute precision. The words you use must be chosen for their precise meaning; the sentences you write must be composed to convey a precise sense. Lack of precision will at best result in a degree of confusion; at worst it may mean you are in effect telling lies.

The more precise what you are writing needs to be, the more carefully you will need to compose it. This takes time and thought. You need to ponder the words and phrases you are using. With experience you will learn to avoid the worst traps and become adept at spotting ambiguities. But it involves setting yourself standards of accuracy beyond those you would regard as sufficient for everyday communication.

2.8 Non-ambiguity

This is a special kind of precision which is of particular importance. Very often in everyday life we use words which mean precisely what we intend them to but which are capable of bearing another meaning if looked at from a different viewpoint or in a different context. We frequently do not notice this alternative meaning because both we and the person we are communicating with share the same fixed viewpoint. Even if we are aware of the possible ambiguity we frequently do not worry about it because we are sure that what we say or write can only be received in the context we intend.

But when you are writing in a legal context you must be aware of all the different viewpoints from which your words might be seen and ensure that what you write is genuinely unambiguous. You should reckon that if what you write could reasonably bear another meaning than that which you intend, someone somewhere will probably try to read it in that way. A quick glance through the law reports will show how many cases arise through an ambiguity in somebody's written words, an ambiguity that obviously never occurred to the person who wrote them. Learn to be aware of and avoid all possible ambiguities. Again, this is particularly important in drafting, but generally true of all a barrister's writing.

2.9 Conciseness

Good writing is concise. This does not mean it should be abbreviated, or even short; rather that it should be succinct and to the point. Try to avoid repetition, waffle, long-windedness or digression. Leave out what is unnecessary or that which obstructs your flow or meaning without adding anything. A good piece of writing should never be a word longer than it needs to be.

But beware of trying to be too concise. If what you are writing merely becomes a summary of what you mean to say, it will not do. Clarity is more important than brevity. Ideas are sometimes more accurately expressed in 20 words than 10. Arguably even elegance should not be sacrificed in the interests of being very concise. Make sure that your writing, as well as being concise, is also always complete.

2.10 Completeness

This is the quality which must be balanced with conciseness. When you write you must express your ideas completely. If what you write has only partially expressed what you are trying to say, or has only set out half the story, or does not explain your full reasoning step by step, then it is incomplete. If incomplete, it is also almost certainly imprecise, ambiguous and unclear.

Just where you draw the line between completeness and conciseness is a matter of fine judgment. You will not always draw the line in the same place. Sometimes you will know that what you are writing will serve its purpose better if you err on the side of conciseness; on other occasions you will realise that it is essential to get everything down in full even if that means you are not as concise as you might have been. But always be aware of the balance that has to be achieved in a good piece of writing.

2.11 Elegance

Good writing is elegant. This is very hard to define since it is a matter of artistic impression, but elegance is nevertheless something we recognise and appreciate when reading a piece of writing. It is certainly an important quality in anything we describe as 'well written'. Elegance cannot be allowed to become the prime objective of a lawyer's writing: if it is in conflict with precision, non-ambiguity or completeness then clarity demands that elegance should to some degree be sacrificed. But it is usually possible, if enough care is taken, to achieve elegance as well as the other qualities of good writing.

No one can tell you how to write elegantly. You will decide what feels and looks elegant for yourself. But obviously you should avoid clumsy phrases, tortuous constructions and jarring words. Elegance is also very much a matter of flow and rhythm. Elegant writing usually sounds good when read aloud as well as carrying the reader easily along the printed page.

2.12 The Reader

You should always have the reader in mind when you write. Just as you only speak to communicate with a particular person or people, so when you write you should always be aware of the person you are writing for. A letter is addressed to a particular individual and must be written in a way that will communicate easily with him or her. Do not use legal terminology if you are writing to a non-lawyer. Do not write to a solicitor as if he or she were a lay client. Do not make jokes that will not seem amusing to the person concerned.

An opinion may be addressed to a solicitor, but frequently a lay client will wish to read it and it should be comprehensible to him or her. Statements of case need to be understood only by other lawyers, but they must make sense to a lawyer who has no other knowledge of the case. Always be aware of the characteristics and background of the likely reader of what you write and gear it to that reader.

2.13 Reading Over

Usually, anything you write will come back to you in printed form, either from a typist or your word processor. Never be satisfied with what you have written until you have read over and checked the printed version. If you care as you should about the quality of your writing, you will care enough to wish to correct typographical errors and to give yourself one final opportunity to improve in any small way you can on what you have written.

THREE

IMPROVING YOUR WRITING SKILLS

To many people, the study of the English language is far from being an interesting topic. However, much of the work of a barrister involves writing. A solicitor who receives an opinion written in poor English will think twice before using the services of the barrister who wrote it.

It is said in *The Complete Plain Words* (Sir Ernest Gowers) that the 'test of good writing is whether you can convey to your readers exactly what you intend to convey'. It is therefore important that a barrister can write in a way that is intelligible to others.

If you write in poor English, there is a risk that you will fail to convey your intended meaning to your reader. Poor English is also likely to distract the attention of your reader.

3.1   The Purpose of this Chapter

The objective of the rules which relate to the construction of sentences (grammar and syntax) is to ensure that the same set of words means the same thing both to the writer and to the reader.

However, this chapter is not meant to be an exhaustive exposition of the 'rules' of English. Instead, its purpose is to try to identify mistakes which are commonly made and to show how those mistakes may be avoided.

3.2   How to Improve Your Writing

(a)   You must practise your writing. Fluency comes, in part, from familiarity with the skill of writing. The more of it you do, the easier it becomes.

(b)   You must read the writings of others. If you spend some of your spare time reading novels, you should find that your own use of English becomes more fluent. If you come across a word which is unfamiliar to you, look it up in a dictionary: this is how to expand your vocabulary. If you read a sentence which is unclear, ask yourself why it is unclear; then make sure that you avoid writing something which is unclear for the same reason.

(c)   You must make sure that you are familiar with the basic rules which govern the writing of the English language.

(d)   Before starting to write a document, make sure that you know what you want to say. The point is made in *The Complete Plain Words* (Sir Ernest Gowers) that 'loose thinking is bound to produce loose writing . . . . It is wise therefore not to begin to write . . . until you are quite certain what you want to say'.

(e) If you are uncertain of the spelling of a particular word, use a dictionary. If you are using a word processor, remember that most spell check programmes will only question words which are not in the programme. This means that the misspelling of 'there' in the following sentence would not be highlighted: 'Their is one complaint about the defendant's work'.

(f) If you cannot think of the word which conveys precisely what you want to convey, use a thesaurus. Most word processors have a thesaurus function.

If you take these steps, you should improve your ability to write in a way which is clear and easy to read.

3.3 The Sentence

Gowers, in *The Complete Plain Words*, writes: 'The two main things to be remembered about sentences by those who want to make their meaning plain is that they should be short and should have unity of thought'.

Ideally, a sentence should convey a single idea. It is sometimes said that, at its simplest, a sentence should include a subject, an object and a verb. For example, 'The barrister [subject] went [verb] into the courtroom [object]'. Most sentences will, of course, contain much more than these three elements, but you should check each sentence to ensure that a subject, object, and verb are all present. If a sentence does not contain all three elements, read it again to check that it makes sense.

3.3.1 INCOMPLETE SENTENCES

A common error is to write an incomplete sentence.

Take these words:

Although liability has been admitted. The question of the amount of damages has still to be decided.

The second sentence is complete, but the first is not.

The construction of a sentence often depends on the word with which the sentence begins. For example, the word 'although' has to be followed by two clauses. The structure of a sentence beginning with the word 'although' should be:

Although [something is/is not true], [something else is/is not true].

The phrase used in the example should therefore be written as follows:

Although liability has been admitted, the question of damages has still to be decided.

An alternative would be to write two sentences:

Liability has been admitted. However, the question of damages has still be to decided

or to create two clauses in a single sentence by means of a semicolon:

Liability has been admitted; however, the question of damages has still be to decided.

3.3.2 CONJUNCTIONS

It is permissible for two ideas to be linked in the same sentence, provided that appropriate punctuation or an appropriate conjunction is used. A conjunction is simply a 'joining' word.

Take this example, in which the conjunction is missing:

The claim form was issued on 1 April, it was not served until 30 June.

This sentence should be written as follows:

The claim form was issued on 1 April, but it was not served until 30 June.

The two clauses in the sentence are joined by the word 'but'.

Another option would be to use a single sentence, but to begin it with the word 'although':

Although the claim form was issued on 1 April, it was not served until 30 June.

Punctuation can also be used to solve the problem. In the example given, a semicolon would cure the defect:

The claim form was issued on 1 April; it was not served until 30 June.

The semicolon is effective in this instance because it is more emphatic than a comma and splits the sentence into two separate parts.

Yet another approach would be to use two sentences instead of one:

The claim form was issued on 1 April. However, it was not served until 30 June.

The words which follow a conjunction must 'harmonise' with the words which precede it.

So, in this example from Gowers, the sentence

A woman who is absent from work because of pregnancy or confinement has the right to return to work in the same grade <u>and working</u> the same hours . . .

is incorrect and should be rewritten because the clause 'to return to work' does not harmonise with the clause 'and working':

A woman who is absent from work because of pregnancy or confinement has the right to return to work in the same grade <u>and to work</u> the same hours . . .

3.3.3   SUBJECT-VERB AGREEMENT

The rule that the subject and the verb must 'agree' simply means that if the subject of the sentence (the doer) is plural, the plural form of the verb (the word which describes what is done) must be used. Similarly, if the subject is singular, the verb must also be singular.

Hence:

The claim form <u>was</u> served.

The claim forms <u>were</u> served.

A common reason for making a mistake is the distance between the noun and the verb. Gowers gives this example:

We regret that <u>assurances</u> given us twelve months ago that a sufficient supply of suitable local <u>labour would</u> be available to meet our requirements <u>has</u> not been fulfilled.

In this example, the verb 'has' (singular) does not agree with the noun 'assurances' (plural).

11

No doubt, the rule about subject-verb agreement seems very obvious. However, difficulties can arise where the subject of the sentence is a 'collective noun'.

Contrast

The witness statements <u>were</u> served three weeks before the trial

and

The bundle of witness statements <u>was</u> served three weeks before the trial.

In the sentence '*the witness statements were served . . .*', the subject is plural ('*witness statements*'); in the sentence '*the bundle of witness statements was served . . .*', the subject is a collective noun ('*bundle*'). The word '*bundle*' is singular (there is only one bundle), even though it consists of a number of objects.

The matter is confused by the fact that some collective nouns are treated as being plural:

A <u>number</u> of witnesses <u>are</u> available to give evidence for the claimant.

The contrast can be explained quite easily. In the sentence which refers to the *bundle of witness statements*, the emphasis is on the bundle (of which there is only one). In the sentence which refers to a *number of witnesses*, the emphasis is on the *witnesses* (of whom there are several).

A further complication is that some nouns may be regarded as being singular or plural. For example, a limited company may be referred to as single or plural. Thus, the writer can choose between

Denby Ltd are manufacturers of widgets

and

Denby Ltd is a manufacturer of widgets.

The same is true of certain other collective nouns such as 'prosecution' and 'jury'.

Where you have a choice whether to regard a collective noun as singular or plural, make sure that you are consistent in your treatment of that noun throughout the document you are writing. For example it is wrong to write:

The Corporation <u>has</u> not asked for any advice . . . and I do not doubt <u>its</u> ability to deal with the immediate situation <u>themselves</u>.

The corporation (which may be treated as either singular or plural) is treated as singular on two occasions ('has' and 'its') but then as plural ('themselves').

Another form of sentence construction which can trap the unwary is where there is a mixture of singular and plural nouns.

In the sentence

The claim form, the affidavits and the draft order <u>were</u> all handed to the judge

the correct form is, of course, plural. Several items *were* handed to the judge. However, it is possible to rewrite the sentence so that the emphasis is not on all the documents, but is on one particular document:

The draft order, together with the claim form and the affidavits, <u>was</u> handed to the judge.

In that case, the subject of the sentence is the draft order and so the verb is singular, not plural.

It should also be noted that where the subject is an 'indefinite pronoun', such as the word 'each', it is regarded as singular:

Each of the documents has been certified as being accurate.

Another complexity is the 'compound subject'. Essentially this is where the sentence has two subjects. The difficulty arises most frequently in the use of 'either' or 'neither'. Where both subjects are singular, the verb will be singular even though there are two subjects:

Neither the Statement of Claim nor the Defence was served within the time limit prescribed by the rules.

Therefore, you should write:

Neither skill nor knowledge is needed

not

Neither skill or knowledge are needed.

Where one of the alternatives is plural, however, a plural verb is appropriate. For example:

Neither my letters nor my report on the case are in the file.

3.3.4   SUBJUNCTIVE FORMS

The subjunctive form of a verb is often used in a phrase containing the word 'that' where the intention is to convey the idea that action is necessary. For example:

I would ask that Mr Jones deal with this in his report.

I suggest that this scheme go ahead.

I am not suggesting that such work be halted.

The subjunctive is also appropriate to express an idea which is conditional. For example:

If he were to be convicted, he would face a sentence of up to five years' imprisonment.

Should he have the chance, Mr Jones should . . .

3.3.5   PRONOUNS

A pronoun is a word which stands for a noun and is used to save repeating the noun.

For example:

The offender's driving licence was endorsed and it was returned to him three weeks later.

This is much neater than writing:

The offender's driving licence was endorsed and the driving licence was returned to him three weeks later.

You must, however, take great care to avoid ambiguities when you use pronouns.

Take this sentence:

If bicycles are chained to these railings, they will be removed.

What will be removed: the bicycles or the railings? To avoid this ambiguity, the sentence should be rephrased:

Any bicycles found chained to these railings will be removed.

Margot Costanzo in *Legal Writing* gives this example:

From the transcript of the evidence it is clear that the bank manager assisted the guarantor to execute the guarantee validly and then he left the room.

There is doubt as to who left the room: the bank manager or the guarantor.

3.3.6   MODIFIERS

As its name suggests, a modifier is a word or phrase which modifies (that is, restricts, limits or makes more exact) the meaning of another word or phrase.

For example, in the sentence

All barristers in private practice must be members of a circuit

the phrase *'in private practice'* modifies the phrase *'all barristers'*. The effect is that barristers only have to be members of a circuit if they are in private practice.

Care needs to be taken with the placing of a modifier to ensure that it only relates to the word or phrase to be modified.

For example, in the sentence

Only solicitors and barristers in private practice may appear as advocates in court

the phrase *'in private practice'* could modify either *'barristers'* or *'solicitors and barristers'*.

The sentence therefore has to be rewritten to remove this ambiguity. If the intention is that the modifier should apply only to barristers, the sentence should be written thus:

Only solicitors, and barristers in private practice, may appear in court as advocates.

The ambiguity is resolved by placing the modifier as close as possible to the word being modified, and by using commas to insulate the modified clause from the rest of the sentence.

If the intention is that the modifier (*'in private practice'*) should apply both to solicitors and barristers, the sentence should be written thus:

Solicitors and barristers may only appear as advocates in court if they are in private practice.

Gowers says that 'words . . . that are most closely related should be placed as near to each other as possible, so as to make clear their relationship'. He gives this example:

No child shall be employed on any weekday when the school is not open for a longer period than four hours.

The phrase *'for a longer period than four hours'* is intended to modify *'employed'*, not *'open'*, and so should be written:

No child shall be employed for a longer period than four hours on any weekday when the school is not open.

The position of a word like 'only' (which is one way of signifying a modifier) can have a dramatic effect on the meaning of the sentence. The following example is given by Gowers:

> *His disease can only be alleviated by a surgical operation*

could mean

> *Only a surgical operation can alleviate his disease* [i.e. the disease cannot be alleviated in any other way]

or

> *A surgical operation can only alleviate his disease* [i.e. the operation cannot cure the disease].

Margot Costanzo in *Legal Writing* gives a further example of ambiguity caused by a misplaced modifier:

> *You could make a tax deductible gift to a school, hospital or community project within the definition of a charitable institution.*

The ambiguity is whether it is only a 'community project' which has to fall within the definition of 'a charitable institution' or whether the school, the hospital and the community project must all fall within this definition.

If the intention is that the modifier should apply to all three, the sentence could be rewritten:

> *You could make a tax deductible gift to a charitable institution (as defined by . . .) such as a hospital, school or community project.*

3.4 The Paragraph

A paragraph is merely a collection of sentences devoted to a single topic. Generally speaking, paragraphs which consist of only a single sentence should be avoided. On the other hand, long paragraphs are very difficult to read and so if you write a very long paragraph you should consider whether it should be split into two or more shorter paragraphs.

Each separate topic should be dealt with in a separate paragraph. Each paragraph should deal with only one topic.

Gowers writes, 'Every paragraph must be homogeneous in subject matter, and sequential in treatment of it. If a single sequence of treatment of a single subject goes on so long as to make an unreasonably long paragraph, it may be divided into more than one. But you must not do the opposite, and combine into a single paragraph passages that [do not have] this unity, even though each by itself may be below the average length of a paragraph.' In other words, a topic may be divided into a number of paragraphs if that topic is too long to be dealt with in a single paragraph, but a number of different topics should not be dealt with in one paragraph.

It is usually helpful if the opening sentence of the paragraphs sets out what the paragraph is about. For example:

> *There can be little doubt that the defendant drove his car negligently. He was driving at 50 mph on a stretch of road governed by a 30 mph speed limit. The road was icy, making it more difficult for the defendant to control his car.*

Finally, related topics should be kept together in the same section of the document.

3.5   Punctuation

3.5.1   THE FULL STOP

The full stop is used to mark the end of a sentence.

When using a full stop check that the sentence which precedes it is complete (see above).

3.5.2   THE COMMA

The comma is used to mark breaks within a sentence. These breaks usually correspond with pauses which would be observed if the sentence were to be read out loud.

Commas are also used to write lists where the presentation of the list in the form of a table would not be appropriate. For example:

The agreement was to supply three photocopiers, a collator, a duplicator and various smaller items.

A comma may also be used after an introductory clause. For example:

Although the defendant admitted that he had been driving his car, he denied that he had consumed any alcohol that evening.

Another use for a comma is to introduce a quotation. For example:

Lord Denning said, 'It was bluebell time in Kent'.

In some instances, commas may also be used in place of brackets. For example:

The claimant's letter, which was received by the defendant on 1 April 1996, sets out the details of the claimant's claim

instead of

The claimant's letter (which was received by the defendant on 1 April 1996) sets out the details of the claimant's claim.

A common mistake in the use of the comma is to write a sentence like this:

A copy of the order made by the judge, must be served on the defendant by the claimant's solicitor.

The comma in that example should be deleted since it is inappropriate to place a comma between the subject and the verb which relates to that subject.

Another common error is to use a comma to link two independent clauses which are not linked together by a conjunction (such as 'and' or 'but'). For example, in this phrase:

On 1 May the company wrote to the engineers to ask them to service the boiler, this was followed up on 14 May by a telephone call repeating the request

the comma should either be preceded by the word 'and' or else should be replaced with a full stop or a semicolon.

Where the subject is followed by a phrase which is intended to modify the subject, the modifier will have to be placed between the subject and the verb. In that case, a comma is put before the modifier and a second comma is placed after the modifier.

For example:

> *A copy of the order, once it has been made by the judge, must be served on the defendant by the claimant's solicitor.*

A common mistake is to omit the second comma. To give another example, in this sentence:

> *The claimant has, in my opinion a good claim against the defendant*

there should be a comma after the word 'opinion'. A good way of remembering the need for two commas in this context is to think of the comma as a bracket. No-one would think of writing

> *The claimant has (in my opinion a good claim against the defendant.*

A slightly more complicated rule is explained by Sir Ernest Gowers. It is that a commenting clause should be placed within commas but a defining clause should not. A commenting clause is one like this: '*Mr Jones, who was here this morning, told me that . . .*'. A defining clause is one like this: '*The man who was here this morning told me that . . .*'. In the first case, the subject of the sentence ('*Mr Jones*') is complete. This means that the sentence would be correct if it just read, '*Mr Jones told me that . . .*'. In the second case, the phrase '*who was here this morning*' is essential to the definition of '*the man*' and without it the subject is incompletely described.

Gowers gives this example:

> *Any expenditure incurred on major awards to students, who are not recognised for assistance from the Ministry, will rank for a grant.*

The commas make the phrase 'who are not recognised' a commenting clause. The implication is that no students are recognised for assistance from the Ministry. If the writer's intention is to say that only some students are not recognised, then the commas should be deleted.

Compare these two sentences:

> *Pilots, whose minds are dull, do not usually live long.*

This sentence means that all pilots have dull minds and therefore do not live long.

If it is written without the comma

> *Pilots whose minds are dull do not usually live long*

it means that only those pilots whose minds are dull do not usually live long.

3.5.3   THE SEMICOLON

A semicolon is similar in effect to a full stop; it is used where a single idea (which could be conveyed in two separate sentences) is conveyed in a single sentence. The semicolon is a useful device where you want to convey two ideas in a single sentence because those two ideas are closely related to each other. It marks a break which is less emphatic than a full stop but more emphatic than a comma.

For example:

> *The writ was issued on 1 April; however, it was not served until 30 June.*

A very common error is to use a semicolon where a colon should be used. For example:

> *It was agreed that the following items would be supplied;*

    (a) three photocopiers

    (b) one collator

    (c) one duplicator.

3.5.4   **THE COLON**

The colon is used to indicate that either a list or a direct quotation follows.

For example:

    It was agreed that the following items would be supplied:

    (a) three photocopiers

    (b) one collator

    (c) one duplicator.

Or

    Lord Denning said: 'It was bluebell time in Kent'.

In the latter case, a comma would serve equally well.

A common mistake is to use a semicolon (;) where a colon (:) should be used (for example to indicate that a list follows, see **3.5.3**).

3.5.5   **THE APOSTROPHE**

The apostrophe has two main uses. The first is to indicate possession.

Where there is one possessor, the apostrophe precedes the s

    The claimant's house

Where there is more than one possessor, the apostrophe comes after the s

    The claimants' house

The second use of the apostrophe is to indicate that something has been omitted. Examples include *don't* and *isn't*. Such words are too colloquial to be used in a formal document such as an opinion.

Probably the most common mistake in the use of the apostrophe is made with the word *it's*:

    it's can only mean *it is*

Where the *it* connotes possession, then the word *its* is written without an apostrophe:

    The company was convicted of manslaughter on the ground that <u>its</u> directors had been negligent.

3.5.6   **THE QUESTION MARK**

The only relatively common error is to use a question mark where a full stop would be appropriate. A question mark is used at the end of a *direct* question, such as:

    Do you wish me to advise on this question?

Where the question is an *indirect* one, then the sentence should end with a full stop:

> *The claimant should be asked where he was standing just before the accident occurred.*

3.6   Simplicity of Language

You should always aim to write in plain English, that is 'in language which conveys its message clearly, simply and effectively' (De Groot and Maxwell, *Legal Letter Writing*).

You will improve your ability to write in plain English if you adopt the guidelines which follow.

Gowers proposes three rules which must be observed in order to write in plain English:

(a)   Use no more words than are necessary to express your meaning.

(b)   Use the familiar word rather than the far-fetched.

(c)   Use words with a precise meaning rather than those which are vague.

However, there are several other principles to be borne in mind if you are to succeed in writing plain English.

3.6.1   USE THE ACTIVE VOICE RATHER THAN THE PASSIVE VOICE

The 'active voice' is where the subject of the sentence does the action; the 'passive voice' is where the action is done to the subject of the sentence.

For example, it is easier to write

> *The claimant sent a letter to the defendant*

than

> *A letter was sent by the claimant to the defendant.*

Using the active voice instead of the passive voice usually results in shorter sentences, which are therefore easier to read.

3.6.2   USE VERBS RATHER THAN NOUNS BASED ON VERBS

It is clearer to write

> *The defendant's lorry <u>collided</u> with the claimant's car*

than

> *The defendant's lorry <u>was in collision</u> with the claimant's car.*

3.6.3   KEEP YOUR SENTENCES AS SHORT AS POSSIBLE

When someone is reading, they usually read sentence by sentence. All the information contained in a sentence is stored up in the memory until the reader reaches the end of the sentence. Only then can the information be processed and the whole message received. It is for this reason that short sentences are easier to read than long sentences. The longer the sentence, the more the reader has to remember before being able to work out what message the sentence is conveying. It follows that short sentences make it easier for the reader to take in the meaning of what is written.

Of course, in any piece of written work the sentences will vary in length. However, if you find yourself writing a long sentence, pause to ask yourself whether it could be split into two separate sentences (or whether it could be split into two parts by the use of a semicolon).

Margot Costanzo in *Legal Writing* gives this example of a sentence which, although not too long, could be split up in order to be more digestible:

Practice of the law today is difficult and successful practice is extremely challenging.

This sentence can be shortened by replacing the 'and' with a full stop:

Practice of the law today is difficult. Successful practice is extremely challenging.

Alternatively, a semicolon could be used:

Practice of the law today is difficult; successful practice is extremely challenging.

Sometimes, the only remedy is to rewrite an unduly long sentence. Take this example of an indigestible sentence taken from *The Complete Plain Words*:

Separate departments in the same premises are treated as separate premises for this purpose where separate branches of work which are commonly carried on as separate businesses in separate premises are carried on in separate departments in the same premises.

It is particularly easy to fall into the trap of writing this sort of nonsense when you are trying to paraphrase the words of a statute. The author suggests rewriting that particular nonsense by starting with the word 'if':

If branches of work commonly carried on as separate businesses are carried on in separate departments at the same premises, those departments will be treated as separate premises.

3.6.4   PUT THE WORDS IN A LOGICAL ORDER

Ideally, the subject should be as close as possible to the verb and the verb should be as close as possible to the object. This keeps the 'action' in one place. Where a modifier is used, the word or words which constitute the modifier should be placed as close as possible to the word or word(s) being modified.

In *Legal Letter Writing*, De Groot and Maxwell (written at a time when a claimant was known as a plaintiff) give this example of a sentence which is difficult to assimilate because of a very long gap between the subject and the verb:

The lawyer, who previously acted for the plaintiff in these proceedings and, in all instances, can be said to have behaved in an exemplary manner (despite allegations to the contrary by the plaintiff), should be awarded her costs without delay.

The authors suggest that the sentence should be rewritten as follows:

This lawyer previously acted for the plaintiff in these proceedings. In all instances she can be said to have acted in an exemplary manner, despite allegations to the contrary by the plaintiff. Accordingly, she should be awarded her costs without delay.

Those three sentences are easier to read than the single, longer, sentence.

Sir Ernest Gowers, in *The Complete Plain Words* gives this example:

The existing Immigration Regulations occasionally — only a very limited number of cases have come to my attention — produce undue hardship as a result of the very strict interpretation.

The reader is kept waiting because the flow of the sentence is interrupted by the comment about the number of cases which have come to the writer's attention.

Gowers suggests rewriting that sentence as follows:

> *The strict interpretation of the existing Immigration Regulations occasionally produces hardship, though I know of only a few cases.*

Gowers gives a further example:

> *These proposals, which it is intended should be effected without requiring police authorities to increase manpower or expenditure although there may be some modest increase in expenditure by the Police Complaints Board, are described in Annex A to this paper.*

It is much easier to read if written thus:

> *These proposals are described in Annex A to this paper. It is intended that they should be effected . . .*

Another problem with the order of the words is that you can convey a meaning other than the one you intend if you do not get the order of the words right.

For example, the sentence

> *When out of work, the state requires you to register as unemployed*

suggests that the state is out of work.

It should be written:

> *When you are out of work, the state requires you to register as unemployed*

or

> *The state requires you to register as unemployed when you are out of work.*

3.6.5 MAKE SURE THAT YOUR USE OF TERMINOLOGY IS CONSISTENT

You must be consistent in the names you give to things and to people. Otherwise, the reader will become confused. So, for example, decide whether you are going to identify a party as 'the respondent', 'the employer', 'the company' or 'Fiddlesticks Ltd' and use the same label throughout.

3.6.6 DO NOT USE LANGUAGE WHICH IS TOO ELABORATE

An extensive vocabulary is a very useful asset to possess, since it enables you to find precisely the right word to convey the meaning which you intend. However, you should try to find the simplest word which says what you want to say. To write, *'The meteorological prognostications were unpropitious'* is pompous in the extreme. It means, *'The weather forecast was poor'*, or you might prefer, *'The weather forecast was unpromising'*.

In the drafting of documents such as contracts and pleadings, the language tends to be very formal. Phrases such as 'the said agreement' and 'hereinafter referred to as' often appear. However, such phrases have no place in documents such as Opinions or in correspondence.

3.6.7 AVOID UNNECESSARY WORDS

In *The Complete Plain Words*, Sir Ernest Gowers complains about the use of 'padding', or 'verbiage' as it is sometimes called. He defines this as 'the use of words, phrases or even sentences that contribute nothing to the reader's perception of the writer's meaning'.

You should make sure that every word you write has a role to play in the sentence of which it forms part. Avoid putting in words which are simply padding. A common offender is the phrase 'as such'.

In the phrase

The claimant has no claim against the defendant as such

the words *'as such'* are meaningless and so should be omitted.

Other offenders include *'it should be noted that'* or *'it should be pointed out that'*: these phrases rarely add anything.

'During such time as' means 'while', 'in all probability' means 'probably', 'in close proximity' means 'near', 'on a temporary basis' means 'temporarily'.

Something else to be avoided is the 'double negative'. Usually two negatives cancel each other and produce an affirmative. To say that something is 'not uncommon' means that it is common. Perhaps the reason for saying 'not uncommon' is to try to convey that the thing is not very common; a better way of doing so would be to say that it is 'fairly common'. The reason for avoiding double negatives is that they can be difficult for the reader to understand. It is also easy for the writer to make a mistake and write the opposite of what is intended. Gowers gives this example:

There is no reason to doubt that what he says in his statement is not true.

What the writer was trying to say was

There is no reason to doubt that his statement <u>is</u> true.

3.6.8   TAKE CARE WHEN USING STANDARD WORDS AND PHRASES

Care needs to be taken when using stock phrases. Examples of phrases which are often written incorrectly include: 'as regards', 'with regard to', 'consists of', 'comprises'.

You must not confuse the word 'counsel' (barrister) with the word 'council' (local authority). Remember that *'advice'* is a noun; *'advise'* is a verb.

Take care when using the word 'however' in the middle of a sentence. If the word 'however' introduces a new clause, then it should be preceded by a full stop or by a semi-colon. For example, do not write:

The claimant has a good case, however there is a need for further evidence to support the allegations that the defendant was negligent.

This should be written:

The claimant has a good case; however, there is a need for further evidence to support the allegations that the defendant was negligent

or

The claimant has a good case. However, there is a need for further evidence to support the allegations that the defendant was negligent.

Where the word 'however' is not introducing a new clause, it may be used thus:

I am of the opinion, however, that the claimant needs further evidence to support her allegation that the defendant was negligent.

3.6.9   **FINAL EXAMPLE**

Margot Costanzo in *Legal Writing* gives this example of a sentence which is too long, contains too many prepositions, and is written in the passive voice:

> *In these circumstances, it is appropriate for the legal profession to assert its right to determine the standards of prospective entrants to the profession by declining to recognise the adequacy of training offered by institutions which are inadequately resourced.*

This unwieldy sentence could be written as follows:

> *In these circumstances, the legal profession should refuse to accept as adequate the training offered by institutions which are inadequately resourced. It is appropriate, after all, for the legal profession to determine the standard of its prospective entrants for itself.*

Further Reading

Carey, G. V., *Mind the Stop*, Penguin Books, 1958.
Costanzo, M., *Legal Writing*, Cavendish, 1993.
De Groot, J. and Maxwell, K., *Legal Letter Writing*, Sydney: Blackstone Press Pty Ltd, 1994.
Gowers, Sir Ernest, *The Complete Plain Words*, 3rd edn, eds Sidney Greenbaum and Janet Whitcut, Penguin 1986.
Eastwood, J. *Oxford Guide to English Grammar*, Oxford University Press, 1994.

FOUR

PLAIN ENGLISH

4.1 Introduction

We have already mentioned plain English in **Chapters 2** and **3**. In one sense 'plain English' simply means English that is clear and well-written. But it has come to acquire a slightly narrower meaning, as the alternative to obscure legalistic jargon, or 'legalese'. This chapter looks at the differences between plain English and legalese, and how you can go about learning to write in plain English as a lawyer.

It goes without saying that plain English is just as important to oral communication as it is to written communication, so do not be misled into treating it purely as a part of Written Word Skills just because this is where we have introduced the topic. Use plain English whenever it is appropriate to do so, in advocacy, in conference, in negotiation, in opinion writing and in drafting, just as you probably use it in everyday life.

4.2 What is Plain English?

Plain English involves the use of 'plain and straightforward language which conveys its meaning as clearly and simply as possible without unnecessary pretension or embellishment' (Richard Wydick, *Plain English for Lawyers*).

4.3 Why Use Plain English?

The Law Reform Commission of Victoria put it this way:

> The language of the law has long been a source of concern to the community. It has been the subject of continuous literary criticism and satire. Critics have highlighted its technical terms, its convolutions and its prolixity. These faults have been noted by judges and by practising and academic lawyers as well. Calls have regularly been made for the use of a more simple and straightforward style. Some improvements have been made in response to those calls. But legal language remains largely unintelligible to most members of the community. It even causes problems for members of the legal profession. In some cases, the obscurity may arise from the complexity of the law and of its subject-matter. In other cases, however, it is due to the complexity of the language in which the law is expressed. Some lawyers do not take sufficient care to communicate clearly with their audience. Letters, private legal documents and legislation itself are still drafted in a style which poses unnecessary barriers to understanding. (*Legal Language*, para. 14.)

The advantage of plain English is that it readily conveys its message to its audience.

4.4 What is the Problem with Legal Language?

The Law Reform Commission of Victoria said:

> Many legal documents are unnecessarily lengthy, overwritten, self-conscious and repetitious. They consist of lengthy sentences and involved sentence construction.

They are poorly structured and poorly designed. They suffer from elaborate and often unnecessary cross-referencing. They use confusing tautologies. . . They retain archaic phrases . . . They use supposedly technical terms and foreign words and phrases. They are unintelligible to the ordinary reader and barely intelligible to many lawyers. (*Legal Language*, para. 17.)

This kind of legal writing presents a barrier to effective communication. It is very easy to fall into the habit of writing like this, because such language is all around you, in precedents, forms, contracts, statutes and even the speech of some lawyers. You can pick it up without thinking about it. But if you do, you will not be writing efficiently, effectively or in the interests of your client. So you must learn to recognise legalese, to avoid it whenever possible and to substitute plain English instead.

4.5 What Is Being Done to Promote Plain English?

The legal establishment, in particular the judges and to a lesser extent the parliamentary draftsmen, are becoming increasingly aware of the need to write in plain English and to insist that others do so as well (where they have the power to enforce this). More and more court orders, standard forms, statutes and regulations are being drafted in plain English. Reform is however, a long process, because old habits die hard, and there is resistance in some quarters.

A major revolution has, however, been brought about by the Civil Procedure Rules which came into force on 26 April 1999. These are all drafted in plain English and are specifically designed to enable a lay person to deal with a civil action in person. The ethos behind these rules is also likely to result in many more documents being drafted in plain English in future, particularly statements of case.

See also reg. 6 of the Unfair Terms in Consumer Contracts Regulations 1994:

> 6. *Construction of written contracts*
> *A seller or supplier shall ensure that any written term of a contract is expressed in plain, intelligible language, and if there is doubt about the meaning of a written term, the interpretation most favourable to the consumer shall prevail.*

This regulation is likely to have a very significant effect on the drafting of consumer contracts.

4.6 Recognising and Rewriting Legalese

The worst examples of legalese are never too hard to spot. Rewriting such passages may, however, present more of a problem. Consider the following examples.

4.6.1 FIRST EXAMPLE — A LETTER

Consider the following (taken from *Yes Prime Minister* by Jonathan Lynn and Antony Jay):

> Dear Prime Minister, *Cabinet Office*
>
> I must express in the strongest possible terms my profound opposition to the newly instituted practice which imposes severe and intolerable restrictions on the ingress and egress of senior members of the hierarchy and will, in all probability, should the current deplorable innovation be perpetuated, precipitate a progressive constriction of the channels of communication, culminating in a condition of organisational atrophy and administrative paralysis which will render effectively impossible the coherent and coordinated discharge of the functions of government within Her Majesty's United Kingdom of Great Britain and Northern Ireland.
>
> Your obedient and humble servant,
> Humphrey Appleby

Reproduced with kind permission of BBC Enterprises Ltd, London.

This is of course a spoof, but it contains the sort of language we are trying to get rid of. The situation behind the letter is that the Prime Minister has locked a door which was previously unlocked and which allowed Humphrey Appleby immediate access from his offices to the Prime Minister's. Try rewriting the letter in plain English. 'Please unlock the door' is tempting, and it is plain English; but it will not do, because it gives no reasons for the demand and because it does not have the tone of a formal protest which is what the writer clearly intends. It is not particularly difficult to do, but you will probably lose the flavour of the original. This is because the original, for all its pomposity, is actually very fluently and elegantly written, and full of character.

4.6.2   SECOND EXAMPLE — A LEASE

The following subclause was in a lease which was the subject of the action in *Inglewood Investment Co. Ltd* v *Forestry Commission* [1989] 1 All ER 1:

> Subject to the provisions of the Ground Game Act 1880 the Ground Game (Amendment) Act 1906 and the Forestry Act 1919 all game woodcocks snipe and other wild fowl hares rabbits and fish with the exclusive right (but subject as aforesaid) for the Appointers and all persons authorised by them at all times of preserving the same (except rabbits) and of hunting shooting fishing coursing and sporting over and on the appointed hereditaments and premises *Provided always* that as regards rabbits the Commission shall have an equal right with the Appointers to kill the same and the Appointers shall not keep or permit to be kept any rabbit warren in or in the immediate vicinity of the appointed lands.

Can you understand it? What does it mean? It consists of over 100 words. It was one of a list of reservations in a schedule, which is why there is no main verb. The plaintiffs (the successors in title to the appointers) were contending that under this clause they had exclusive rights to shoot deer on the land. The court held however that they did not, because 'game' meant only those animals listed, and 'preserving . . . hunting shooting fishing coursing and sporting' also covered only the game listed. Can you rewrite it (a) to make it say what the plaintiffs were contending it said and (b) to give it unambiguously the meaning that the court gave it?

The difficulty is that the original is trying to say too many things all at once. Your aim will be to say one thing at a time. You will probably want to break it down into several sentences; maybe also into several subclauses. Even then it is very difficult to do. Do not expect what you draft to be shorter than the original. In situations like this the plain English version, though clearer, is often longer.

4.6.3   THIRD EXAMPLE — A STATUTE

This is s. 7(11) of the Small Landholders (Scotland) Act 1911:

> *The Land Court shall thereafter determine, with due regard to the provisions of the Landholders Acts, and by order or orders declare—*
> *(a)   In respect of what land, if any, specified in the scheme, one or more holdings for new holders may respectively be constituted, and up to what date the power to constitute them otherwise than by agreement may be exercised;*
> *(b)   What is the fair rent for each new holding;*
> *(c)   What land, if any, specified in the scheme is to be excluded therefrom; and*
> *(d)   Whatever else may be necessary for the purpose of making the scheme effective and of adjusting the rights of all parties interested in or affected by the proceedings:*
> *Provided that, where the Land Court are of opinion that damage or injury will be done to the letting value of the land to be occupied by a new holder or new holders, or of any farm of which such land forms part, or to any tenant in respect that the land forms part or the whole of his tenancy, or to any landlord either in respect of an obligation to take over sheep stock at a valuation or in respect of any depreciation in the value of the estate of which the land forms part in consequence of and directly attributable to the constitution of the new holding or holdings as proposed, they shall require the Board, in the event of the scheme*

being proceeded with, to pay compensation to such amount as the Land Court determine after giving parties an opportunity of being heard and, if they so desire, of leading evidence in the matter: Provided always that, where within twenty-one days after the receipt from the Land Court of an order under this subsection a landlord or a tenant, as the case may be, intimates to the Land Court and to the Board that he claims compensation to an amount exceeding three hundred pounds and that he desires to have the question whether damage or injury entitling him to compensation as aforesaid will be done, together with the amount of such compensation (if any), to be settled by arbitration instead of by the Land Court, the same shall be settled accordingly; and, at any time within fourteen days after the said intimation, failing agreement with the Board as to the appointment of an arbiter, it shall be lawful for him to apply to the Lord Ordinary on the Bills for such appointment, and the Lord Ordinary shall, forthwith on receipt of such application, nominate a single arbiter to decide the questions aforesaid, whose award shall be final, and binding on the Board, in the event of the scheme being proceeded with; and, if no final award be given within three months from the date when the arbiter is nominated, the questions aforesaid shall be decided by the Land Court as herein-before provided:

Provided that the Arbitration (Scotland) Act, 1894, shall not apply, and the Second Schedule to the Agricultural Holdings (Scotland) Act, 1908, shall apply to any such arbitration with the exception of paragraphs one, five, ten, eleven, and sixteen thereof, and with the substitution of the Lord Ordinary for the sheriff and the auditor of the Court of Session for the auditor of the Sheriff Court: And provided further that, in the event of the scheme not being proceeding with, the expenses of parties reasonably incurred in connection with the arbitration as the same may be allowed by the auditor of the Court of Session shall be paid by the Board.

In determining the amount of compensation under any provision of this Act, no additional allowance shall be made on account of the constitution or enlargement of any holding being compulsory.

This is perhaps a slightly unfair example: no modern statute would have a single subsection as long as this. The very length of it is daunting. Can you see how it might be rewritten and restructured today? It may well be you will want to turn it into ten or more separate subsections.

4.6.4   FOURTH EXAMPLE — A COURT ORDER

Before *Practice Direction* [1994] 1 WLR 1233; [1994] 4 All ER 52, a freezing injunction might have looked a bit like this:

UPON hearing Counsel for the Plaintiffs ex parte AND UPON reading the affidavit of MILES KING, sworn herein on 11th June 1996 AND UPON the Plaintiffs by their Counsel undertaking:

(1)   To abide by any order this Court may make as to damages, in case this Court shall be hereafter of opinion that the Defendant should have sustained any loss and damage by reason of this order for which the Plaintiffs ought to pay.

(2)   To indemnify any person (other than the Defendant, his servants or agents) to whom notice of this Order is given against any costs, expenses, fees or liabilities reasonably incurred by him in seeking to comply with this Order.

(3)   To serve upon the Defendant as soon as practicably possible the Writ in this action, this Order and the affidavits specified above.

(4)   To notify the Defendant as soon as practically possible of the terms of this Order.

(5)   To notify and inform any third parties affected by this Order of their right to apply to this Court for this Order to be varied or discharged insofar as this Order affects the said third parties.

IT IS ORDERED THAT:

(1) The Defendant, whether by himself, his servants or agents or otherwise, be restrained until trial or further order from removing any of his assets out of the jurisdiction, or disposing of or charging or otherwise dealing with any of his assets within the jurisdiction so as to deplete the same below £44,809.

(2) Without prejudice to the foregoing, the defendant be restrained until further order from drawing from, charging or otherwise dealing with the account standing in his name at the Threadneedle Street branch of Barclays Bank at Threadneedle Street, London EC4, except to the extent that any credit balance on it exceeds £44,809.

(3) Provided nothing in this Order shall prevent the Defendant from expending:

    (i) up to £300 per week on living expenses;

    (ii) reasonable sums in respect of the legal expenses of this action;

    (iii) such sums as shall have been previously approved in writing by the Plaintiffs.

(4) Liberty to apply on 24 hours' notice to the other party.

(5) Costs reserved.

Would an ordinary lay person have much chance of understanding this? Would he or she know what was the effect of not complying with the order? Or what steps now needed to be taken? Probably not, without the help of a solicitor. Look now at the Annex to the Civil Procedure Rules 1998 (CPR) Part 25 *Practice Direction* — Interim Injunctions.

You will notice that the meaning and effect of the order is set out in plain English, such that a lay person who takes the trouble to read it would understand his or her position. But, not surprisingly, this takes much longer than the old fashioned order.

4.7   Writing Plain English

Your aim in writing plain English is to write concisely and clearly so that the reader can understand easily what you are saying.

What is plain English and the extent to which you need to write in plain English does therefore depend on who your reader is. If your reader is another lawyer then you may use legal terminology and words that draw fine distinctions because your reader will understand them and appreciate them. If your reader is a lay person it may be unwise to use legal jargon and unnecessary to draw fine distinctions: you will not help, but cloud his or her understanding by using such words. Where you are writing for a mixed readership, as for example when you are writing an opinion, you will need to strike a balance. You want your opinion to be accessible to your lay client, while at the same time to be professional and precise for your instructing solicitor.

Most lawyers, even when they are trying to write in plain English, do not write as plainly as they could in their first draft. If you are determined to write plain English you will usually need to go through several drafts. The more you write, the more you can see how it could be made simpler and clearer. The more you simplify and clarify your words, the more precise and clear the thought behind them becomes, which in turn leads to even plainer language. It takes longer to write good plain English than it does to write legalese.

The biggest danger, certainly when drafting, is to sacrifice precision for the sake of simplicity. You must take great care to avoid this. Often what looks simple is only simple because it is more general and imprecise than what you started with.

4.8 Basic Rules of Plain English

It is not possible in this Manual to cover all the rules of plain English, or all the good and bad words and phrases that exist. There are other books that go into this more fully. Especially recommended is *The Complete Plain Words* by Sir Ernest Gowers. See also **Chapter 3**.

However, some very basic rules can be identified and they are these:

4.8.1 USE SHORT SENTENCES

Everyone has their own idea of how short a short sentence is, and what is short for lawyers may be long for journalists. We suggest you regard a sentence of 25 words and under as short. Try to write for the most part in short sentences. You can usually achieve this if you do not try to express more than a single thought in each sentence. But do not go out of your way to avoid longer sentences when they are appropriate. Good and elegant writing usually requires that sentences should vary in length rather than all have about the same number of words. Variety maintains the reader's interest.

4.8.2 USE CORRECT GRAMMAR AND PUNCTUATION

Although it may sometimes be more concise, or more like everyday speech, to use bad grammar, in written English grammatical errors can only mean a lack of clarity. For most people correct grammar is instinctive, and mistakes only occur when we do not conceive a sentence as a whole. Always read through whole sentences, trying to phrase them as you would if speaking them aloud, and any grammatical errors will probably leap out at you.

Punctuation is also important. It is essential to plain English that you should take care over punctuation, since it is part of the structure and clarity of your sentences. You can often spot the need for punctuation marks, or the need to remove them, if you speak or think your sentence through aloud.

4.8.3 USE EVERDAY ENGLISH

We have already seen that there is a place for legal terminology and a time to avoid it. Jargon, and other technical terms, should be dispensed with wherever possible. There are many occasions when there are perfectly clear and straightforward alternatives to jargon words. Only occasionally is the technical term the only suitable word.

Legalese at its worst goes beyond simply using legal terminology and uses totally obscure or archaic words and phrases that nobody uses in everyday English. There really can be no excuse for these in ordinary writing.

It is also important to resist all the other absurd jargons that creep into written and spoken English from time to time, and are known variously as, e.g. 'computerspeak', 'Haigspeak', 'Socialese' etc. Such language only makes what you are writing sound obscure and pompous. A student once complained in a letter that there was 'a comprehension dissonance' between his tutor and himself. He wanted to know why his written work had been marked down for lack of clarity!

4.8.4 USE SIMPLE STRUCTURES

Avoid putting an idea in a complicated or roundabout way when it can be put in a simpler one. Almost everything you write at a first attempt can in fact be put more simply and in fewer words. Avoid in particular compound structures which use three or four words to express a single concept, double negatives and the passive rather than the active voice.

Of course this cannot be an absolute rule. The compound structure or the double negative may occasionally carry a shade of meaning or precision which the alternative does not. The passive voice may give the sentence the correct subject (e.g. 'The defendant was sued by the claimant' tells the reader that you are writing about the defendant. The alternative 'the claimant sued the defendant' introduces a sentence about the claimant).

Avoid word-wasting idioms and phrases like 'The fact that it was raining' (since it was raining) or 'In the region of' (about). Also make sure you get rid of redundant words, as in 'null and void', 'totally and utterly'.

4.8.5 USE THE FIRST AND SECOND PERSON

Wherever appropriate it is always clearer to talk in terms of 'I' and 'You' rather than in the third person or in a wholly impersonal way. There are certain formalities in opinion writing and drafting that must be observed and do not allow for the use of 'I' and 'You', but these apart, never be impersonal when you can be personal. It is clearer, shorter and more honest.

4.8.6 ARRANGE WORDS WITH CARE

A great deal of poor English can be improved simply by changing the arrangement of words and phrases. If you put clauses in a better order, the meaning of a sentence often becomes much clearer. If you reduce the gap between a subject and the verb or the verb and its object you can often make a sentence much easier to understand. Always try to arrange your material so that the reader is assisted through it and it is easy to absorb. If the reader ever has to stop, go back and re-read, then you have not written plain English.

4.8.7 USE A GOOD LAYOUT

Although a lot of what a lawyer writes will be in conventional paragraphs, there are many occasions when a barrister writes in numbered paragraphs, clauses and sub-clauses. If these are well marked, they will be easier to read. If a contract term consists of 200 words for example, it will be more easily understood if broken up and subdivided than if it appears as a solid block of text. Even conventional paragraphs are often easier to read if they are numbered and subtitled; and it goes without saying that several shorter paragraphs are usually easier to read than a few very long ones.

Further Reading

Gowers, Sir Ernest, *The Complete Plain Words*, 3rd edn, eds Sidney Greenbaum and Janet Whitcut, Penguin, 1986.
Rylance, Paul, *Legal Writing and Drafting*, Blackstone Press Ltd, 1994.
Wydick, Richard, *Plain English for Lawyers*, 2nd edn, Durham NC: Carolina Academic Press, 1985.

FIVE

EXERCISES

5.1   Exercise 1

Consider these eight qualities of good writing from **Chapter 2**:

clarity,
grammar,
punctuation,
precision,
non-ambiguity,
conciseness,
completeness,
elegance.

Suppose these were the assessment criteria for marking a piece of writing. How many marks would you allocate to each if you had 100 marks to distribute:

(a)   If you were assessing a letter from a lawyer to a lay client?

(b)   If you were assessing a draft contract?

5.2   Exercise 2

Consider the following sentences. What is ambiguous, vague or inaccurate about them? How can that ambiguity or vagueness be removed or the inaccuracy corrected?

(1)   Room 6 is for the use of barristers and their pupils.

(2)   The landlord and his agent may enter the premises at any time.

(3)   I gave £1,000 to John and Mary.

(4)   This table is only to be used for reading and writing.

(5)   My trustees may give the money to such benevolent and charitable institutions as they see fit.

(6)   The defendant agreed to replace any units found to be defective within three months.

(7)   No more than six books or files may be taken into the examination room.

(8)   All prisoners with a conviction for theft on 31 January 2000 will be released.

(9)   Students were deemed to have passed any examination they had failed to pass by 31 August 1999.

(10) The head of chambers shall be a member of the Bar Council.

(11) Money was to be paid to John only by Mary.

(12) No smoking, eating or drinking allowed.

(13) By a contract made on 10 December 1998 between the claimant and the defendant the claimant agreed to purchase 1,000 light bulbs at a price of 30 pence.

(14) The claimant was driving her Ford Sierra car in Piccadilly at 9 a.m. on 13 April 1999 when she was struck by the defendant in a Vauxhall Astra car.

(15) The defendant denies that he was in breach of contract as alleged by the claimant.

(16) It is denied that the claimant's accident was caused by the defendant's negligence.

(17) The defendant does not owe the claimant £3,621.85.

(18) John Smith went to Leicester to start college on 30 September 1999.

(19) The claimant swerved to avoid the defendant who had strayed onto her side of the road and collided with a wall.

(20) The claimant was walking on a greasy marble floor when she slipped and fell over and was injured.

(21) The claimant did not deliver the goods to the defendant on 18 April 1999 as agreed.

(22) The defendant did not take adequate precautions to prevent the accident.

(23) The claimant claims damages for the death of John Smith for his dependants.

(24) The claimant seeks an injunction restraining Mrs Jones from building her home extension on the claimant's land.

(25) Notice must be received between 13 and 15 January 1999.

(26) Replies must be received within 28 days of this notice.

(27) Notice may be delivered any weekday until 28 February 1999.

5.3 Exercise 3

Rewrite the following in plain English:

(a) Turning to the request which has been made by the claimant for the grant of injunctive relief. With respect to this request, the argument is put forward by the defendant that injunctive relief is not necessary because of the fact that the exclusionary clause is already null and void by reason of a prior judgment given in a similar case by the court. This being the case, the exclusionary clause can have no further force or effect, and the defendant argues that in such an instance the case can be fully and properly resolved without the issue of an injunction. For these reasons it is argued that injunctive relief is not suitable in this case.

(b) It shall be a breach of the terms of this agreement for any member to fail to post a notice in a prominent place that is in no way obscured from public view listing that member's retail prices for all items offered for sale, saving only that those items offered at a special sale price for a period not exceeding seven days need not be listed on the said notice.

(c) In consideration of the performance by the contractor of all the covenants and conditions contained herein and contained in the plans and specifications annexed hereto, the owners agree to pay to the said contractor an amount equal to the cost of all materials furnished by the contractor, and the cost of all labour furnished by the contractor, to include the cost of tax and insurance directly connected to such labour, together with the amounts payable to subcontractors properly employed by the said contractor in completion of his obligations herein set out. In addition to the amount hereinbefore specified, the owners agree to pay to the contractor a sum equal to 10% of the value of the construction on completion, the total amount payable to fall due only on satisfactory completion of the said construction. It is specifically agreed by the parties hereto that notwithstanding this term the owners shall not be required under the terms of this agreement to pay to the contractor an amount in excess of the sum of Fifty Thousand Pounds.

(d) It shall be and is hereby declared to be unlawful for any person to expel, discharge, or expectorate any mucus, spittle, saliva or other such substance from the mouth of the said person in or on or onto any public pavement, street, road or highway, or in or on or onto any railway train, bus, taxicab or other public conveyance, or in or on or onto any other public place of whatsoever kind or description, and any person who does so expel, discharge or expectorate any such substance as defined above in any place herein delineated shall be guilty of an offence.

5.4 Exercise 4

Humpty Dumpty sat on a wall,
Humpty Dumpty had a great fall;
All the King's Horses,
And all the King's Men,
Couldn't put Humpty together again.

(a) Ask Humpty and your instructing solicitor a series of questions which will elicit the further information required for you to determine whether he has an action for damages for personal injury and if so against whom and on what basis.

Compose your questions on the basis that the specific question you ask will be answered, not any question you may think you are asking — your questions must be precise.

(b) Having acquired all the information you need, state the facts of the case in such a way that if they are proved, then whoever you consider to be liable must be found liable.

5.5 Exercise 5

Figure 5.1 shows two different building techniques for a stone wall. Write a paragraph or two explaining the difference between coursed random rubble and squared uncoursed rubble.

Figure 5.1

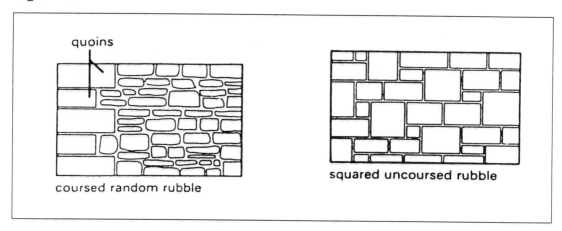

quoins

coursed random rubble

squared uncoursed rubble

5.6　Exercise 6

Describe in writing the design and construction of a spiral staircase, being as concise and clear as possible.

5.7　Exercise 7

Rewrite the following particulars of claim so as to state the facts more clearly and remove ambiguities. If in doubt as to the sense intended, make a sensible choice.

(1)　The claimant rents the first floor flat of 24 Lockwood Grove, London W17. The defendant is on the floor above.

(2)　The defendant is always making a lot of noise day and night. It started in December 1998. It gets into the flat below and the claimant cannot bear it.

(3)　He plays loud music all night four or five days a week and when he was asked to turn it down he refused. He was asked three times but the defendant turned it up.

(4)　When he was asked to turn it down the defendant deliberately stamped on the floor for about half an hour, all five of them.

(5)　They sang as well several times, in the early hours.

(6)　It is disturbing the claimant's family which is a nuisance and he will go on doing it unless he is stopped.

(7)　The claimant cannot sleep and has suffered damages.

5.8　Exercise 8

You are instructed by Homewood Garden Centre Ltd. As part of its business Homewood undertakes the service and repair of motor mowers. Recently it repaired and serviced a mower on behalf of a long-standing customer. A few days later the mower's throttle return spring came adrift, with the result that the mower was stuck at full throttle, ran out of control and smashed into a greenhouse causing damage to the greenhouse itself and to the plants inside, which were being grown for sale. Homewood was obliged to settle a claim by the customer for the cost of repairing the mower, damage to the greenhouse, damage to plants and loss of profit.

The company now wishes to incorporate into all its service and repair contracts a standard term which would prevent it being liable to such an extent again. It feels that it was reasonable that it should be liable for the cost of repairing the mower, but not for any of the other damage or loss. You are asked to draft a suitable clause to be inserted into your client's standard-form contract which will limit its liability in the way it wishes. It should cover the service and repair not only of motor mowers, but any other mains-, battery-, petrol- or diesel-driven garden tool. It should be written in plain intelligible language to comply with reg. 6 of the Unfair Terms in Consumer Contracts Regulations 1994.

SIX

INTRODUCTION TO OPINION WRITING

6.1 Summary of Materials

In this, the main part of the Manual, you will find materials for the opinion writing course. These materials explain how to go about writing an opinion, deal with specific aspects of opinion writing and cover several different types of opinion. You will find a large number of sample opinions taken from real cases in practice, which illustrate the skill and enable you to see what you are working towards.

Chapter 7 deals with the background, purpose and method of opinion writing as well as the content and style of opinions. It is concentrating largely on the opinion on the merits of a case. You should regard this chapter both as your starting point and your bible of opinion writing. Read it carefully before you start the opinion writing course, and re-read it several times again once you have gained some experience.

Chapter 8 goes into more detail on one important aspect of opinion writing — the use of law, especially case law.

Chapter 9 gives you a practical illustration of the process of writing an opinion. It begins with some instructions to counsel, then goes through the analysis of facts and law, the preparation and planning of the opinion, and finally sets out the completed opinion. There then follows a critique of the opinion and an alternative opinion in the same case by another author.

Chapter 10 consists entirely of sample opinions taken from real cases in practice, written by different barristers, which individually illustrate different aspects of opinion writing and types of opinion, and collectively give you an overview of the skill as it is practised in chambers.

Chapter 11 concentrates on a very specific type of opinion — the opinion produced largely for the benefit of the Legal Aid Board. It outlines counsel's duties when advising a legally-aided client and gives some examples.

Chapter 12 deals with another distinctive type of opinion, the advice on quantum in a personal injury case. The chapter needs to be read in conjunction with your work on the Remedies course and **Chapter 11** of the *Remedies Manual*.

Chapter 13 introduces a major type of opinion — the advice on evidence. There is a full explanation of how to go about writing an advice on evidence in a civil case, together with practical examples.

Chapter 14 covers the advice on evidence in a criminal context, once again with text and examples.

Chapter 15 takes a very specific and technical type of civil advice on evidence — the advice on evidence relating to assessment of quantum in a personal injury case. Like

Chapter 12, this chapter should be read in conjunction with Chapter 11 of the *Remedies Manual*.

Chapter 16 contains assessment criteria: the standard criteria by which you should judge your opinion writing skills, and which will be applied as appropriate by assessors on the course.

Lastly, Chapter 17 contains 17 exercises for use on the opinion writing course.

6.2 The Opinion Writing Course

To a very large extent, opinion writing is a skill learned by practice and experience. Most of the opinions you write during the course will be in the context of practical training exercises or assessments. However, we will not require you to write a full opinion immediately. There are numerous sub-skills involved in opinion writing, all of which can and should be isolated and developed separately before they are employed together. The course will therefore start by looking at the skills of:

(a) analysing instructions;

(b) thinking practically;

(c) ascertaining the needs of the client;

(d) getting to grips with the facts;

(e) identifying the issues;

(f) using the law in a practical way;

(g) giving advice;

(h) answering questions;

(i) reaching conclusions;

(j) exercising judgment;

(k) encapsulating a long thought process in a single paragraph;

(l) clear expression;

(m) structuring an opinion;

and maybe other sub-skills also. This will be done by means of a series of short exercises. Only then will you be asked to write a complete opinion for yourself.

6.3 Objectives of the Course

By the end of the course you should:

(a) Understand the context of an opinion in a barrister's work and in a case.

(b) Understand the purpose of an opinion in different contexts.

(c) Appreciate the qualities of a good opinion.

(d) Know and be able to make use of the basic principles of opinion writing.

(e) Understand how to plan an opinion.

(f)   Be able to write a clear structured opinion.

(g)   Have developed some skill at exercising your judgment on legal and factual issues.

(h)   Have developed some skill at giving reasons for your opinions.

(i)   Have developed some skill at expressing both your opinions and your reasons for them clearly and in written form.

SEVEN

OPINION WRITING

7.1 Why Learn to Write Opinions?

Opinion writing is something that all barristers do. It is a common misconception that a barrister's work consists solely of appearances in court, advocacy, or advising clients orally, in a face-to-face situation. In fact a considerable part of most barristers' work, for some the most part, is done in chambers and in writing.

Barristers usually think of their work as falling into two categories: court work and chambers work. For court work, they are using their interpersonal and expressive skills: their skill at advocacy, their communication skills, their ability to think and speak at the same time, their skill at questioning, and occasionally their negotiating skills. For chambers work they are using their writing and thinking skills: their ability to manage factual information, to carry out legal research, to draft, to advise. Surprisingly few barristers would identify opinion writing as a skill in itself.

But they would be wrong not to do so. In reality neither a barrister's work nor a barrister's skills can be divided so neatly into those two categories. Giving advice to a client in conference, that is, in a face-to-face situation, may happen either at court or in chambers. A negotiation may be conducted anywhere, even by telephone. A barrister is just as likely to have to write an opinion on a train returning from court or at the kitchen table as at his or her desk. Communication skills form an important part of opinion writing; thinking skills, fact-management skills, even drafting skills are an important part of advocacy. In learning opinion writing, you are actually learning skills, aptitudes and a way of thinking that prepare you for all aspects of a barrister's work.

7.2 What is Opinion Writing?

7.2.1 PAPERWORK

As well as (rather mistakenly) dividing his or her work into court work or chambers work, a barrister will usually identify (more accurately) a specific category of chambers work: 'paperwork'. All barristers have paperwork to do. Some have more of it than others, depending on the nature of their practice, but none will ever get away from it entirely. 'Paperwork' is a relatively self-contained aspect of a barrister's work; it consists of two things: opinion writing and drafting.

7.2.2 INSTRUCTIONS

Paperwork arises in response to a written set of instructions. 'Instructions' come from solicitors, called your instructing solicitors, and look like a brief, tied up with red ribbon, but rather than containing instructions to appear before some tribunal (a brief) they contain instructions to advise in writing, draft documents or both. If you are instructed to draft a statement of case, or other documents, you do so. If you are asked to advise in writing, what you write and send back is called an 'opinion'. An opinion is therefore your written response to instructions to advise.

These instructions are likely to be your first contact with the case or dispute. Instructing solicitors have sent the papers to you because the time has arisen when they can no longer advise the client or handle the client's case without reference to counsel. It may be that they want a second opinion; it may be that the case is in an area in which you can give specialist advice; it may be that the case is bound to result in court proceedings and they consider it best therefore to bring in counsel at the earliest possible moment; it may be that a statement of case needs to be drafted: it does not make sense to ask you to draft without also advising; it may be that a favourable counsel's opinion is required in order for the client to be granted legal aid. However, there are many other situations, and later stages, at which counsel's opinion may be sought.

7.2.3 CONTENTS OF INSTRUCTIONS

Included in the instructions will be (a) a document from your instructing solicitor, setting out what you are asked to do, the background to the case, possibly a description and analysis of the issues, maybe even the solicitor's own answer to the problem; (b) all other relevant documents, plans, photographs etc. These are likely to include copies of any claim form which has been issued, statements of case which have been served, documents which have been drafted; copies of any contract, conveyance, lease, will or other instrument out of which the dispute arises; copies of all correspondence which has passed between the parties and their solicitors and/or insurers; statements of any witnesses, including your client(s) or representatives of your client company; expert reports, medical reports etc.

The instructions, when analysed, consist broadly of a question, or, more likely, a series of questions. These questions are asked by your instructing solicitor, on behalf of the client. Your opinion is your answer to these questions. An answer must always tell the questioner what he wants to know (not necessarily what he wants to hear!). Since your questioner is the solicitor, the answer is basically addressed to him or her. But since the solicitor is only asking the questions so as to be able to advise the client, the answer must also concern the client specifically and the advice given must be advice to the client, not just to your instructing solicitor.

Probably the most common questions asked in instructions are: 'Does the client have a good case? If so what remedies are available to him? How much would he recover in damages?' or 'Is there a good defence to this action? If not, how can liability be minimised?' 'How much is the client likely to have to pay in damages?' Your opinion answers these questions, gives advice, and is returned to your instructing solicitors with the instructions.

7.2.4 ADVISORY CHARACTER OF OPINIONS

Once again: an opinion is your response to instructions to *advise*. It follows that it must contain advice. In learning to write opinions, you are more than anything else learning to *advise*. Advising is not just an activity, something you do. You do not advise someone simply by telling them what to do. You do not advise someone by writing a lengthy essay and putting 'That is my advice' at the end of it. Nor is it just a way of saying things: you do not give advice simply by starting every third sentence with the words 'I advise that'. Advising is inextricably bound up with and is part of the mental attitude with which you approach opinion writing, with the thinking process that precedes that actual writing of the opinion, and with the writing process itself. We need therefore to look at opinion writing in these three aspects: the mental attitude, the thinking process and the writing process.

7.3 The Right Mental Attitude: the Practical Approach

The mental attitude required to write a good opinion, or give good advice, is that of a practitioner as opposed to an academic. The approach required is a practical as opposed to an academic approach. Practical rather than academic thought is needed.

7.3.1 ABANDONING AN ACADEMIC ATTITUDE

Whatever course in law you followed at the academic stage, and however practical it appeared to be, it is inevitable that your approach has been largely academic so far. This is because at the end of the course you were going to be examined not on what you did, but on what you knew. Practitioners are not much concerned with what they know, but with what they do. So long as your concern has been knowledge of the law, seeking to understand the law, considering what the law is or should be, rather than solving problems, advising people, deciding what to do next, your approach has been fundamentally academic.

The most academic academics tend to have a theoretical approach to the law, studying it for its own sake. If confronted with a legal problem they will regard the research and the analysis of the law as an end in itself and may even regard the reaching of conclusions or the answering of the problem as something of an irrelevance. To the academic, the problem is more important than its answer.

The practitioner abhors a problem with no answer. He or she will always seek to reach a conclusion, to provide the best possible answer to the problem. The practitioner will regard the law as relevant only insofar as it helps to find an answer. His or her mind will be focused on the client rather than the law. However academic or practical your approach has been hitherto, it must now become more practical.

None of this has actually defined the right mental attitude or the practical approach. Even if a definition is possible, it is probably not desirable. The practical approach is something to be developed and acquired, and defining it does not necessarily help. But it is possible to give some guidance on how you can develop the right mental attitude. Here are four fundamental principles to remember at all times:

(a) You are dealing with a real situation.

(b) The facts are more fundamental than the law.

(c) The law is a means to an end.

(d) Answer the question.

7.3.2 YOU ARE DEALING WITH A REAL SITUATION

It goes without saying that every case in practice involves a real situation. You must deal with every case in training as if it were a real situation too, even though it may not be easy: some of the problems can be slightly artificial, deliberately simplified; events may seem somewhat contrived. But you should treat the case as real.

In a real situation there is a real client with a real problem who wants your advice. Imagine, if it helps, that a client, Mr Smith, is sitting opposite you. What would you say to him? How could you help him? This focuses the mind on what Mr Smith actually wants, or the reason he is seeking your advice.

Mr Smith has not come to see you so that you can show off your knowledge. He has a problem and wants help in finding the right answer. He does not specifically want to know what the law says, but rather how he stands in relation to the law. He wants to know what his legal position is and what he ought to do about it. That's the problem. It's *his* problem. And it's a real problem.

But where does the reality of the problem lie? It does not lie in the questions of law that the problem raises, or even in the questions of fact which you will have to answer. It lies in the facts themselves. It is not because of the law that the problem exists, but because of the facts. The facts are the reality. So the second principle is:

7.3.3 THE FACTS ARE MORE FUNDAMENTAL THAN THE LAW

Because they come first. It follows that in dealing with a case, in advising a client, in writing an opinion, your starting point will always be the facts. This may seem obvious and you may protest that you have always taken the facts as your starting point. But have you?

During the academic stage, when confronted with a problem, what thoughts first ran through your mind? Quite possibly, thoughts like: 'Is this a tort case or a contract case?' 'What's the point of law in this case?' — legal questions, rather than factual questions.

The first thoughts that run through a practitioner's mind in reading instructions are questions like 'What's happened?' 'What's the situation?' 'What's the problem?' 'What does my client want?' 'What should be done?' 'What advice can I give?' Such questions address the facts, not the law. The facts are fundamental because they give rise to the problem and to any questions of law that may be answered in order to achieve a solution to the problem.

So if the facts are more important than the law, where does the law fit in? The answer lies in the third principle:

7.3.4 THE LAW IS A MEANS TO AN END

And frequently a very important means, but not an end in itself. The law is what you consult, and use where appropriate, to help you produce a solution to the problem. The law provides a framework which enables you to shed light on the facts, organise the facts, analyse the facts, and interpret the facts, and within which you are able to form an opinion on the facts and answer questions of fact.

The golden rule is: use the law to help you form an opinion on the facts, not the facts as an excuse to form an opinion on the law. This becomes clear when you look at what your client is actually asking. For example, the claimant company in *Photo Production Ltd v Securicor Transport Ltd* [1980] AC 827 would not have asked its legal advisers, and did not want to know the answer to the question 'In what circumstances can a party in fundamental breach of contract rely on an exclusion clause?' The question it would have asked, and wanted an answer to, was 'Can Securicor, in the events which have happened, rely on this exclusion clause?' or even, quite simply, 'Is Securicor liable to pay this company the cost of rebuilding its factory?' So an answer expressed in the form of, 'In my opinion the decision of the House of Lords in *Suisse Atlantique* was correct' is quite meaningless. What your client wants is an answer expressed in the form: 'In my opinion Securicor can rely on its exclusion clause and the claimant will fail to recover damages'. In other words, since the question arises out of the facts of the case and not the law, the answer must address the facts and not just the law.

The lawyer who, when consulted by a client, investigates the law and answers only the questions of law, is like a doctor who, when consulted by a patient, investigates the symptoms, informs her what she is suffering from and packs her off without prescribing treatment. The law must also be used to help your client attain his or her objectives. This leads into the fourth principle:

7.3.5 ANSWER THE QUESTION

Your instructions are a series of questions, all of which need to be identified and answered. Not only must you answer all the questions, you must answer the actual questions asked and not those which have not been asked, as illustrated above. You will not tend to answer the right questions if your mental attitude is wrong, and if you don't answer the right questions you will not be advising your client properly.

This is not as easy or as obvious as it sounds. It is very rare that you will be able to say yes or no, win or lose. But what the practitioner cannot do is say, 'I can give no answer'. There may be no *definite* answer, but there *must* always be *an* answer. Just how you do this is described below (see **7.4.6** and **7.7.1**). But as far as the mental attitude goes, the essential principle is that you should always be seeking to answer every question as clearly and as completely as you can, and this means not only questions where the answer is clear, but also those where it is unclear; not only questions of law, but questions of fact as well. Dealing with questions of fact is likely to be something you have not yet been asked to do, or have avoided doing, at the academic stage. A barrister, in writing an opinion, has to deal with questions of fact. All of them. As clearly and completely as it is possible to do. There may be no definite answer to them, but they must still be dealt with.

7.4 The Thinking Process: Preparing to Write an Opinion

If you can appreciate and adopt the four principles of the practical approach, then you will be in the right frame of mind, an advising frame of mind, to start the first stage of writing an opinion, which is the thinking process.

The thinking process can be divided into seven stages, but you should note that these seven stages are not separate such that stage 2 only begins when stage 1 is complete, and so on. Rather they overlap, and your thoughts will be going on to later stages even while you are completing the early stages. They are set out here in the logical order in which they first come in to your thinking process. The first step, obviously is:

7.4.1 STAGE 1: READ AND DIGEST YOUR INSTRUCTIONS

Surprisingly, this does not necessarily mean, at this stage, reading every word of them. In practice they could be hundreds of pages thick, and it will not be productive to plough through them page by page only to discover that half of them are irrelevant. What you are trying to do in reading your instructions is to find out exactly what your instructions are, what is required of you, what the case is about, what are the basic facts, and what your client actually wants to know.

In fact you will find that your instructions frequently set out quite expressly what you are asked to do. In reading your instructions, you will begin with that, but will start gathering the facts from whatever documents seem appropriate, referring back and forth through your instructions all the time. You will frequently find, for example, that if there are statements of case enclosed, that is the best place to start, because they will encapsulate the story; then you may find that your client's proof of evidence is the best thing to read next, followed by your solicitor's comments on it, but always referring to items of correspondence whenever they are mentioned. There is no best rule: you will quickly develop skill at assimilating your instructions fast. While you are doing this, you will in fact also have started stages 2 and 3: you are likely to discover the answer to the primary question fairly early on, and you will be absorbing and organising the facts even as you read. Stage 2 is:

7.4.2 STAGE 2: ANSWER THE PRIMARY QUESTION: WHAT DOES MY CLIENT ACTUALLY WANT TO KNOW?

This is very important. You must have a clear idea of what your client wants to know if you are to address your mind to the right issues and give proper advice. Your objective is, after all, to tell your client what he or she wants to know.

As we have seen, your client does not really want to know the law. He or she does not even primarily want to know the answer to questions like, 'Has there been a breach of contract?' 'Was the driver of the other car negligent?', though these are questions you will certainly have to address your mind to and give an answer to. Your client, at the end of the day, is interested in the *result* as it affects him or her and the questions he or she is seeking an answer to in reality are, for example:

NOT	*BUT*
Will the claimant establish liability?	Will I have to pay damages to the claimant? If so how much?
Will my claim under the Fatal Accidents Act succeed?	Can I get compensation for the death of my husband? Will it be enough to maintain my standard of living?
Is the restraint of trade clause valid?	Can I take my new job or can't I?
Is the gift in clause 3 of the will valid?	How much do I give to Mary and how much to John?

Until you have accurately identified what your client wants to know, you have no basis on which you can tackle stage 3, which is:

7.4.3   STAGE 3: ABSORB AND ORGANISE THE FACTS

This is a process of fact management, a skill which is central to any lawyer's work and which you must acquire. It requires a clear, logical and incisive mind.

The facts must be absorbed: everything that is important or relevant in the case must be at your fingertips. You must make sure you have a comprehensive grasp and understanding of all the material facts. This cannot be done simply by absorbing or memorising facts: they must also be organised or marshalled. There are many different ways of doing this: note making, schedules, time plans, charts, diagrams etc. are all useful, both on paper and in your head.

As you organise the facts, you will discover that a great many facts included in your instructions — a lot of the information provided — will in the end turn out not to be relevant to the questions you have to answer or to the issues in the case. Such irrelevant material can be discarded from your thoughts. There will also, inevitably, be gaps in your instructions, facts that are not included, information or documents not provided. You will need to identify these and formulate the right questions to ask which will elicit precisely the further information you require.

Your instructing solicitor may well have expressed a view on what are the material facts. That view may well have affected his or her decision as to what information to provide. Your instructing solicitor may also have identified the issues which he or she thought were important in the case. If this has been done well, you will find your solicitor's work very helpful when you are organising the facts and identifying the issues for yourself. But do not regard your instructing solicitor's view as definitive. You may well take a different view of the case, and regard different facts and issues as important. You may even see different issues arising altogether. It is important to keep an open mind and not to assume that you have to agree with your instructing solicitor's view of the case.

The process of organising the facts must inevitably be coloured by, and therefore takes place to a considerable extent in parallel with, the next stage, which is:

7.4.4   STAGE 4: CONSTRUCT A LEGAL FRAMEWORK

At this point the law comes into your thinking. Eventually, you are going to apply the law at two stages and for two different purposes. The one you might think of first, to help you answer the question, or even to provide the answer to the question, comes later. At this stage you apply the law to help you to organise the facts and to discover the questions which need to be answered, to identify the issues of fact and law involved in the case and to put them into a proper order.

What you are in fact doing is constructing a framework for the case and for your opinion in the case. This framework consists of a sequence of issues, each issue basically encapsulating a single question. The issue arises, and the question needs to be posed, because, from your knowledge of the law or your research, you have identified it as an essential ingredient in the chain of questions of law and fact all of which have to be answered to determine the answer to the question your client is asking. Two examples of well-established frameworks may help to illustrate the point:

(a)   In a personal injury action, based on negligence:

   (i)   Did D owe C a duty of care?

   (ii)   Was D in breach of that duty (i.e., was he or she negligent)?

   (iii)   What are C's injuries and losses?

   (iv)   Were they caused by D's negligence?

   (v)   Was C contributorily negligent?

   (vi)   Is the damage reasonably foreseeable?

   (vii) What is the quantum of damage?

(b)   In a claim for damages for breach of contract:

   (i)   Was there a contract?

   (ii)   What were its terms?

   (iii)   Has D acted in breach of the contract?

   (iv)   What damage has C suffered?

   (v)   Was that damage caused by D's breach?

   (vi)   Was it within the parties' contemplation?

   (vii) How much is it in financial terms?

Every case has such a framework, either a standard one, like these examples, or a standard one adapted to exclude issues that do not arise or include other issues that do arise, or a framework specially constructed for the unique facts of the case.

Such a framework can only be constructed by an application of the law. You may know the law, or you may have to research it. If research is required, this may be a lengthy process, involving reading many cases, textbooks and statutes. Inevitably, when you are doing that research you will not only have in your mind the sequence of issues you are trying to construct, but also the search for an answer to them. However, identifying the issues logically comes first.

It is very important when looking up or researching the law to do so with the facts of the case that you have absorbed and organised clearly in your mind. You should never, ever conduct legal research without knowing what question you are seeking the answer to, otherwise it will be without purpose or direction. In constructing your framework, you will have in mind such questions as: What must be established before the claimant can succeed in this case? In what circumstances will I advise the executor to give the money to John, and in what circumstances to Mary? Research without such questions in your mind is likely to be lengthy, disorganised, academic and fruitless.

Identifying your sequence of issues and constructing your framework will also help you in the process of organising facts. It will tell you which facts are relevant and what is the relative importance of various pieces of information. It will show you how the facts fit together, what depends on what.

As well as identifying the specific issues upon which your client's case depends, you must also identify all the questions upon which an answer is required. Some of these questions will have been specifically posed in your instructions. But other questions are only implied. Some examples of the sort of implicit questions you might find are:

(a) Do I have a good case?

(b) What are the chances of success?

(c) How strong is the evidence?

(d) Is it worth proceeding in this matter?

(e) What's the procedure?

And one question which you should regard as implicit in every set of instructions:

(f) What is the next step?

Every implied question must be identified and given a place in your sequence of issues to be answered.

A place will very probably also have to be found in your framework for issues relating to the case for the other side. You cannot consider your client's case without considering the likely opposing case. Possible defences that might be raised give rise to additional issues. The likely evidence that the other side will produce will give rise to evidential issues. These evidential issues belong in your structure just as much as legal or factual issues.

By the time you have organised the facts and produced your legal framework, you should have arrived at stage 5, which is:

7.4.5 STAGE 5: LOOK AT THE CASE AS A WHOLE

Before you can go further, it is important that you should be able to see the case as whole, see how everything hangs together, where each question leads. You will see the starting-point in your line of reasoning and where your reasoning will lead. All the issues involved in the case, and all the material facts, interrelate. The case is a unity which you understand and can find your way around. It has shape and structure. This structure will, incidentally, almost certainly provide the skeleton plan for your written opinion.

It is at this point, also, when you should clearly see what gaps there are in the information and evidence available to you. You must identify these gaps and make a request for any additional material required to be provided, bearing in mind what it is realistic to expect your solicitor to provide. You must also be ready to answer the issues you have raised in alternative ways, depending on how any additional evidence or facts turn out.

You may have started on the next stage already, even while you were organising the facts and constructing your framework, but you can only really deal with it when you have seen the case as a whole.

7.4.6 STAGE 6: ANSWER ALL THE QUESTIONS

Every question in your sequence of issues must now be answered. Every question has an answer. The answer may not yet be clear, it may have to be determined by a court, but nevertheless you can give your answer. You do this by forming an opinion.

A few of the issues that need to be dealt with will have a clear answer, yes or no, A or B. Such an answer can only be given where the facts and law are so clear that there can be no real doubt or where there is only one answer in law. If, for example, you are dealing with a case involving a collision between two motor vehicles, you can state categorically that the defendant driver owed a duty of care to the claimant; that is not a matter for your opinion. Where you have a written contract between two parties, neither of whom has challenged its validity, you can state that that is the contract; to express the 'opinion' that it is 'probably valid' would be ridiculous.

But it is unlikely that you will be able to answer many of the issues in this way: certainly not major issues around which the dispute turns, unless your research into the law provides a definite answer. If the overall answer, or the answer on a central issue were so clear, it is unlikely that instructing solicitors would have sought your opinion at all. Most of the issues will not be able to be answered in a definite way. There can be no conclusion of certainty on a question of fact. Rather, you will have to reach a conclusion of uncertainty, where you exercise your judgment to form an *opinion*.

You may have to exercise your judgment to form an opinion on questions of law or fact, questions of mixed law and fact, or all three. Your research into the law may have provided a clear legal answer to any question of law, but more likely you will have to form an opinion on the law itself, or its applicability to the facts of the case. Hence the necessity only to carry out your legal research knowing what question you are trying to answer. The judgment you use in forming an opinion on the law is your lawyer's judgment, using your skill at legal understanding and interpretation.

But more importantly you will use your judgment to form opinions on questions of fact as well. There can be no certain answers to questions like, 'Was the driver negligent?' 'Did the claimant behave reasonably?' 'Is this piece of evidence convincing?' 'Is this version of events credible?' No statute or reported case can ever answer such questions. And yet you must answer them. You must reach your own conclusion insofar as the law and facts allow, even though your conclusion is a conclusion of uncertainty. You exercise your judgment to form an opinion. The judgment you use in answering such questions is not just a lawyer's judgment, but your judgment as an experienced practitioner, as a man or woman of the world, as a decision-maker. One of the qualities that is most respected in good barristers is their ability, when exercising their judgment, almost always to be right. It is a quality you should cultivate.

It is important to emphasise at this point that you are exercising your judgment, not giving judgment. You are not the final judge of the case, deciding who should win and lose, resolving questions of fact with findings of fact which cannot thereafter be challenged. In exercising your judgment you are weighing up all the information you have before you, and forming an opinion about what would be the likely decision of a judge on *that information* alone. You are exercising your judgment for the purpose of giving advice, not for the purpose of determining the case. You cannot see yourself as the final judge; and you must remember that there is a case for the other side that must in the end go into the balance as well.

It follows that you cannot answer all the questions asked simply by looking at your instructions and the facts as presented to you and exercising your judgment on them. You will need also to use your powers of inference or even your imagination to examine the likely case for the other side. Just because your client appears to have a good case does not mean your client will succeed. The other side doubtless think they have a good case as well. In the end a court is likely to have to resolve disputes of fact; there will be a conflict of evidence. There can only be a clear case when the facts are virtually certain or agreed between the parties. A good *answer* to a claimant's or the prosecution case does not mean the *defence* will succeed. Your client may turn out to be an unreliable or an incredible witness. It is important therefore to look at what the other side may say in court and take this into account in exercising your judgment.

Your instructing solicitor may have expressed a view as to what the answer to one or more questions is. While you should have due regard for his or her opinion, you must not substitute it for your own. You may disagree.

So you must answer all the questions in your sequence of issues, exercising your judgment where necessary, deciding what your opinion is, what you think. This is all part of advising your client. Having answered all the questions in your sequence of issues, you will have found your answer also to the central question of what it is your client actually wants to know, and you can come on to the final stage, which is:

7.4.7 STAGE 7: CONSIDER YOUR ADVICE

In other words, you do not just form an opinion on your client's case or problem, you also advise your client what he or she should or could do. If your client has a problem, he or she does not only want to be told the solution, he or she wants to be shown how to go about obtaining that solution. What your client needs is good practical advice, so you should consider also the practical steps that you advise your client to take. This will be a very important part of the written opinion.

7.4.8 THE SEVEN STAGES

These seven stages of the thinking process are not, to a practising barrister, conscious stages which he or she goes through. But they are all logically present in the thinking process and every competent barrister goes through them subconsciously, bringing them in in the order set out above, even if he or she has never actually thought about them! They are all necessary in order to be prepared for the actual writing of the opinion.

7.5 The Writing Process: the Opinion Itself

You have now been through the thinking process: everything is clear in your mind. You know what your answers are, what advice you are going to give. You have to: you cannot possibly write an opinion until you know what your opinion is. But simply knowing your opinion, knowing the answer, does not mean the writing process is a mere formality. You have to know how to express yourself in an opinion, how to transfer the thinking process on to paper. What you do *not* do is simply write out the thinking process itself. Rather, you set out the *fruits* of the thinking process. We need to look a little more closely at what an opinion is and what it is for.

7.5.1 THE PURPOSE OF THE OPINION

We have already seen what your opinion is in essence: it is your response to instructions. Your response has, however, three different aspects, all of which we have touched on, but which we can now state more clearly ((a), (b) and (c)), and an objective (d):

(a) *Your opinion is your answer* to a series of questions asked of you by your instructing solicitor on behalf of your client. Therefore every question must be identified and answered. We have already seen the necessity of this, and discussed how you identify issues and answer them as part of the thinking process. We shall shortly consider how you actually express your answers in writing.

(b) *Your opinion is a kind of interim judgment* on your client's present position as you see it. You must be objective, as a judge would be. Although, at the end of the day, if the case is to proceed, it will be your duty to do the best you can for your client, to fight the case on his or her behalf, to show his or her case in the best possible light, to win the case so far as the law and facts allow, you have not reached this stage yet. At this point you are not trying to fight a case, win it or show it in the best possible light: that would be to mislead your client. You may consider *how* the case may be fought and won, and assess the chances, but nevertheless you must judge the strength or weakness of your client's case coolly and dispassionately. We have already considered the importance of exercising judgment. This is always an objective process. The only subjective element is that you are judging the case put to you by one side only, rather than the case put to you by both sides, as a judge would at trial. But, again remember, you are *not* the judge. You are not *deciding* the case.

(c) *Your opinion is a piece of advice* to your client regarding his or her position and what he or she should do. This *is* subjective: you are obviously trying to help your client as opposed to anyone else and to solve that client's particular problem. Advising is not just a matter of advising someone what to do, but is closely bound up with the whole process of answering questions and exercising judgment.

(d) *Your objective in writing the opinion* is to lead your client to the clearest possible understanding of his or her position, so that he or she can decide, on your advice, what to do about it. So your opinion should be clear, complete, unambiguous, easy to read, easy to follow, and an accurate representation of what you actually think. It should be definitive, rather than discursive, but it must be a *reasoned* opinion. An opinion is incomplete if no reasons are given. It must also look to the future and indicate the way forward.

7.5.2 SOME THINGS THAT AN OPINION IS NOT

(a) An opinion is not an *argument.* Arguments seek to persuade somebody of something and there is no element of persuasion in an opinion. You are not arguing your client's case, presenting it to a court, or trying to prove anything. You may well *rehearse* the arguments for and against your client's case: but that is part of the reasoning for your opinion, which is your view on those arguments.

(b) An opinion is not an *essay.* An essay discusses, explores, considers; it is discursive rather than definitive. An essay, typically, sets out the thinking process, rather than the fruits of the thinking process. Your opinion should never resemble an essay. It should be shorter than an essay covering the same ground would have been.

(c) An opinion is not a *submission.* When making a submission, you are putting forward an argument, or a theory for someone else's judgment. In an opinion you are exercising your own judgment, giving your own advice. Your opinion should *never* contain the words 'It is submitted that' or 'I submit that'. Such words betray a fundamental misunderstanding of the whole concept of opinion writing. If you find yourself writing them, cross them out and write what you really mean, which is, 'It is my opinion that' or 'I think that'.

(d) An opinion is not an *instruction.* Although your opinion is definitive, and you are giving judgment, in layman's terms 'laying down the law', you cannot go too far. You can tell your client what his or her position is and advise your client what to do; you can tell him or her how to go about things and give instructions about the conduct of a case. But you cannot *tell* your client to bring an action or abandon one; *tell* him or her whether to enter into a contract or not; *tell* him or her to plead guilty or not guilty. Decisions such as these are your client's to make (except in very rare circumstances): your task is not to make the decision for your client, but give him or her all the information and advice needed in order to make the right decision.

We can at last come on to the questions of how you actually set out the opinion and express yourself in it.

7.5.3 FOR WHOM IS THE OPINION WRITTEN?

One thing you will find quite hard to sort out in the early stages of learning to write opinions is whether you are really writing for the instructing solicitor or for the lay client. The strict answer is that you are writing for the instructing solicitor. He or she has sent you the instructions and posed the questions; it is to him or her that you are replying. A more complete answer is that you are writing for both the solicitor and the lay client, but in different ways and to a different extent in different cases. You should ask yourself 'Who is going to act on this advice?'. If it is the solicitor, then you are writing primarily, or occasionally exclusively, for his or her benefit. But if it is the lay client, you must make sure that your opinion is written in such a way as to be intelligible and helpful to him.

However, writing for the lay client does *not* mean that you should avoid legal terminology or explain legal principles in layman's terms. To the extent that you are giving legal advice, you are writing as one professional lawyer to another, and you should assume that your instructing solicitor has the same knowledge of general principles as you do. Just take care to avoid unnecessary obscurity and jargon. It is where you are giving practical advice which will affect your lay client that you should make sure the lay client can understand the advice you are giving, and the reasons for it.

There is a balance to be struck, which is not easy to explain, but which comes quite naturally once you have read a few opinions and had some practice.

7.6 How the Opinion should be Set Out

The first thing to be clear about is that there is absolutely no correct or incorrect way to write an opinion. You may do it however you wish. Every barrister has to a greater or lesser extent their own individual style. However you write your opinion, there will always be a barrister who will say 'I don't like your style, I wouldn't write it like that'. During your training you will hear contradictory views forcefully expressed.

Nevertheless, there are undoubtedly such things as good opinions and bad opinions. We have already examined quite thoroughly the qualities that a good opinion should have and the functions it should serve, and you cannot give it those qualities or fulfil those functions simply by writing it any old way that happens to take your fancy. In the interests of clarity, it *must* have a clear structure; in the interests of completeness, it must have clear reasoning; in the interests of readability it must follow a clear line. In the end, you will discover your own style and write your own opinions as you wish, but it is good to have a starting point.

The following structure is therefore a suggested starting point. It is safe, mildly conventional and unoriginal: but if followed it should lead to a good rather than a bad opinion.

Before you start writing your opinion, you must have a skeleton plan. This plan will have evolved during the process of thinking and analysing the issues. Without such a plan (which may be on paper or in your head) your opinion is bound to be disorganised, rambling and poorly structured. Having prepared that skeleton plan, try as hard as you can to stick to it. Do not wander off at a tangent, or allow yourself to drift into discussing an issue you had decided to take at a later stage, unless it is clear to you that this is an improvement on your original plan.

7.6.1 BACKSHEET AND HEADING

Your opinion has a backsheet on which should be printed the title of the case as it appears in your instructions. This may be a full court heading (as in pleadings) or it may just be the name of the client. Use whatever your instructing solicitors have used. Underneath appears, in capitals, underlined, 'OPINION' or 'ADVICE' as the case may be. Thus:

<u>Mary Smith v International Pancakes Ltd</u>

<u>OPINION</u>

The same heading, or an abbreviation of it, will usually appear also on the inside, immediately above your first paragraph.

Your opinion may be called 'Opinion' or 'Advice'. There is not a hard-and-fast distinction. Traditionally, it is an opinion when you are advising on law, questions of fact, liability, merits, quantum of damages etc.; and an advice where the emphasis is on evidence or procedure or the practical steps to be taken. Try to differentiate, but do not worry too much if you cannot. As a rough guide, call it an opinion in civil matters (except for an advice on evidence) and an advice in criminal matters. But many barristers will disagree with this.

After the heading, there follows the body of the opinion, written in numbered paragraphs. You write in the first person, that is to say, you refer to yourself as 'I' not as 'counsel'. But you refer to your client and your instructing solicitor in the third person, 'he, she, it or they', rather than in the second person, 'you'.

7.6.2 THE OPENING PARAGRAPH(S)

The opening paragraph(s) should contain a brief statement of what the case is all about, and your objectives. In other words, you identify the fundamental facts, the key issues and what you are asked to do.

Some barristers will say that the opening paragraph(s) should contain all the material facts. There are good reasons why this may be useful in some instances, but generally speaking the facts are well known to the client and the instructing solicitor and little purpose is served by setting them all out. What you should certainly not do, is simply copy out your instructions at great length or regurgitate all the facts unselectively and uncritically. The introduction to the opinion should be concise.

Next, you may decide to state your main conclusions and give your overall opinion on the case. Most barristers actually put their conclusions at the end of the opinion, but you are encouraged to put them at the beginning while learning the skill. It is helpful to both the solicitor and client and an aid to clarity. If the overall conclusion is already stated one can read the subsequent reasoning knowing where it is leading. It is also a very good discipline to make yourself state the opinion at the outset, as it ensures that you cannot start writing without having decided what your opinion is.

If the conclusions are not stated at the beginning, they must be clearly stated at the end of the opinion.

7.6.3 SUBSEQUENT PARAGRAPHS: YOUR REASONS

Use however many paragraphs you need. This is where you set out the reasoning that has led you to your overall conclusions. You do this by taking each issue in its logical order, saying what you think on that issue and why; that is, stating your opinion and reasons, and giving advice.

The logical order should be clear once you have applied the correct legal framework and put the problem into shape (as part of the thinking process). So, for example, if your overall conclusion is that in your opinion Mary Smith has a very good chance of establishing that International Pancakes Ltd is liable to her for her injuries and that she is likely to recover damages in the region of £25,000, your reasoning might go like this:

1 International Pancakes owed her a duty of care, because . . . [identify the specific facts and why they gave rise to a duty, applying the appropriate law].

2 The company was in breach of duty, i.e., negligent, because . . . [identify the acts and omissions that constitute negligence and if necessary explain why].

3 There is some difficulty about causation, but in my view this can be overcome because . . . [give reasons].

4 Most of the loss and damage suffered by Mary Smith is recoverable but one or two small items were not reasonably foreseeable, because . . . [give reasons].

5 The heads of damage are . . . [set out] and in my opinion they will be quantified as follows . . . [give your quantification and reasoning on each head].

This is a very simple example. Many of the above issues may well subdivide, in which case you might state your overall opinion on the issue of negligence before going on to deal with each sub-issue in turn, indicating the reasoning that has led you to the opinion that International Pancakes was negligent.

On any issue where your opinion is required, you should state it. Do not leave it to be deduced or inferred; do not hint at it or obscure it. Ten pages of waffle with the words 'That is my opinion' at the end will not do. Use phrases such as 'I think that' 'It is my opinion that' 'I have come to the conclusion that'. And whenever you express an opinion, you must always give your reasons for it. This applies not just to your overall conclusion, but to each separate issue as well. For the reasons explained above, it is a good idea to state the opinion first and give the reasons for it second.

Giving reasons is not always something which comes easily. It may be relatively straightforward to give reasons for an opinion on the law, because the reasons will then be reasons of law. But when you express an opinion on a question of fact, you cannot use the law as your reason. It is nonsense, for example, to say 'The defendant was negligent because he owed the claimant a duty of care' or 'Clause 6 is unreasonable because the Unfair Contract Terms Act 1977 applies'. Your reasons for an opinion on a question of fact can only come from the facts themselves. For example, 'The defendant was negligent because he had read the instruction manual which stated quite clearly that the machine should never be switched on without the safety guard in place and nevertheless he did so'; or 'Clause 6 is unreasonable because in effect it makes the claimant responsible for checking the quality of the defendant's workmanship, which she would have neither the skill nor the knowledge to do'.

Another common fault is the reasoning which simply repeats the conclusion. It is meaningless to write an opinion which states, expressly, or in effect, 'The defendant was negligent because he failed to take reasonable care for the claimant's safety' (i.e., he was negligent because he was negligent); or 'Clause 6 is unreasonable because it fails to satisfy the test in section 11 of the Unfair Contract Terms Act 1977' (i.e., it's unreasonable because it's unreasonable). Make sure you avoid such circular statements.

Giving reasons actually constitutes the bulk of your opinion. It can be a lengthy process, especially if the issues are complex or there is a lot of law involved. It is important therefore that your reasoning should be easy to follow. It must follow a clear line; the reader should always know where that line has come from, where it is going to, and what stage along the line he or she has reached. This is why it is impossible to write a good opinion without having prepared a skeleton plan first, and why you should stick to it.

It is to help you stick to your plan that it is suggested you write in numbered paragraphs. This was always the traditional way of setting out an opinion, though nowadays some barristers write in unnumbered paragraphs. However, it is a useful discipline and recommended, at least while you are learning to write a good opinion. Other helpful aids are subheadings: put a title to each section of your opinion, as some judges do to their judgments in the law reports. Subheadings tell the reader at once what issue you are dealing with at each stage, and help you to stick to it. Also useful are short linking sentences explaining the structure of your opinion, for example, 'So for the reasons stated I think that clause 2 was a valid term of the contract and I come on now to consider whether the defendants were in breach of it'.

The worst enemy of clear reasoning, apart from muddled thinking, is irrelevance. Your opinion must of course be complete, so everything relevant must be included; but it should also be as concise as possible, and so it should contain nothing irrelevant. It should be fairly easy to identify what is relevant and irrelevant if you ask yourself three questions:

(a) Is it part of my opinion in this case?

(b) Is it a necessary step along my line of reasoning?

(c) Is it part of the advice I am giving to this client?

If the answer to any of these questions is yes, then it is obviously relevant. You may get more than one yes, but if you get no three times, then it is almost certainly irrelevant.

Irrelevance is likely to creep in if you fall into the trap of setting out your thinking process or all your research into the law rather than the fruits of your thinking process or legal research. Other common examples of irrelevance are:

(a) Simply setting out the facts of the case or copying out your instructions without comment. You may well need to examine and analyse the facts with great care and in some detail, but only as part of the reasoning process.

(b) Giving an elementary law lecture; e.g. 'A person owes another a duty of care if there is a sufficient relationship of proximity between them and it is reasonably forseeable . . . etc.'. This makes you sound like a first year undergraduate, not a professional lawyer.

(c) General exposition of the law in a particular area, quite irrespective of whether it actually touches on the facts of the case you are dealing with.

(d) Detailing all the case law you have researched. You may well have read a lot of cases, and having read them, come to a conclusion on the facts of this case. But it is most unlikely that every single case you have read forms part of your reasoning. You do not need to mention every case just because you read it. A general examination of case law is part of the thinking process, not part of your opinion. Do not describe your research in writing. State the conclusion you have come to and set out your reasons.

(e) Following blind alleys of reasoning. Do not take an issue, discuss it for several paragraphs and come to the conclusion at the end of it that it is irrelevant or makes no difference to your opinion. Such a discovery should have been made before you started writing, so you can simply state, 'Such and such is irrelevant because . . .'.

(f) Seeking to distinguish cases that are so wholly different that nobody would ever have thought of comparing them in the first place; similarly, discussing statutory provisions which obviously do not apply.

(g) Wasting time on hypothetical cases: 'If the facts were not as they are but something else', followed by several paragraphs of irrelevant discussion, concluding 'but that is not the case here so I do not need to concern myself with this possibility'.

(h) Advising your client of what he or she already knows.

Overall: keep your reasoning clear, sharp and to the point.

7.6.4 RULES OF STRUCTURE

7.6.4.1 Liability and quantum
One rule of structure that should never be broken is that liability is dealt with first, then quantum. Never mix the two together, or jump between them.

So, for example, if you are considering the liability of two potential defendants arising out of the same facts, the correct order of issues is:

(1)   Liability of D1

(2)   Liability of D2

(3)   Quantum against D1

(4)   Quantum against D2

and NOT, as students frequently attempt, (1), (3), (2), (4).

7.6.4.2   Separate parties
If you are considering the liability of two defendants, take each of them in turn, and consider possible causes of action against each of them separately. The correct order of issues, for example, might be:

(1)   Liability of D1 for breach of statutory duty

(2)   Liability of D1 in negligence

(3)   Liability of D2 for breach of statutory duty

(4)   Liability of D2 in negligence.

It might possibly, but rarely, be more appropriate to take the issues in the order (1), (3), (2), (4). But in no circumstances should you merge (1) and (2) or (1) and (3) into a single issue.

7.6.5   SUBSIDIARY POINTS

Having stated your overall conclusions, set out your reasoning and given advice, the main part of the opinion is complete. However, there may well be some subsidiary points to deal with and your next paragraph or paragraphs will deal with these. There may well be some specific questions put to you in your instructions, which, while not being part of the overall opinion, must nevertheless be answered. There are also likely to be some implied questions to be dealt with. Every implied question must be identified and given a clear and complete answer, just as express questions must be. Some may be answered as part of your overall opinion, but others will be answered when you are dealing with subsidiary points. Remember that one question is always implicit and must be dealt with: What is the next step?

A major matter which may well need to be dealt with at this stage is evidence. Sometimes you will be asked specifically to advise on evidence, in which case you will either write a separate 'advice on evidence' or deal with it fully in your opinion. Even if you are not asked specifically to advise on evidence, however, it would be odd to make no mention of it in your opinion. You cannot consider your opinion on the strength of a case, or your advice to your client on what you think he or she should do without reference to evidence. It is in the end on the evidence that a case is won or lost. So you should be addressing your mind to what can be proved and cannot be proved on the evidence you have; and to what further evidence is required. Anything important must be mentioned in your opinion. It is no good advising your client that he or she has a good case if, say, a piece of machinery was not properly serviced, if in fact you do not have any evidence to show that it was not properly serviced. Indicate what evidence is missing, and from where it might be obtained.

Points of procedure may need to be dealt with. You may, for example, want to advise that a request for further information should be made, or that an application should be made to the court. You may want to advise for or against making a Part 36 offer, or accepting a Part 36 payment. You may want to advise that an attempt should or should not be made to settle the action. All these are examples of matters that should properly be dealt with in your opinion.

Also important is reference to any issue involving costs. In your client's mind there will always be an overriding question: 'How much is all this going to cost me?' You should make sure you are aware of your client's financial position, eligibility for legal aid etc. You should *never* advise that any step should be taken which might have implications in terms of costs, without advising your client what those implications are.

7.6.6　FURTHER ADVICE

It may well be that having dealt with all the issues, having answered all the questions and advised your client, there will still be other helpful advice you can give, in which case give it. Only give it if it is relevant and helpful. To decide whether it is helpful, remember your overall objective: to lead your client to the clearest possible understanding of his or her position, so that the client can decide, on your advice, what to do about it. Any advice which fulfils this objective, whether by clarifying the position or advising on the steps to be taken, is likely to be helpful.

7.6.7　THE CONCLUSION

The most common way to conclude the opinion is to have a paragraph headed 'summary of advice' or 'summary of conclusions', setting out the main points of advice once again in shortened form. This is certainly essential if you have not stated your overall opinion at the outset of the opinion, because it is important that your client and instructing solicitor should be able to extract your advice easily. Your advice should always be plain to see, not buried. It may also be a good idea if, for example, you have a corporate client and it is likely that your opinion will be summarised for a board or committee rather than presented in its entirety. In such a case it is wise that the summary should be yours rather than anyone else's. A summary of conclusions at the end may also serve a stylistic purpose.

Your final paragraph should round your opinion off in some way. This is actually more a point of style than of content. Barristers like to think that a good opinion is not just a functional piece of writing, but a work of good literature as well. In the same way as no good literature just suddenly stops, but rather rounds itself off neatly or tellingly, so should an opinion. It needs an end as well as a beginning and a middle. You can do this in any way you like, according to your literary abilities, but if you can think of nothing better, a conventional solution is to finish with the summary of advice mentioned above. This may be unnecessary, if you have already stated your conclusions at the outset, but it does at least solve the stylistic difficulty. You may alternatively finish with a restatement of what the solicitor and/or client should do next.

If you have also produced some other piece of writing, usually a statement of case, note this also in your final paragraph.

7.6.8　COUNSEL'S SIGNATURE

At the bottom of the opinion, counsel's name and signature appear, with date, and usually chambers address.

7.6.9　VARIATIONS IN PRACTICE

Please remember that the above description of the structure and content of an opinion is only given as a starting point. You will probably not find a single barrister who agrees with every word of it. Do not expect every opinion you see to follow it precisely. Different opinions serve different purposes and their structure and layout will vary as the content varies.

There remain a few points of content and style to be dealt with.

7.7 Points of Content

7.7.1 ANSWERING QUESTIONS THAT HAVE NO DEFINITE ANSWER

The importance of answering questions is something we keep coming back to, and we have seen how most questions do not have a definite answer, a conclusion of certainty, but can only be answered by a conclusion of uncertainty, where you exercise your judgment to form an opinion. We must now look at the difficulty of expressing an opinion when you cannot be certain. The answer you give has got to be clear and complete. It is quite possible to give such an answer, and be helpful, without being definite. You must reach *conclusions,* i.e., you must be conclusive, but you do not need to be definite in your answer. It is understood by all concerned that the barrister's opinion is only an opinion: infallibility is not expected. The rule is to be as definite as you can be but no more than you can be. It is a difficult balance to strike. The most common complaint of pupil masters is that their pupils tend to be too definite: to say 'The case will succeed' when they should say 'The prospects are good'. On the other hand, another common failing of beginners is not to be definite enough: to say 'The claimant may or may not succeed in his action, depending on how things turn out'. Sometimes this vagueness is couched in definite terms: the opinion which, on close analysis, in effect states: 'In my opinion the claimant will succeed in this action if the judge finds in his favour'!

You have to strike the right balance between certainty and uncertainty. If the question is 'Will the claimant succeed in his action?', do not answer 'yes' when you mean 'probably'; 'probably' when you mean 'possibly'; 'possibly' when you mean 'unlikely'; 'good chance' when you mean 'fair chance', 'reasonable chance' when you mean 'remote chance'; 'some chance' when you mean 'no'; or 'no' when you mean 'slight chance'. What you do is find a form of words which seems to you exactly to express your feeling about the strength of the case. For example:

> I do not think that Mrs Jones has any good prospects of establishing liability in this case, but there is enough evidence before me to justify serving particulars of claim on the other side to see what response it provokes.

> There are numerous obstacles to be overcome in establishing liability in this case, but on balance I think they can be overcome and if they are, Mrs Jones's prospects of success are good.

Take care, also, when expressing your opinion on a subsidiary question of fact. For example, 'In my opinion the driver of the car was negligent' sounds very definite. In this case it would probably not be understood as being quite so definite, because what you really mean is 'In my opinion a court would find him to have been negligent'; but take care. Phrases like 'In my opinion he was negligent' can appear in opinions, but they can mislead others and even you into treating as definite a question of fact which has yet to be decided. It is much better to say 'I think a court would find him liable'. Beware also of saying 'I would award the claimant damages of £50,000', when all you mean is that £50,000 is your estimate of a likely award by a court.

But, of course, a conclusion of uncertainty must not only be expressed, it must also be reasoned. This may be a lengthy process: probably the less certain you are able to be, the more reasoning you will need to justify your conclusion. To give your reasons for a conclusion of uncertainty, and to give advice in so doing, you will probably need to go through the following points. You will need to set out fairly fully the client's position as you see it, not just the legal position but the factual position, the position the client finds himself or herself in in the light of the law; you will need to consider the pros and cons, weigh up the evidence, assess the chances (not necessarily numerically); you should certainly make clear the circumstances in which your client would succeed and the circumstances in which he or she would not. You may well need to explain your view of what the other side's case is likely to be and the strength of it. All in all you identify and explain everything that has gone into the balance as you have weighed up your opinion, and let your client know exactly where he or she stands.

7.7.2 CITING CASES AND OTHER AUTHORITIES

Cases are mentioned, discussed, applied and distinguished in your opinion, just as they are in a judge's judgment. But whereas judges are obliged to deal with the arguments they have listened to and so need to discuss most of the cases they have been asked to read, in your opinion you should only cite a case where it is relevant to your opinion, reasoning or advice. Do not try to get in as many cases as you can. Do not mention every case you have read. Apply the relevancy test. Not every opinion needs to have cases in it. In practice a great many opinions are written which mention no case law at all. If no case is relevant, put none in.

Cases may be properly cited where they are authority for a point of law, where they form part of your reasoning or where they have helped you to reach your conclusion. They should not be cited just to show you know them. You should not, for example, put '(*Donoghue* v *Stevenson*)' every time you write the word 'negligence'. When you cite a case, cite it in the proper manner. If you simply put a case name at the end of a sentence, you are citing it as authority for what you have just said. Make sure you do not cite a case like this as if it were authority on a question of fact: for example, 'In my opinion the defendants were in fundamental breach of contract (*Photo Production Ltd* v *Securicor Transport Ltd*)'. If the case is simply being cited as the source of a proposition, or as an illustration or as part of your reasoning, this should be made clear. Cases that form part of your reasoning, either because they have led you to your conclusion, or because they need to be distinguished in order to justify your conclusion, can and should be cited for this purpose: use them in such a way that their relevance is clear. Otherwise do not cite them at all.

It will usually be sufficient simply to mention the name of the case in an appropriate and relevant way. It will only occasionally be relevant to set out the facts and *ratio* of a reported case, in which case try to make it part of your reasoning, rather than simply setting it out descriptively, like a chunk from a textbook. Never copy out headnotes of cases in your opinion.

Wherever you cite a case, or refer to a textbook, give the full reference, so that your instructing solicitor can look it up, and for your own future use.

7.7.3 DEALING WITH LACK OF INFORMATION

You will never receive a set of instructions that contains every single point of information you could possibly want. There will always be some gaps. What you cannot do is use lack of information as an excuse for not advising. You must *never* say, 'I cannot advise on this point because I have not been told whether . . .' and then go no further.

You must always advise as fully as you can on the information you have. Even if there is something absolutely central to your opinion missing, you can still follow this rule. Sometimes the less information you have, the longer your opinion needs to be, because you will have to advise in such a way as to cover several eventualities. If your opinion depends on whether the claimant did or did not know that he had a flat tyre, you must say what your opinion would be if he did know and what it would be if he did not.

Where there are gaps in your instructions, it is essential that you should identify them and point them out to your instructing solicitors in your opinion. If there is information you need, you ask for it. In practice, if you could obtain it by telephoning your instructing solicitor, you should do so. Otherwise ask for it in your opinion. But do not ask for information just for the sake of it. Always make it clear what you want that information for and how it will affect your opinion. If it will not make any difference to your opinion, do not ask for it.

7.7.4 LENGTH

The question of the right length for an opinion is a tricky one. Some barristers write at greater length than others. Excessive length and excessive brevity are both common faults in students' opinions.

The aim must be to write an opinion that is just the right length in all the circumstances. A balance must be struck between completeness and conciseness, both as a matter of content and as a matter of style. But in fact the right length for an opinion is more an issue of content. Differences simply of *style* do not affect the length of an opinion all that much.

An opinion that is too short is usually too short because of inadequate analysis of the issues, inadequate thought or inadequate reasoning. In other words it is superficial. Only occasionally is excessive brevity the result of over-enthusiastic pruning. More usually an opinion which is too short fails to say all that needs to be said and does so because the writer has failed to identify what needs to be said.

An opinion that is too long is usually too long because of an over-academic approach by a writer who has failed to distinguish between an opinion and an essay. The essence of an opinion is that it sets out the fruits of the research and thinking process, not that process itself. You should not bring in to the opinion every avenue of thought and reasoning that you have pursued. You should set out the conclusions you have reached at the end of the day and the advice you accordingly wish to give. If the case is complex, you do not 'do it justice' by writing a complex opinion, but rather by penetrating to the core of the matter, stripping it down to its bare essentials, unravelling all the complexities and encapsulating the result in a clear and concise opinion.

For this reason, if for no other, opinion writing is a skill in a way that essay writing is not.

7.8   Style

It goes without saying that your opinion should be written in clear, stylistic, fluent English. This will, however, inevitably be of your own individual style. Some barristers tend to write in short, punchy sentences; others prefer immaculately constructed, mellifluous sentences of 100 words or more. Either will be fine, if the opinion has all the qualities of a good opinion. Short, punchy sentences must not result in inaccuracy, or incomplete reasoning; long sentences must still be grammatical and easy to read. Your opinion ideally should be complete, but not a word longer than necessary. If you have the ability to be concise, brief and snappy without any sacrifice of content, this is ideal.

Within the opinion, try to stick to ordinary, everyday language, and avoid archaisms and pomposities like 'the said motor vehicle', 'the matters aforementioned', 'hereinafter referred to as the relevant date'. Phrases like this are derived from statements of case, and even there they are somewhat out of date. They have no place in an opinion, where there is no need for excessive formality or pedantic accuracy. Use the plain English you would use to write a letter. Perhaps not any kind of letter, but the kind of letter you would write, say, to your bank manager. You would not say, 'I am enquiring about the balance of my account (hereinafter referred to as my overdraft)'. Don't say it in an opinion either.

The one and only formality which remains conventional and which you should adopt is to refer to your instructing solicitors as 'Instructing Solicitors', usually with capital initials, and in the third person rather than the second person throughout. But do not refer to yourself in the third person: write 'I advise that', not 'Counsel advises that'.

Be polite, both to your client and to your instructing solicitor. Address your client as you would address him or her face to face: 'Mr Jones', not 'Jones' or 'Jack'; it is preferable to call him or her by name rather than to refer to him as 'the claimant'. Do not suggest that your client may be lying. Do not pass moral judgments upon him or her. Do not start an argument with your instructing solicitors, or accuse them of incompetence. Treat them with respect, as fellow professional lawyers.

Finally remember what has already been said: there is no one right way to write an opinion. Strive for perfection, but do not expect you will ever achieve it, or that there can ever be such a thing in reality. No two barristers will agree about the perfect opinion.

7.9   When you have Finished your Opinion

When your opinion has been typed, sign the typed copy, put a cross through the title of the action on the backsheet of your advice and on the backsheet of your instructions. Endorse the backsheet of your instructions 'Opinion enclosed', and sign it.

Then hand your opinion, tied up in the red tape on the outside of your instructions, to your clerk, who will (a) note the fee that you are going to charge for your opinion, and (b) let your solicitors know that the papers are ready and take their instructions as to whether they will collect the papers or would like them to be sent back by post or document exchange.

Remember also that the instructions may come back to you in the future. If so your original opinion should be included. But it may not be: so make sure you keep a copy just in case!

Further Reading

Blake, Susan, *A Practical Approach to Legal Advice and Drafting*, 4th edn, Blackstone Press Ltd, 1993.

EIGHT

THE USE OF LAW IN AN OPINION

8.1   Introduction

The purpose of this chapter is to explore further the part played by law in an opinion.

It is in the use of law that the difference between writing an essay and writing an opinion becomes clearest. In essay-writing the main object is to write about the law. In opinion writing the main object is to advise a client what to do next. In opinion writing, the law is simply a means to an end; it is never an end in itself. The law is merely part of the reasoning process.

Whilst it is impracticable to draw up a list of hard-and-fast rules, this chapter is intended to provide some guidance on how law should be used in opinion writing.

8.1.1   DO NOT GIVE A LAW LECTURE

Even though an opinion may require legal research and will have to contain advice given within a legal framework, the opinion must not give abstract advice. It must, in other words, be firmly anchored in the facts of the case with which you are dealing. It follows that the law must be related carefully to the facts of the case.

The opinion must be written in a way which is practical, not academic. Neither your instructing solicitor nor your lay client wants to read a legal treatise. They want advice which is specific to the instructions with which you are dealing. It is therefore important that you do not try to give a law lecture in your opinion. If you find yourself setting out the law in the sort of detail to be found in textbooks and articles, you will almost certainly be writing an essay, not an opinion.

For example, if you are advising on damages in a case involving breach of contract, the following text would need considerable pruning:

> *The object of the award of the damages in a case of breach of contract is to put the claimant in the position, so far as money can do so, he or she would have been in had the contract been properly performed. It was held in* Hadley v Baxendale *(1854) 9 Exch 341 (followed in* Victoria Laundry v Newman *[1949] 2 KB 528) that loss would only be recoverable if it was within the contemplation of the parties at the time they entered into the contract. This will be the case in one of two circumstances:*
>
> > *(1)   The damage is such as may fairly and reasonably be regarded as arising naturally, i.e. in the ordinary course of things, from the breach; or*
> >
> > *(2)   the defendant was aware that this particular type of loss would flow because of the breach of the contract because of special knowledge which he had at the time of making the contract (usually derived from something the claimant has said to the defendant).*
>
> *For example, if A contracts with B that A will repair a piece of machinery belonging to B and A fails to repair the machinery properly and B thereby loses an exceptionally*

lucrative contract, A would only be liable for the resulting loss of profit, insofar as it exceeds the loss of profit which could be expected to arise in any event, if he knew of its existence.

In tort, on the other hand, the test of remoteness (see The Wagon Mound *[1961] AC 388 and* The Wagon Mound (No. 2) *[1967] 1 AC 617) is whether the type of loss sustained by the claimant was a reasonably foreseeable consequence of the tort committed by the defendant. If the type of loss is a reasonably foreseeable consequence, it does not matter that the degree of loss is much greater than expected (Smith v Leech Brain [1962] 2 QB 405).*

The law is set out in too much detail (especially in light of the fact that the principles being set out would be well known to your instructing solicitor already). The paragraph about tortious damages is of course irrelevant to a case where the only possible liability is contractual. It would have been much better to write something like this:

The first loss which the company sustained was the loss of profit on its contract with Widgets Ltd. The repairer had visited the company's premises on three occasions and must have seen that the company had only one moulding machine. It must therefore have been within the contemplation of the repairer that if this machine were to be out of action for longer than anticipated, the company would be unable to manufacture goods produced by that machine. The consequent loss of profit must therefore have been within the repairer's contemplation.

8.2 Dealing with the Well-known Principle of Law

There is no need to set out basic principles of law with which instructing solicitors will be familiar.

Example: Suppose that you are writing an opinion in respect of a claim arising from a road accident. To write, '*Following the neighbour principle established in* Donoghue v Stephenson *[1932] AC 562, one road user owes a duty of care to another road user*' is unnecessary. It is obvious that one road user owes a duty of care to another, and so the point does not have to be made expressly. The appropriate starting point would be to say that the defendant was (or was not) in breach of the duty of care owed to the claimant because . . .

8.3 Only Cite Authorities on Points of Law

Do not make a statement of fact and then cite a case to support it.

Example: Suppose that you are writing an opinion in respect of a claim arising out of the alleged negligence of a doctor. It would be wrong to include a sentence which reads, '*In my view, the court will find that the doctor was in breach of the duty of care he owed the patient: see* Bolam v Friern Hospital Management *[1957] 1 WLR 582*'.

The relevance of the *Bolam* test is that it establishes that a doctor is to be judged according to the standard of what a reasonable doctor would do. It follows that this authority should be dealt with like this:

In Bolam v Friern Hospital Management *[1957] 1 WLR 852 it was held that a doctor is to be judged according to the standard of what a reasonable doctor would do. In the present case, the doctor failed to do what a reasonable doctor would have done in the circumstances in that . . .*

8.4 How to Cite Cases

Where it is necessary to cite a case, you should always give a citation for that case, for example *Caparo* v *Dickman* [1990] 2 AC 605.

The rest of this section is concerned with deciding which case or cases to cite.

8.4.1 DEALING WITH A MINOR POINT

Where you wish to refer to a point of law with which your instructing solicitor may well be familiar but where you also wish to show that there is support for the proposition of law you have just set out, it is usually sufficient to set out the proposition of law and then cite the authority for that proposition. In this instance, you are summarising the effect of the earlier decision, not relying on a specific dictum. Here, it is sufficient to set out the proposition of law and then give the name of the case, together with its citation.

For example:

> *An accountant is only liable for negligently prepared accounts if reliance by the claimant on those accounts was reasonably foreseeable* (Caparo v Dickman [1990] 2 AC 605).

8.4.2 DEALING WITH A MORE IMPORTANT SOURCE

Where the source plays a more important role in your reasoning process, you generally need to deal more carefully with that source. In this instance, you should set out the basis of the decision you are relying on. Then apply the law you have stated to the facts upon which you are asked to advise.

Example: You are asked to advise someone who was prosecuted by the police because the police had been given incorrect information by an informant who bore a grudge against your client. One of the possible causes of action you consider is a claim for malicious prosecution. Your legal research reveals a case called *Martin* v *Watson* [1995] 3 All ER 559, decided in the House of Lords.

That part of your advice might read as follows:

> *In* Martin v Watson *[1995] 3 All ER 559 it was held by the House of Lords that, for the purposes of a claim for malicious prosecution, the person who supplied the information on which the police acted may be regarded as the prosecutor. However, this will only be so where the prosecution is brought by the police as a result of information received from the informant, the informant agrees to give evidence against the accused, and the informant is the only person who could give evidence against the accused (there being no other witnesses).*
>
> *In the present case, the evidence of the informant was supported by that of another witness. Thus, the prosecution in this case did not result exclusively from information supplied by the informant; there was other evidence upon which the police were able to base their judgment to arrest the accused. It follows that the informant in the present case cannot be regarded as the prosecutor, and so a claim for malicious prosecution against her would be bound to fail.*

8.4.3 SET OUT THE FACTS OF THE CASE AND THEN PARAPHRASE OR QUOTE PART OF A JUDGMENT

In many instances, it is sufficient to refer to the overall effect of the case without referring to a specific dictum. If a case is central to your reasoning, however, it may well be appropriate to quote from the judgment(s) in the report of the case. The words you are relying on will only make sense if the context of those words is made clear and so some of the background to the case has to be set out. When setting out the words you rely on you should paraphrase rather than quote from your source if you can shorten the text by so doing.

Example: You are asked to advise someone accused of murder. Your client admits killing the victim but wants to rely on the defence of provocation. At the time of the incident, your client was suffering from the effect of an hallucinogenic drug and was taunted by his wife for allowing himself to be in such a state. One of the cases you find in your legal research is *R v Morhall* [1995] 3 All ER 659. When dealing with this authority, you need to make it plain that the defendant in that case acted under the influence of glue-sniffing, rather than hallucinogenic drugs. You might say something like this:

> In *R v Morhall* [1995] 3 All ER 659 the defendant had been glue-sniffing. The deceased chided him about his glue-sniffing and a fight ensued in which the deceased was fatally stabbed with a knife by the defendant. It was held by the House of Lords that the general rule is that the effect of intoxication (whether alcohol, drugs or glue) is to be disregarded in assessing whether the accused acted as a reasonable person might have done. However, where the accused is 'taunted with his addiction . . . or even with having been intoxicated (from any cause) on some previous occasion . . . it may where relevant be taken into account as going to the gravity of the provocation' (per Lord Goff at p. 667).
>
> In the present case, the provocation was closely connected with the fact that the accused had been taking an hallucinogenic drug. The jury should therefore be directed that the effect of the drug is to be taken into account when considering whether the accused responded to the provocation in a way that a reasonable person might have done.

If you wish to paraphrase rather than quote, then you could do so thus:

> In *R v Morhall* [1995] 3 All ER 659 the defendant had been glue-sniffing. The deceased chided him about his glue-sniffing and a fight ensued in which the deceased was fatally stabbed with a knife by the defendant. The House of Lords affirmed the general rule is that the effect of intoxication (whether alcohol, drugs or glue) is to be disregarded in assessing whether the accused acted as a reasonable person might have done. However, Lord Goff (at p. 667) held that intoxication may be taken into account where the accused is taunted with the fact of his intoxication or with the fact that he is addicted to drink or drugs as the case may be. Lord Goff said that such taunts could be relevant to the gravity of the provocation.

8.5 Show the Relevance of the Case

Whichever of the methods suggested in **8.4** you decide to adopt for a particular case, it is essential that you make it clear *why* you have chosen to cite a particular case. In other words, you must make clear what statement or principle of law you have derived from that case.

This is good discipline. If you are unable to show why you have cited the case, then either that case is irrelevant or you have not properly understood the effect of that case. In either situation, it has no part to play in the chain of reasoning which leads to the conclusions you have reached.

8.6 Which Case(s) to Cite

If there are several cases which appear relevant, you do not need to cite them all. Certain general principles may be applied:

(a) Cite the case which is the most authoritative: if a House of Lords decision is on point, you should cite that in preference to a later decision of the Court of Appeal which merely applies the law stated in the House of Lords case.

(b) Where a later case interprets, or seeks to resolve, an ambiguity in an earlier case, you will need to cite both if the later interpretation is relevant to the case in which you are advising.

(c) You should generally cite only the case which lays down the general principle; do not cite cases which merely apply that general principle without adding to it in any way. For example, when dealing with the requirement of confidentiality which is implied into contracts of employment, it is usually enough to cite the leading case, *Faccenda Chicken* v *Fowler* [1987] Ch 117.

However, there will be instances where one case sets out a general principle and a later case then applies that principle to a set of facts which are very similar to those of the case in which you are advising. For instance, *Caparo* v *Dickman* [1990] 2 AC 605 sets out the general principle that liability for economic loss due to negligent advice is usually confined to cases where the advice has been given for a specific purpose, of which the giver of the advice was aware. In *Spring* v *Guardian Assurance plc* [1994] 3 All ER 129 the House of Lords had to consider whether a person who supplies a character reference to a prospective employer owes a duty of care to the job applicant to ensure the accuracy of the reference. If you were to be instructed in a case involving an inaccurate employment reference, or something analogous to such a reference, it would be appropriate to cite *Spring*, rather than *Caparo*.

(d) Do not cite earlier cases if a later case sets out authoritatively the principle to be applied. So, where one House of Lords case restates a principle set out in an earlier decision of the House of Lords, you need only refer to the later decision. For example, in the provocation example (above), *R* v *Morhall* may be cited in preference to *DPP* v *Camplin* [1978] AC 705.

(e) In some instances, the law which is relevant to the opinion you are writing is based on a series of cases. This will be so where an area of law is being developed by the courts, so that each of a series of cases adds something new to the case which preceded it. Sometimes, it is appropriate to refer to the cases all together; sometimes you should deal briefly with each case, showing what each case adds to the principles established by the earlier cases. But remember that you must always focus on the principles that are relevant to the case in which you are advising.

(f) You must avoid giving a history lesson, for example by referring to a source which no longer represents the law. An example of this fault would be to write:

In Hollington *v* Hewthorn *[1943] 1 KB 587 it was held that evidence of a conviction in a criminal court could not be tendered in evidence in a civil case based on the same facts. The effect of this decision was reversed by the Civil Evidence Act 1968, s. 11, which states that evidence of a conviction is admissible in civil proceedings if it is relevant to an issue in those proceedings.*

The effect of *Hollington* v *Hewthorn* is irrelevant (since it was reversed by the statute) and should be omitted: you should set out the law as it is, not as it was.

It would have been much better to write:

Civil Evidence Act 1968, s. 11, states that evidence of a conviction is admissible in civil proceedings if it is relevant to an issue in those proceedings.

(h) It follows from these general guidelines that some of the law which you find in the course of your legal research should be omitted from your opinion. The following summary should help to remind you of some of the pitfalls:

(i) Do not cite several cases which all say the same thing.

(ii) Do not go off at a tangent (ask yourself whether you are writing things which are relevant to your instructions).

    (iii)   Do not try to show off your legal research abilities. Remember that all the law you cite must be relevant to the case in which you are advising. It will often be the case that you spend a considerable length of time finding some law, only to decide that it is not sufficiently relevant to merit use in the opinion you eventually write.

8.7   Using Statutory Materials

Much of what has been said about the use of case law applies equally to statutes. In particular:

(a)   Only cite a statutory source if it in an integral part of the reasoning which supports your conclusions.

(b)   Only cite the statutory source which is in force at the time when the facts of the case in which you are advising took place.

(c)   If you can paraphrase the statutory wording, so as to make it shorter or clearer, then you should do so.

For example, Theft Act 1968, s. 6 says that:

> *A person appropriating property belonging to another without meaning the other permanently to lose the thing itself is nevertheless to be regarded as having the intention of permanently depriving the other of it if his intention is to treat the thing as his own to dispose of regardless of the other's rights; and a borrowing or lending of it may amount to so treating it if, but only if, the borrowing or lending is for a period and in circumstances making it equivalent to an outright taking or disposal.*

It would be better to paraphrase this fairly long and convoluted provision:

> *Theft Act, s. 6 provides that a person can still appropriate property even if he does not intend the owner to lose the property permanently. This will be the case where the appropriator treats the property as his own, regardless of the other person's rights. If a person borrows property belonging to someone else, the borrower can still intend to deprive the owner of the property permanently if the borrowing in fact amounts to an outright taking.*

If you decide to paraphrase rather than to quote from a statute, you should take care that your paraphrase is accurate.

Statutes should be referred to by their short titles: for example, the Criminal Appeal Act 1995. Statutory instruments should be cited with both their title and number: for example, the Magistrates' Courts Rules 1981 (SI 1981/552).

Where a statute (or statutory instrument) has been amended, you should only cite it in its amended form (assuming that the amendment was in force at the relevant time). For example, it would be appropriate to write: 'The Children and Young Persons Act 1933, s. 49(5) (as amended) provides that . . .'.

8.8   Which Sources to Cite

Usually, you should cite only primary sources (that is statutes, statutory instruments and cases). However, the citation of textbooks and articles is acceptable in exceptional cases. For example, where there is no authority on a point, academic opinion may be a useful guide to the answer; similarly if there are conflicting decisions and the conflict cannot be resolved by applying the doctrine of precedent (*stare decisis*), as where the only relevant decisions are conflicting decisions of the High Court, academic opinion may well be of assistance.

8.9   Apply the Law to the Facts

A common fault is to cite a case but not show how the case supports the proposition for which it is cited. If a source (such as a case) is worth citing, the relevance of that source should be made apparent. You should show how any source you have cited helps you reach your conclusion.

There is a test which you can apply to make sure that you are doing this. After you have made a statement of law, apply it to the facts. This is a good way of ensuring that you are not writing an essay.

For example:

In Alcock *v* Chief Constable of South Yorkshire *[1992] 1 AC 310 the House of Lords held that one of the preconditions to a claim for nervous shock by a bystander who suffered psychiatric illness as the result of injuries negligently caused to someone else, was that the bystander should witness the accident or its immediate aftermath. In the present case, Mrs Jones did not see the injuries sustained by her son until she saw him in hospital some six hours after the accident. In my view, this was not sufficiently close in time to the accident to satisfy this requirement.*

8.10   Producing Sound Conclusions

If you are writing an essay, there is often no need for that essay to set out a firm conclusion; it is enough for there to have been a wide-ranging discussion of the law. In an opinion, of course, the same does not hold true. Conclusions must be expressed; otherwise your instructing solicitor and your lay client will not have been advised what to do next.

If the result of your legal research is that there is clearly a right answer to a particular question, that answer must be stated and the reason why it is the right answer must be made apparent. If the result of your legal research is that there is no single right answer, as where there is no statutory provision or case law directly on point, the possible answers should be set out and the opinion should suggest which answer is most likely to be right and must give reasons for that view.

For an opinion to be of an acceptable standard, the conclusions it contains must be sound and must be supported by sound reasoning. In this context, the word 'sound' may be taken to mean 'the right answer or, if there is no single right answer, an answer which may be argued with a reasonable prospect of success'.

When you are writing an opinion, you must remember that you are no longer writing an essay for a law tutor but you are learning to write an opinion for a real client with a real problem. This means that your advice must be realistic. It is not appropriate to advise a client that they have a strong case if the weight of authority goes against your client's case but you think that the House of Lords may ultimately support it. So it would in the vast majority of cases be wrong to say that your client has a good case on the basis that a previous decision of the Court of Appeal is incorrect. It follows that you should not base your opinion on a dissenting judgment in the Court of Appeal, even if you think that the dissenting judgment would ultimately be approved by the House of Lords; similarly, dissenting speeches in the House of Lords should not form the basis of your conclusion.

8.11   Examples

For some examples of opinions involving law in their reasoning, see **10.9–10.11**.

NINE

AN ILLUSTRATION OF THE OPINION WRITING PROCESS

This chapter endeavours to set out the process of moving from a set of instructions to the writing of an opinion, looking both at the mental process and the preparatory work required. As in much skills work, this guide is not intended to be mandatory, but to provide a suggested basis on which you can build good working practices. This chapter picks up and illustrates many of the points made in **Chapters 7** and **8**.

9.1 Instructions to Counsel

JACKIE RUSSELL

v

WATCHDOGS LIMITED

Counsel is instructed on behalf of Mrs Jackie Russell, who is the owner of Falstaff Farm, Gadshill, Kent where she breeds and trains racing greyhounds.

At night the greyhounds are locked into the kennel compound, which consists of two kennels, each housing about ten dogs, in a courtyard enclosed by a high wall with a single iron gate. Outside the courtyard is an exercise area entirely surrounded by a wire-mesh fence. To keep watch, Mrs Russell hires a security company, Watchdogs Ltd ('Watchdogs'). By a contract made in January 1995 Watchdogs agreed, for a fixed charge (at the material time £70.50 per week), to provide a night patrol service whereby a patrolman would visit and check the kennel enclosure four times a night between the hours of 9.00 p.m. and 7.00 a.m. The contract contained the following clause:

> Under no circumstances shall the company be held responsible for any loss suffered by the customer through burglary, theft, fire, criminal damage or any other cause, except insofar as such loss is attributable to the negligence of the employees of the company acting within the course of their employment.

Throughout the period of the contract the regular patrolman has been Mr Harry Prince, whom Mrs Russell and her family have got to know quite well. However, on occasions (e.g., when prowlers have been seen, or the night before a major race meeting) Mrs Russell has felt that additional security is necessary and has telephoned Watchdogs which has provided an all-night watchman at a fixed fee of £94.00 per night. There is no mention of this service in the contract.

On 18 April 1999 Mr Prince reported to Mrs Russell that on two occasions the previous night he had seen prowlers near the perimeter fence who had run off when challenged. Mrs Russell asked him to be particularly vigilant the next night and immediately telephoned Watchdogs to ask for an all-night patrol that night, which was agreed. No payment in advance was requested and indeed nothing was said about money.

That night, Mrs Russell's daughter, Elizabeth, was in the Boar's Head Inn, which is 100 yards away from Falstaff Farm, and saw Harry Prince drinking with a companion.

He was there at 9.00 p.m. when she arrived and was still there at 11.30 p.m. when she left. Believing an all-night patrol had been arranged, she thought nothing of it. In fact it seems no all-night patrolman arrived.

The next morning, 19 April, Mrs Russell found that raiders had broken into the kennels. Two greyhounds, Pistol and Poins, were missing and a third, Peto, was dead. A veterinary surgeon found that he had been strangled and put the time of death at around midnight. The police found evidence that two men had cut a hole in the wire fence, sawn through the padlock on the iron gate and picked the lock on the kennel door. All had been left open. The police estimate that it would have taken the raiders about one hour to get in.

Pistol has never been found and it appears that he was the raiders' target. Poins apparently escaped through the open fence and roamed the countryside for two days. He was shot dead by a local farmer when he attacked the farmer's sheep.

Pistol had just retired from racing and was now at stud. He was expected to earn around £10,000 a year over the next five years in stud fees. Poins and Peto were both successful dogs each of whom was expected to win races worth £5,000 in all in 1999 and again in 2000. They would then have retired. Poins would have gone to stud. The estimated value of the three dogs is: Pistol £20,000; Poins £17,500; Peto £8,000. Mrs Russell was deeply distressed at the loss of her three favourite dogs and suffered from depression for several months.

Instructing Solicitors have received the following letter from Watchdogs:

Dear Sirs,

We must inform you that we have no record of any telephone conversation with your client on 18 April 1999 and we deny that any agreement to provide an all-night watchman service on that night was entered into. Mr Prince's log for that night shows that he made four visits, at 12.30, 2.30, 4.30 and 6.30 a.m. Your client's loss is plainly not attributable to any negligence on the part of our employees and we must accordingly deny any liability.

Yours etc.

Mrs Russell on 3 July 1999 received a bill from Watchdogs containing the following items:

	£
Night patrol service 1 April to 30 June 1999 12 weeks at £70.50	846.00
All-night watchman service 3 nights at £94.00	282.00
	1,128.00

Mrs Russell says she arranged for an all-night watchman on three occasions in the period covered by the bill: on 2 and 18 April and 31 May.

Counsel is requested to advise Mrs Russell as to liability and quantum.

9.2 Preparing to Write an Opinion

9.2.1 READ THE BRIEF THOROUGHLY

Your first step is to read the instructions in *Jackie Russell* v *Watchdogs Ltd* slowly and carefully. This brief consists only of instructions with no enclosures, so this is quite straightforward. There is no need to order papers before you start to read.

Be careful of forming strong views about the case on first reading, or you may prejudice the depth and width of your analysis in the following stages. In reading this brief the point is not to label the case 'breach of contract' as soon as possible, but on initial reading only to absorb as much of the factual background as possible. At this stage your mind should be asking questions about what caused the dogs to be lost, which is clearly the client's central problem, rather than starting to take decisions. The brief should provide counsel with all essential information or the solicitor may be found to be in gross dereliction of duty (*Locke* v *Camberwell Health Authority* (1989) *The Times*, 11 December 1989), but for reasons of time and cost it will rarely be very comprehensive.

9.2.2   CLARIFY YOUR OBJECTIVES

What do your instructions ask you to do? The instructions will never ask you to write all you know that is vaguely legally relevant, but will set you specific tasks, which are normally set out at the start or the end of the instructions. Here you are asked to advise on liability and quantum — whether the client can sue and if so how much she will get.

Having read the brief once and clarified your objectives, it is useful to read it again and annotate it. Annotating on first reading can be dangerous as what you are being asked to do may not be clear in your mind, especially in this case where your tasks are only set out at the end of the instructions. In annotating you should underline or highlight those points which are most relevant to whether there is a cause of action and to what has been lost, perhaps using a separate coloured pen for different aspects of the case, such as cause of action and damages.

9.2.3   ANALYSE THE FACTS

Before you form views on the appropriate legal solution you will need to carry out a thorough fact management exercise. The legal argument must be based on the facts, not twisted to fit your preconceived legal theory.

Methods of fact management are dealt with in the fact management chapters of **Case Preparation**. Written notes of facts will be part of preparing to write any opinion. The following is a very basic analysis of the *Russell* case.

People   Mrs Russell. Client. Claimant.
Watchdogs Ltd. Employed to keep watch on premises. Potential Defendant?
Mr Prince. Employee of Watchdogs Ltd. Regular patrolman. Witness? Potential Defendant?
Elizabeth Russell. Daughter of client. Witness?
Police. Report on break-in.
Vet. Report on death of dog.
Those who broke in. Seems they cannot be traced.

Places   Mrs Russell's kennels. A plan would be useful.

Dates   January 1995. Contract for patrol service made.
18 April 1999. Prowlers suspected.
Mrs Russell calls to book all-night service.
9.00–11.30 p.m. Mr Prince in the pub.
12.00 a.m. Break-in.
12.30, 2.30, 4.30, 6.30 a.m. Mr Prince visits.
19 April 1999. Loss discovered.
July 1999. Quarterly bill for April–June sent.

Figures   Cost of patrol service. £70.50 per week
Cost of all-night watchman. £94.00
Loss of dogs. Capital value of Pistol, Peto, and Poins £45,500
Income. Loss of stud fees for Pistol £10,000 per year × 5 years
Loss of winnings for Poins and Peto £5,000 per year × 2 years each

Having analysed the basic facts, three further stages of factual analysis are important in preparing to write an opinion, because they are all closely related to exercising your judgment on the chances of the case succeeding.

(a) *Identify any gaps in the facts* Almost certainly your instructions will not give you all the facts, as it would be very expensive and time consuming for instructing solicitors to collect everything before sending a case to a barrister. Your opinion will have to be based on the facts that are available. Gaps in the facts are important first because they may prove a weakness in developing a legal case, and secondly because in your opinion you will need to indicate to instructing solicitors what extra information should be sought. The main gaps in the facts in this case are:

   (i) limited information about the agreement for an all-night watchman on 18 April;

   (ii) limited information about the actions of Mr Prince that night;

   (iii) limited information about the break-in;

   (iv) limited information about the ability of the dogs to win races.

(b) *Identify which facts are probably agreed, and which are probably in dispute* The point is that a case can be most firmly founded on facts that are agreed. Where facts are in dispute, your case is open to challenge and is less strong. Again this will be directly relevant to exercising your judgment on the case. In this case the facts which are probably agreed are:

   (i) the existence of the original contract;

   (ii) that the dogs were lost.

   The main facts which are likely to be in dispute are:

   (i) whether there was an agreement for an all-night watchman to come on 18 April;

   (ii) what Mr Prince did on the night of 18 April;

   (iii) precisely when the break-in occurred;

   (iv) loss and damage.

(c) *Identify which facts you have evidence of* This is especially important in relation to facts in issue — if you have a fact in issue on which you have little or no evidence your case is very weak! Again this will be important when you come on to exercise your judgment. Also, your opinion should indicate to instructing solicitors where evidence is required.

   In this case, the evidence which we have is:

   (i) the original contract;

   (ii) Mrs Russell's oral evidence;

   (iii) Elizabeth's oral evidence (but query if some of this is hearsay);

   (iv) Mr Prince's oral evidence (but query if he would appear as a witness for our client or for Watchdogs, and how useful his evidence would be if he is still employed by Watchdogs);

   (v) the police report about the break-in;

    (vi)   the evidence of the quarterly bill (which is not very clear as it does not give dates for the all-night service);

    (vii)   evidence on death of dogs.

(d)   *Identify which facts you need evidence for*   The further evidence we will need is:

    (i)   all possible evidence about the making of the contract for an all-night watchman on 18 April;

    (ii)   evidence about what Mr Prince did on the night of 18 April;

    (iii) evidence of the capital value of the dogs (you cannot simply assume the figures in the brief are correct);

    (iv) evidence of the income the dogs will lose, which may be pure conjecture.

An important point about analysing the facts in the brief. When students start learning to write opinions it is very common for them to say that they feel they cannot proceed until they know all the facts. Such an attitude shows a failure to appreciate what the role of the barrister is and how cases must be put together in real life. Of course it is right that in practice one can telephone a solicitor to get further information, or even have a conference with a client, but this is not a reason for failing to write an opinion at an early stage, for several reasons:

(a)   It is unrealistic to think that you will ever have all the facts about a situation. Some information is lost or destroyed, and other things are simply never recorded in any form.

(b)   Some information is just not available to a client or his representatives as it is known only to the other side or to someone else.

(c)   Only limited information will be available at an early stage in a case when initial advice must be given.

(d)   Information takes time to collect, and it may well be that a client wants a general opinion without waiting.

(e)   Information costs money. Costs should only be incurred gathering information when it is clear that this is necessary.

(f)   Solicitors will normally not wish to take time and money gathering substantial factual information before sending a case to counsel. They will wait for counsel's directions as to what is really required.

Therefore you must get used to dealing with gaps in factual knowledge in a positive way. Do identify precisely what information is needed and why and also build up confidence in using professional judgment.

9.2.4   ANALYSE THE LEGAL ISSUES

Once the facts are fully analysed it is safe to start to analyse legal issues. This is where the professional ability of the barrister begins to come into play, deciding what legal possibilities there are, and which is strongest. The first question here is whether there is a cause of action, and it is best to try to consider every possibility, even if some are then dropped.

(a)   *Breach of contract*   The fact that there is a contract makes this an obvious possibility, but you must define precisely the contract and the breach. The contract in this case might be either the written contract signed in 1995, or a separate contract for an overnight watchman made orally on 18 April 1999.

As for the breach, start first by considering the express terms and how they might have been broken. There may be a breach of an express term, if it could be proved that Mr Prince never visited the premises at all on the night in question, or if there was a contract for an all-night watchman, and no all-night watchman came.

Go on to consider possible implied terms, remembering that you need to find terms that the court would be prepared to imply, and which you can show have been breached, leading to your client's loss. This needs professional ability. It is not easy in this case as a number of terms that might be implied would not give rise to a claim, because the theft of the dogs would still not have been prevented.

(b) *Negligence* The fact that there is a contract should not lead you to think that only a contractual action is possible. This is the sort of error that results from taking quick decisions when reading instructions. Because the loss may arguably have been caused by a failure to act properly, negligence is clearly an alternative. However, because in this particular case the duty of care that might give rise to a negligence claim is basically contractual, it may well be better to argue there is an implied term in the contract that the watchman should act with reasonable care and skill, rather than to argue negligence as a separate cause of action.

(c) *Other tort actions* As the central problem is the loss of the dogs, suing those who killed or took the dogs for conversion or trespass is an option. The difficulty here is obviously that these people cannot be traced. It is important to think widely in this way in planning an opinion, even if the option is dropped immediately as not being feasible.

Having looked for the range of possible causes of action, there is also the need to consider who should be sued. As has already been said, suing those who broke in is impossible here. The suggested defendant is Watchdogs Ltd, and this appears to be justified as the contract is with them. There is also the possibility of suing Mr Prince for negligence, but the case against him personally might be difficult to prove, and he is unlikely to be able to pay a substantial amount of damages. Professional judgment would therefore suggest simply relying on the vicarious liability of the employer.

9.2.5 ANALYSE THE CASE AGAINST YOU

The case against you needs to be analysed in factual terms and in legal terms. Factual points were dealt with in **9.2.3** above, with the need to identify gaps in facts, facts in issue, and evidential difficulties. All of these are directly relevant to deciding whether the case will succeed.

In legal terms it is necessary to consider possible defences. Here the first possible defence is simply to argue that there was no contract to provide an overnight watchman, which means that factual and evidential difficulties on this are particularly important. The second possible defence is to argue about what terms might reasonably be implied, which will require the preparation of good legal arguments on this point. The third line of defence is the exclusion clause, the effect of which will therefore require full consideration.

9.2.6 CARRY OUT ANY NECESSARY RESEARCH

It is important to take careful decisions as to what areas to research, or you will waste a substantial amount of time. **Do not start any research until you have fully analysed the facts and the law and can therefore draw up an appropriate research plan.** This cannot be over-emphasised. It is all too easy when first learning to write an opinion to do far too much legal research, for reasons that are not hard to see:

(a) academic study of law does require looking at the law in great detail, and it can be difficult to get away from this approach;

(b) if your knowledge of a particular area of law is limited or a little rusty it is very tempting to seek to re-learn the entire area;

(c) it is easy to be lured into feeling that reading a lot on an area may reveal a small point that will make a lot of difference to a case.

However, excessive legal research simply reveals a lack of good analytical powers and a lack of professional ability to work efficiently. This is not to say that detailed legal research of appropriate areas is not important, but it should be limited to what you have identified as being important for the case. The client does not want to know fine legal details but wants a result, and it is not reasonable to expect a brief fee to cover many hours of research that are not really necessary.

In this case you should not need to carry out any substantial research into contract law, as much of the law is basic principle. The legal analysis outlined in **9.2.5** might suggest that you would wish to research two areas:

(a) The circumstances in which a court will imply a term into a contract and what sort of term it might imply.

(b) The validity and effect of exclusion clauses.

9.2.7 USE YOUR PROFESSIONAL JUDGMENT

Now the professional ability really comes into play! You have a number of factual and legal pieces to fit together in a way that gives the client and the solicitor clear guidance. There is no easy way to explain how to do this — the proper exercise of professional ability can only come with practice — but what you are trying to do is to unite all the areas that have already been outlined:

(a) to assess all the legal possibilities;

(b) in the light of the facts, and

(c) in the light of the evidence, and

(d) in the light of what you know of the case for the other side,

(e) to weigh up which course is best;

(f) to meet the client's objectives.

Learning to use professional judgment is not easy. It is almost a chicken and egg situation. You cannot use judgment without professional experience, and you will not have the experience until you have had plenty of practice on cases. Thus to some extent a leap in the dark is required. However, confidence is an essential quality in a barrister, so you must have the confidence to start experimenting with using judgment to fill in gaps in a case and take decisions.

The first task in this case is to advise on a cause of action. From the points outlined above it would seem that the correct decision is that an action should be brought for breach of contract, relying on implied as well as express terms. The terms implied must be carefully chosen, and arguments must be found to avoid the operation of the exclusion clause.

The second task is to advise what the client can recover. This requires drawing up a comprehensive list of the heads of loss, looking at the arguments on each from the legal and practical point of view. The heads of loss are:

(a) The capital value of the three dogs.

(b) The lost prize money of all three.

    (c)   The lost stud fees.

    (d)   Mrs Russell's depression.

    (e)   The damage to the premises.

The difficulties are:

    (a)   Whether all loss is foreseeable.

    (b)   Whether all the loss can be proved.

    (c)   Whether there is any element of double recovery in claiming lost income and lost capital.

Figures for each head, collected together in analysing the facts, should be fully analysed here, with any appropriate calculation carried out.

9.2.8 DECIDE HOW TO EXPRESS YOUR OPINION

This is a professional skill that may require substantial practice and may well only come with experience. The difficulty is that you need to satisfy various requirements in expressing your opinion:

    (a)   Your opinion must be absolutely clear.

    (b)   If there are any options, they must be clear.

    (c)   Your opinion needs to weigh up and express the chances of success.

    (d)   Your opinion should avoid being too dogmatic or authoritarian. Give guidance on the law, but decisions on the case must finally be those of the client.

Combining these requirements is not easy, as they in some ways conflict. Guidance on expressing your opinion and giving your reasons is provided in the previous chapter. Do practice trying to find appropriate words and expressions.

9.2.9 DRAW UP A SKELETON OPINION

Before actually writing your opinion, you should draw up a framework of all the elements to be included. This should ensure that everything is covered, and that a clear structure is followed. It is a false economy to start by going straight into writing an opinion without drawing up a skeleton, as you will often find that you miss something out or get confused and have to start again. *You should never have to waste time writing an opinion out twice. The properly planned opinion will be right first time.*

In drawing up the framework, you should be synthesising, summarising and choosing from all the preparatory work you have done. *A good opinion is a summary of all the work you have done on the facts and the law; it should never include details of fact management or legal research.* Thus much of the analysis carried out in this section would never appear in the finished opinion.

The following suggested framework amalgamates the points discussed above in a way that forms the basis for the opinion that follows.

<u>OPINION</u>

1   Introduction

    (a)   Summarise briefly main facts of contract and loss.

    (b)   Summarise conclusion.

(i)   Action for breach of contract to provide all-night watchman.

(ii)   Action for breach of implied term of reasonable care and skill.

(iii) Will get damages for loss of dogs, but problems with causation and foreseeability, and with distress.

2   Causes of action

(a)   Discuss whether one contract or two, one for regular service and one for all-night watchman on 18 April. Conclude better to allege two for clarity and to help avoid problems with exclusion clause.

(b)   Express terms and breaches:

(i)   That there would be an all-night watchman. Provided prove contract for all-night watchman, which may be difficult, clear breach.

(c)   Implied terms and breaches:

(i)   That visits would be regular and/or sufficient for security. Implied to give contract business efficacy. Can probably show visits not sufficient for security, though note other side argues four visits made.

(ii)   That watchman would act with reasonable care and skill. Can rely on Supply of Goods and Services Act 1982, s. 13. Can probably show breach of this, not only in that break-in, but in that should have discovered it quickly (they claim Prince visited at 12.30).

3   Defences

(a)   Other side may argue that no contract for overnight watchman/no implied terms. Importance of evidence on the former, and legal argument and detailed wording on the latter.

(b)   Other side may seek to rely on exclusion clause. We should refute this by arguing:

(i)   not part of contract for all-night watchman;

(ii)   on proper construction does not apply, *Photo Production Ltd* v *Securicor* [1980] AC 827;

(iii) there was negligence so liable anyway.

Can't get rid of clause under Unfair Contract Terms Act 1977 since not dealing as consumer.

4   Quantum of damages

(a)   Capital value of dogs. Will need proof of value. May be causation and foreseeability problems with Peto and Poins.

£20,000 + £17,500 + £8,000 = £45,500

(b)   Loss of winnings. Can get damages for loss of a chance, *Chaplin* v *Hicks* [1911] 2 KB 786. However, may not get full loss as might not have won anyway. Need evidence of ability. Also problem of double recovery, as capital value partly based on ability to win. Also mitigation, deduct cost of keeping dogs.

£5,000 × 2 years × 2 dogs = £20,000

(c)   Loss of stud fees. Similar arguments.

Pistol £10,000 × 5 = £50,000

Poins the same?

(d)   Depression. Can't normally get this for contract action, but see *Jackson v Horizon Holidays* [1975] 1 WLR 1468. Just a chance if argue security of mind part of contract, *Hayes v Dodd* [1990] 2 All ER 815.

(e)   Damage to premises. Should be able to get damages for this. Need to establish figure.

5   Conclusion

Enclose draft. Offer further advice if appropriate.

Signed

Address

Date

9.3   Sample Opinion

JACKIE RUSSELL v WATCHDOGS LIMITED

OPINION

1   I am asked to advise Mrs Russell with regard to the loss of three dogs from her kennels at Falstaff Farm, Gadshill, Kent, where she breeds and trains racing greyhounds. This loss was suffered on the night of 18/19 April 1999, when following a break-in, one dog was taken, one escaped and one was killed. I am asked to advise whether Watchdogs Limited, a security company, can be held responsible for this loss for failing to keep adequate surveillance on her premises, and if so, what sum may be recovered by way of damages.

2   In summary, I would advise that Mrs Russell can sue Watchdogs Limited, alleging breach of the ageement to provide an all-night watchman, and breach of implied terms that the watchman would be present for sufficient periods to provide security, and would carry out his job with reasonable care and skill. There is a good chance that this action would succeed, and that Watchdogs would not be able to rely on the exclusion clause in the contract. I would anticipate recovering a substantial figure in damages, based primarily on the capital value of the lost dogs, though there may be some difficulty with causation as regards Poins. Arguments of foreseeability, double recovery and mitigation will almost certainly prevent full recovery of figures for lost winnings and stud fees, and I have some doubt whether a claim for distress suffered by Mrs Russell will succeed.

The contract(s)

3   The first issue is the precise contractual basis on which Watchdogs were employed. While I am sure that Instructing Solicitors have brought to my attention all the relevant terms of the written contract that Mrs Russell made with Watchdogs in January 1995, I would be grateful for a full copy of it. It is not clear whether the service on the night of 18/19 was provided under this contract and/or under an oral ageement made by telephone on 18 April.

4   It appears to have been the understanding of the parties that all services were provided under one contract. There appears to have been no separate negotiation of

terms beyond the mentioning of a price when an all-night watchman was provided previously, and the fact that Watchdogs appear to have understood all services to be provided under one contract is evidenced by their sending a single invoice for all. Perhaps instructing solicitors could check with Mrs Russell if this was her understanding.

5   However, the possibility that there was a separate contract for the all-night watchman is supported by the basic contractual principle that once a contract is reduced to writing it will normally be taken to include all the terms agreed between the parties. I am told that there was no provision at all for the all-night service in the written contract, and it seems that Mrs Russell did not even know that such a service was available until after she signed the contract. There is clearly a separate fee for the all-night service. Although it makes relatively little difference whether there was one contract or two, I would advise arguing that there were two contracts, both for the sake of clarity, and so that it can be argued that the terms of the written contract, in particular the exclusion clause, do not apply to the oral contract.

The breaches of contract

(a)   The agreement for an all-night patrol

6   The obligation under the oral agreement was to provide an all-night watchman for the evening in question. If we can establish this, there is a clear breach as it is admitted that no such watchman was supplied. The difficulty is to establish the agreement, as it was purely oral and has now been denied by Watchdogs. The evidence of Mrs Russell herself will be vital — could instructing solicitors please ascertain details of the telephone call she made. When did she make the call? Who did she speak to? What did she say? What was the reply? Can instructing solicitors also ascertain from Mrs Russell for what hours such a watchman would normally remain on the premises.

7   Evidence to support the making of an agreement for an overnight watchman on the night of the 18/19 would be very valuable. The difficulty here is of course that anyone who simply overheard the telephone conversation or was merely told about it will almost certainly only be able to provide hearsay evidence. It appears that the all-night watchman was sought following a conversation with Mr Prince. His evidence of this conversation might assist, but it is not clear whether we could or should lead his evidence. If Mr Prince is still employed by Watchdogs, he may well be called as a witness by them, and he may in any event not prove to be a useful witness for us due to a possible fear of losing his job. Even if he is not still employed by Watchdogs, our allegations cast doubt on his ability to do his job properly.

8   It may be possible to use the bill sent by Watchdogs as evidence of the agreement for the all-night watchman, though it does not specify the dates for which the charge is made. We might seek clarification from Watchdogs as to the dates involved now, or there may be some tactical value in waiting until trial and pursuing this in cross-examination. In any event, Mrs Russell should pay this bill, as it is the consideration for the contract on which she seeks to rely! There may be other evidence, perhaps provided by Watchdogs' records on discovery, and cross-examination seeking to establish that their office is not very efficiently run might prove effective.

(b)   The written contract to provide a night patrol service

9   The obligation under the written contract was to provide a regular night patrolman, his duty being to visit the kennel enclosure four times during the night between the hours of 9.00 p.m. and 7.00 a.m., and I understand that the regular patrolman making such calls was Mr Harry Prince. I assume he would not be the person to act as an all-night watchman when one was requested. As Watchdogs claim that Mr Prince did visit four times on the night in question there would seem to be no breach of any express term (but can instructing solicitors check with Mrs Russell whether she has any knowledge whether he did visit at the times alleged).

(i)   Breach of implied term to spread visits over whole night

10   The first possibility is to imply a term that the patrolman should visit regularly, or at least spread his visits so as to provide reasonable security. It could be argued that there is a breach in spreading visits over only six hours rather than over the full ten hours from 9.00 p.m to 7.00 a.m. I would advise that such an implied term be alleged on the basis that it would give business efficacy to the contract, though I have some doubt whether we would succeed in establishing it, not least because it would undermine the purpose of security if the watchman always came at the same time as a result of spreading his visits evenly. It may be that we will need to get evidence of the business practice of security firms if this issue proceeds to trial.

(ii)   Breach of implied term to act with reasonable care and skill

11   The alternative is to allege that there is an implied term that the watchman should do his work with reasonable care and skill. Such a term is implied by the Supply of Goods and Services Act 1982, s. 13, and it will be easier to establish breaches of it, not least in that Mrs Russell had asked for particular vigilance on the night of the break-in. Watchdogs have admitted in their letter that Mr Prince was the regular patrolman for the evening in question, so a breach would arise when he spent at least two and a half hours drinking before doing his night's work — thus undermining his ability to do his job properly. Could instructing solicitors please get a full statement from Elizabeth Russell to establish the details of this. What was Mr Prince drinking? How many drinks did he have?

12   A further breach would arise in that Mr Prince totally failed to realise that the premises had been broken into although he apparently called four times after the break-in occurred! As there is only one gate he can hardly have been doing his job properly. Although I am grateful for the description of the premises provided by the Instructing Solicitors, I would like to have a detailed plan of the premises, with measurements. A statement from the vet as to time of death of Peto will be required to prove the time of the break-in.

The exclusion clause

13   Instructing solicitors rightly draw my attention to the exclusion clause in the contract. While on the face of it this clause presents difficulties, as Watchdogs will certainly seek to rely on it, I feel that there are three ways of arguing that the clause should not apply. I do not think it can be argued that the clause should not apply as being unreasonable under the Unfair Contract Terms Act 1977, s. 3, since it seems unlikely that Mrs Russell was dealing as a consumer.

14   Firstly, if it is argued that the oral contract is separate from the written contract, it can be argued that the written term does not apply to the agreement for the all-night watchman. However, Watchdogs might argue that the clause does apply as a result of the course of dealing between the parties. Alternatively, it can be argued that on a proper construction the clause simply does not apply at all: *Photo Production Ltd* v *Securicor Ltd* [1980] AC 827. Such an argument would be based on the exact circumstances of what happened, and on the reasonableness of the term: *George Mitchell (Chesterhall) Ltd* v *Finney Lock Seeds* [1983] AC 803. Finally, it can be argued that even if the exclusion clause does apply it does not prevent recovery, as on its own wording there is no restriction of liability where loss is caused by the negligence of an employee of Watchdogs. Clearly Mr Prince was negligent if he failed to notice the break-in during one of his four admitted visits, and if whoever took the phone call booking the all-night watchman failed to properly record it, they were negligent.

Measure of damages

15   In general terms, if it is established that there was an agreement for an all-night watchman, then the failure to provide one can be said to have caused all the loss

84

suffered by Mrs Russell. If an all-night watchman had been present there would presumably have been no break-in at all. If only breaches of implied terms are established, however, causation may present more difficulties, as it may be difficult to show that proper performance of duties would have prevented the break-in. However, it may be argued that at least the break-in would have been detected soon after it occurred, when it might have been possible to pursue the raiders and recover at least two of the dogs.

(a) The capital value of the dogs

16   The capital value of all three dogs should be claimed, but in addition to causation there may be arguments on the foreseeability of the loss of all three dogs. It seems that Pistol (£20,000) was taken by the burglars, but Poins (£17,500) merely escaped and was later shot by a farmer. I anticipate that we can successfully argue that it is foreseeable that a dog may escape following a break-in, may get hungry and attack animals, and may therefore properly be shot by a farmer, but we must be prepared for some difficulty. As regards Peto (£8,000), it appears that the dog was strangled, but it is not clear why. I can only presume that the dog barked or tried to bite one of the burglars, and it should be possible to argue that it is foreseeable he might be killed as a result.

(b) Winnings and stud fees

17   I anticipate difficulty in recovering the full sums lost under these heads. As regards the potential winnings of the dogs, £10,000 each for Poins and Peto, it will be necessary to provide expert evidence on the potential of each dog. There must be some doubt over how often each dog would have won, so while damages for loss of a chance are recoverable (*Chaplin* v *Hicks* [1911] 2 KB 786), it is highly unlikely that the full figure will be awarded for each dog. In *Chaplin* v *Hicks* the plaintiff was only awarded damages of 25% of the prize she might have won. The potential earnings at stud (£50,000 Pistol and a similar figure for Poins) are affected by similar arguments. Again expert evidence of the potential stud earnings will be required, and as it is possible that either dog might have failed to realise its full potential, a substantial reduction is likely to be made. Damages for the loss of both stud fees and winnings would also have to be reduced to take into account the cost of keeping the dogs.

18   There is a further problem with the figures for prizes and stud fees — they involve a strong element of double recovery in that the capital value of the dogs is presumably high simply because their potential winnings and earnings were good. At first glance it may seem better to go for loss of income (potentially £120,000) rather than capital values (£45,500), but the court is most unlikely to award anything like the full amount of income loss for the reasons already given. I would therefore advise that it is preferable to go for the loss of the capital value of each dog which can be more easily proved and is recoverable in full. However the client must be consulted about this.

(c) Mrs Russell's depression

19   As for Mrs Russell's depression at the loss of her dogs, I am of course sympathetic, but as instructing solicitors will appreciate, the recovery of damages for distress is by no means an easy matter in a contractual action. Damages may be awarded (*Jackson* v *Horizon Holidays* [1975] 1 WLR 1468) but generally only when personal enjoyment is an element of the contract. In *Saunders* v *Edwards* [1987] 1 WLR 1116 damages for disappointment were awarded in a case where it was represented that a flat had a roof terrace when in fact it had not. However, in *Hayes* v *James Charles Dodd* [1990] 2 All ER 815 the plaintiff got no damages for distress when his garage did not have the rear access that had been represented to him as the court held that a commercial contract was involved. It might be possible to argue that Mrs Russell was buying peace of mind with the contract, but as the contract is really a business contract I am no more than 20% confident of success. It would be necessary to get medical evidence of Mrs Russell's depression, and she may well feel that she does not wish to go through with this with a low chance of success.

(d) Damage to the property

20 Some damage was caused to the kennel enclosure by the burglars, and damages may be claimed for this. Figures should be sought for the cost of repairing the enclosure.

(e) Taxation and insurance

21 Mrs Russell should be made aware that since the damages awarded compensate her for a loss in her trade of breeding greyhounds, any income damages awarded will need to be entered into her trading accounts, and will be liable to income tax. This might be an additional reason for seeking the capital value of the dogs, though then the possibility of liability to capital gains tax may arise, unless the money is used to purchase other dogs.

22 My instructions do not make it clear whether Mrs Russell was insured against the loss of her dogs. Perhaps instructing solicitors could investigate. While insurance would not affect the basis of this action, it might mean that Mrs Russell could recover from her insurers any sums she cannot recover from the defendants.

Conclusion

23 In conclusion, I would advise that an action for breach of contract be commenced forthwith, and I enclose Particulars of Claim for that purpose. It may be that Watchdogs Limited will wish to settle the matter rather than proceed to trial, and I would be happy to advise further if this would be of assistance.

ANN O'NIMOUS

3 Stone Court
Temple EC4

8th September 1999

9.4   Feedback on Sample Opinion

The above opinion is in many ways quite good. It is practical and realistic, it addresses the facts rather than the law, but uses the law where appropriate to substantiate the reasoning. Were it to have been written by a student, it would most probably be graded very competent.

However, there are some weaknesses and errors, which might be validly criticised. If you did not notice any when you were reading it, go back and read it again with a view to identifying where it could be improved. Then read the following points of criticism.

(a) The overall length is excessive. The complexity of the case does not justify an opinion of this length. There are various reasons why it has turned out to be so long. There are some matters that are really rather peripheral and could be left out. There are some issues which are dealt with in unnecessary depth. There seems to be a general desire to be a little over-thorough in reasoning and explanation.

(b) Paragraph 2 is probably trying to set out too many conclusions. What Mrs Russell and the instructing solicitor want to know at this point is simply whether liability could be established and whether Mrs Russell would recover in full for the loss of the dogs. The various bases of liability, the various heads of loss and the complications with regard to quantum could be dealt with later. A summary of conclusions at the end could be as detailed as this; an overall conclusion at the beginning need not be.

(c) The section on 'The contract' (paragraphs 3–5) is long-winded and to a considerable extent unnecessary. Since the conclusion at the end of paragraph 5 is that 'it makes relatively little difference whether there was one contract or two' and advises treating them as two, the preceding paragraphs are largely redundant. One could simply say that there is some doubt, but it doesn't much matter and leave it at that.

(d) Paragraphs 6–8 deal with the issue of whether it can be established that there was an agreement for an all-night patrol. Since this is so central, the writer is right to deal with it fairly fully. But this section lacks the most important ingredient: *a conclusion* as to whether this can be established, or at least an assessment of the chances. The issue has been left undetermined, and so not properly advised upon.

(e) The statement in paragraph 7 that anyone who overheard the telephone conversation will only be able to provide hearsay evidence is misleading. If someone overheard Mrs Russell asking for an all-night watchman, this will be perfectly admissible direct evidence that she did so. It will only be hearsay as to whether Watchdogs agreed to provide an all-night watchman.

(f) It is hard to see what tactical value there could be in not disclosing the Watchdogs bill until trial, as suggested in paragraph 8. Surely the best tactic would be to confront Watchdogs with it at the earliest possible moment and ask what dates they allege it refers to. If Mrs Russell is correct in her dates, then with luck Watchdogs may concede that they agreed to provide an all-night watchman on 18/19 April. If they still insist that there was no such agreement, then at least we will have notice of the defence we have to meet.

(g) In paragraph 10 the writer advises that we should allege an implied term that 'the patrolman should visit regularly, or at least spread his visits so as to provide reasonable security'. This advice is inconsistent with the advice in paragraph 2 that the implied term to be alleged should be that 'the watchman would be present for sufficient periods to provide security'. It is not just a matter of saying the same thing in different words. In paragraph 2 it is suggested that the term should relate to the duration of the visits, whereas in paragraph 10 the writer seems to have changed her mind and be thinking of an implied term which relates to the spacing of the visits. Doubtless the draft Particulars of Claim will clarify the writer's opinion, but it does not look good to offer contradictory advice in this way.

(h) Also in paragraph 10 the writer advises that it might be argued that the term can be implied to give business efficacy to the contract, without explaining what the argument might be. If there is no argument, it might be better to go straight to the conclusion which follows, namely that there is not much chance of such a term being implied.

(i) The statement in paragraph 11 that Mr Prince would put Watchdogs in breach of contract simply because he spent two and a half hours drinking before doing his night's work, is too sweeping and incautious. Of course he would be negligent if he were too drunk to do his job properly, but we would need more evidence of this. Elizabeth does not say *what* or *how much* he was drinking. Even if it was alcohol, it does not follow that drinking in moderation would make him unable to perform his duties with reasonable care and skill.

(j) In paragraph 12 the writer deals with the possibility that Mr Prince was negligent in failing to notice a gaping hole in the fence. As dealt with at this point, the advice seems to be that this might be a sound basis for liability. Only in paragraph 15 does the writer point out that there is a problem with causation. It seems a bit perverse to separate breach and causation so misleadingly in this way. The issue clearly needs to be dealt with as one.

(k) The exclusion clause is dealt with in paragraphs 13 and 14. The same fault appears as in the section on the all-night contract: there is no conclusion on the issue of whether the exclusion clause could or could not be relied upon by Watchdogs. Only the arguments are rehearsed — there is no advice.

(l) The subheading 'Measure of damages' above paragraph 15 is wholly inappropriate: the paragraph is dealing with the issue of causation.

(m) The point in the last sentence of paragraph 15, that if the break-in had been discovered early there would perhaps have been a greater chance of recovering the dogs, is a valid one. But it will be very difficult to produce evidence to show this. The writer treats it as a matter of argument rather than evidence, which is misleading and speculative.

(n) Paragraph 17 deals with the recoverability of the lost winnings, and although it rightly points out the evidential difficulties, seems to express the view that these losses are recoverable. But then in paragraph 18 the writer seems immediately to contradict this opinion by pointing out, again correctly, the problem of double recovery and in the end advising that the claim is in reality for the value of the dogs. It would surely be better to raise the double recovery point at the outset, and then reach the same conclusion. This will save time.

(o) The advice in paragraph 19 is actually unsound in law. The writer has confused distress and depression. It is correct to conclude, for the reasons given, that Mrs Russell is unlikely to recover damages for distress. But the instructions refer to depression, which is in many cases a medical condition. If Mrs Russell suffered from clinical depression, then this was a personal injury, and damages would in principle be recoverable, if not too remote. Further instructions are needed.

9.5   An Alternative Opinion

JACKIE RUSSELL

v

WATCHDOGS LIMITED

OPINION

1   On the night of 18/19 April 1999, thieves broke in to the kennel compound at Falstaff Farm, Gadshill, Kent, where Mrs Jackie Russell breeds and trains racing greyhounds. Three of Mrs Russell's favourite dogs were lost: Pistol was stolen, Poins was allowed to escape, and was later shot by a farmer, and Peto was strangled. Mrs Russell was distressed and suffered from depression for several months.

2   Security was supposed to be provided at the compound by Watchdogs Limited ('Watchdogs') at two levels and under two separate agreements. There was a written agreement to provide a regular night patrol service, under which a patrolman (Mr Harry Prince) was to make four visits a night between the hours of 9.00 p.m. and 7.00 a.m. There was also an oral agreement, made by telephone on 18 April, to provide an all-night watchman for just that one night. But Mr Prince seems not to have made any of his four visits until after the thieves had departed; and the all-night watchman never turned up.

3   I am asked to advise Mrs Russell as to liability and quantum in any claim that might be made against Watchdogs for the loss of the dogs.

4   In my opinion a claim based on the failure of Watchdogs to provide an all-night watchman would have good prospects of success, assuming it can indeed be established that such a contract was made, and Mrs Russell should be able to recover by way of damages a sum representing the value of all three dogs.

LIABILITY

The all-night watchman agreement

5 Watchdogs are denying that they agreed to provide an all-night watchman on the night of 18/19 April 1999. They claim they have no written record of the telephone call made by Mrs Russell on 18 April. However, they sent a bill charging Mrs Russell for an all-night watchman on three occasions between 1 April and 30 June, and Mrs Russell says that those three occasions include the night of 18 April. Unless Mrs Russell has forgotten some other occasion when she used the service in this period, this bill should provide good evidence of the existence of the agreement. I advise that a copy should be sent to Watchdogs, or their solicitors, inviting them to say on what dates they allege the all-night service was provided, and to admit that one of the dates referred to is 18 April. It would also be useful to find out if any member of Mrs Russell's family (Elizabeth perhaps?) overheard her asking for an all-night watchman on the telephone. Unless any evidence to the contrary appears, I think it likely that the existence of the all-night watchman agreement can be established.

6 Once it has been shown that Watchdogs agreed to provide an all-night watchman, liability should be established without difficulty. Watchdogs admit that no such service was provided on that night. I think a court would have little difficulty in concluding that if it had been, the break-in would probably not have occurred. Watchdogs' only possible defence would be to rely on the exclusion clause referred to by instructing solicitors. They would have to show that it was incorporated into the oral agreement. I think this unlikely. The night patrol contract makes no reference to the all-night watchman service, and I do not see how it can be argued that this service was provided under the written contract. It was oral and separate. Could it be implied that the exclusion clause should be incorporated into the all-night contract? Only if this is evidenced by the previous dealings between the parties, which is very unlikely if the arrangement has always been made by telephone, as I am instructed (though could Mrs Russell confirm this?). Or the clause might be incorporated if it is contained in a separate document comprising standard terms and conditions which is merely referred to in the night patrol agreement. If so, it might be argued that the standard terms affect all agreements made between the parties. I would like to see a copy of the relevant documents, in order to ascertain if this might be the case.

7 But even if the clause is incorporated into the oral agreement, I do not think Watchdogs will be able to rely on it. Applying the principle of *Photo Production Ltd* v *Securicor Transport Ltd* [1980] AC 827, it cannot have been the parties' intention, on a true construction of the contract, that the exclusion clause should protect Watchdogs in the event of their failing to perform the contract altogether.

8 In my opinion, therefore, the chances of establishing liability for breach of the all-night watchman agreement are good.

The night patrol agreement

9 I think it is unlikely that liability could be established for any breach of the night patrol agreement. There is no evidence to suggest that Mr Prince did not make the four visits he was supposed to make, except perhaps the surprising fact that he apparently never noticed the hole in the fence. But I do not think this alone would prove his failure to appear, and there is no more. The times of his visits did not apparently coincide with the probable time of the raid. It could be argued that there must be an implied term in the agreement that there would be a reasonable space between the patrol visits — all four visits in the space of an hour between 6.00 a.m. and 7.00 a.m., for example, would surely defeat the purpose of the agreement. But I do not think Mr Prince's pattern of attendance that night (as alleged by Watchdogs) could be said to be unreasonable, given the need not to be too consistent, and the very low cost (about £10 per night) of the service.

10   There is of course also an implied term in the agreement to the effect that Mr Prince would patrol with reasonable care and skill (Supply of Goods and Services Act 1982, s. 13). It might be shown that Mr Prince was negligent either in having consumed too much alcohol or in failing to notice the hole in the fence, or both (the two might be connected). But no causation would flow from such a breach. If the raid occurred before midnight, no amount of vigilance on Mr Prince's part could have prevented it. The only faint possibility of establishing liability on this basis rests on being able to show that if Mr Prince had noticed the break-in at 12.30 a.m. and raised the alarm, Pistol and Poins would have been saved. But it is hard to see where evidence to support this could come from, and I do not think a court would find it inherently probable.

11   I do not therefore think there is much chance of establishing any liability for breach of the night patrol contract. Even if the problems I have mentioned could be surmounted, I think Watchdogs probably would in this instance be able to rely on their exclusion clause (unless liability was based on Mr Prince's negligence). It is not in my opinion an unreasonable exclusion given the very limited amount of security Watchdogs were supposed to provide and the low cost of the service.

QUANTUM

The loss of the dogs

12   Mrs Russell would in my opinion be able to recover damages for the loss of all three dogs. I do not think there is any problem of remoteness in respect of Pistol or Peto, but it might be argued that the death of Poins was too remote. However, I think this argument would not succeed. It was plainly within the contemplation of the parties that if there was no security provided at the compound, a dog could be stolen or harmed or escape. It was foreseeable that a dog that escaped might come to harm. It does not matter if the precise manner in which Poins met his death was not within the parties' contemplation providing the type of harm was contemplated (*Parsons (H) (Livestock) Ltd* v *Uttley Ingham & Co Ltd* [1978] QB 791).

13   The question arises whether Mrs Russell can recover damages based on the value of the dogs, their likely earnings, or both. On the assumption that their market value reflects their profit-earning potential, it will not be possible to recover the lost earnings in addition to their value, as that would amount to double recovery. There is no doubt that Mrs Russell will be entitled to the market value of the dogs; that is the normal basis of assessment for the loss of goods (even such treasured goods as Pistol, Poins and Peto). But where the goods are profit earning, it is sometimes possible to recover instead the loss of profit. On the face of it, that seems to be a significantly larger sum — maybe £70,000 or more as against £45,500. But the figures I have for likely earnings are presumably gross, and must be reduced to take account of the costs of keeping, training, guarding and insuring the dogs. Doubtless this would bring the loss of earnings down substantially. There would also be the difficulty of proof. Mrs Russell would have to produce evidence as to the likely earnings of the dogs over the rest of their lives, which may not be easy, and would require some speculation. I think it likely that the court would prefer expert evidence of value, taking account of earning potential, in any event. I therefore advise Mrs Russell to claim on the basis of value, unless she is able to obtain strong evidence to show a probable level of net profit significantly greater than these sums.

Distress and depression

14   I do not think Mrs Russell can recover damages to compensate her for her grief or distress. Such damages may be recoverable in contract where the contract is one to provide peace of mind, or personal enjoyment, as in the spoilt holiday cases. But however much she loved her dogs, Mrs Russell is essentially running a business, and I think the court would treat this as a commercial contract, in which case damages for distress are almost certainly irrecoverable: see for example *Hayes* v *James Charles Dodd* [1990] 2 All ER 815.

15   On the other hand if Mrs Russell's depression was a depressive illness requiring medical treatment, then she has a potential claim for personal injury. If instructing solicitors could arrange for a medical report to be obtained substantiating this, then I advise that such a claim can be made. However, I do not have great confidence in its success. The difficulty would be remoteness. I think Watchdogs might well argue successfully that personal injury was not a foreseeable consequence of their failure to provide an all-night patrolman.

Damage to property

16   In addition, Mrs Russell should be able to recover damages for the cost of repairing the fence and replacing the padlock, any veterinary bills in connection with Poins' and Peto's deaths and any other incidental expenses resulting from the break-in.

Conclusion

17   I advise accordingly that a claim should be pursued against Watchdogs for their breach of contract in failing to provide an all-night watchman and that it has good prospects of success. The claim should provisionally be for the market value of the three dogs, plus incidental expenses and possibly also for Mrs Russell's depression, but this last may not be recovered. I would be happy to advise further and draft Particulars of Claim if so requested.

JOSEPH BLOGGS

4 Gray's Inn Place
8th September 1999

TEN

FURTHER EXAMPLES OF OPINIONS ON THE MERITS

The eleven opinions in this chapter are all real opinions or advices written by barristers in real cases. Only names, places and dates have been changed. They will hopefully serve to give you some idea of differences in style, and how opinions can be tailored for different circumstances.

10.1 Liability and Damages — Personal Injury

This first opinion is a fairly typical practical example. Note the absence of any law.

<u>STEVEN REED v JAMES TELFORD and MAURICE JONES</u>

<u>OPINION</u>

1   On 3rd December 1998 Mr Steven Reed was driving his Rover 400 south along a section of dual carriageway along the A1 in Durham. It was early morning at about 6 a.m. and it was still dark. Mr Reed says that he had been travelling at between 50 m.p.h. and 70 m.p.h., overtaking a number of cars in the inner lane of the carriageway. The speed limit was 70 m.p.h. As Mr Reed approached the junction of the Al Moxon Lane (the 'Green Man' junction) he was confronted with a trailer of an articulated lorry straddling the southbound carriageway. The lorry was stationary as the driver had driven across the southbound carriageway from Moxon Lane and was waiting for a break in the northbound traffic to enable him to complete his turn into the northbound carriageway. Such was the length of the lorry that there was insufficient width in the central reservation to accommodate it.

2   Mr Reed attempted to steer round the rear of the lorry but was unable to avoid it. He struck the trailer towards its rear end (probably at the rear wheel) at some speed causing appreciable damage to the front of the Rover particularly the offside. The Rover spun out of control down the southbound carriageway, and ended up approximately side-on to oncoming traffic, the front of the car facing the central reservation. Following the collision, apart perhaps from a brief moment when he remembers someone telling him that he would be all right, Mr Reed lost consciousness. Apparently the driver of the lorry, Mr Telford, completed his turn to the northbound carriageway, parked, and then returned to assist Mr Reed. Mr Telford released Mr Reed from his seatbelt. A few minutes later, this being about 10 minutes after the initial collision, a Ford Escort car driven by Mr Jones collided with the Rover hitting it approximately midway down the offside. Mr Reed was still in the Rover when the second collision took place.

3   Mr Reed made a short statement on 7th January 1999 giving a brief description of the events leading up to the first collision. Given the seriousness of his immediate injuries however and his loss of consciousness it cannot be expected of Mr Reed that he remember the events of that morning well, and certainly not what happened between the first and second collision. We have a reasonably clear impression of what

Mr Telford will say from the expert report of Mr Roulston. In addition there are police statements from John Ackford, George Davis, Elizabeth Jones (the second driver's wife), Maureen Morden and Brenda Kent, together with statements of the present parties to the proposed civil proceedings. The statements are handwritten. I would be grateful if my Instructing Solicitor could arrange for them to be typed up for the trial.

4   I need not analyse these statements in this Opinion. The facts of both collisions are reasonably clear and the main issues the Court will have to consider are the speeds of Mr Reed and Mr Jones before their respective collisions, and the visibility of the lorry as they drove towards it. Mr Telford has to accept that he was stationary straddling the southbound carriageway. Paragraph 112 of the Highway Code states:

112.   When going straight across or turning right into a dual carriageway treat each half as a separate road. Wait in the central reservation until there is a safe gap in the traffic on the second half of the road. *If the central reservation is too narrow for the length of your vehicle, wait until you can cross both carriageways in one go.*

As part of everyday driving experience Mr Telford's manoeuvre is perhaps understandable. It may take some while for there to be a simultaneous gap in both northbound and southbound traffic, and it is a very patient driver who waits for as long as it takes for there to be a clear road both ways. Nevertheless the motorist who straddles a carriageway in the hours of darkness is plainly subjecting other road users to unnecessary risk. In my view Mr Telford will be held liable for the first collision.

5   Whether Mr Reed is held contributorily negligent would depend upon the view taken by the Court of his speed and his ability to see the lorry ahead of him. Mr Ackford will be the witness most pressed on this question of speed at trial. He says in his police statement that he cannot say what Mr Reed's speed was, and I hope he is not persuaded to suggest Mr Reed was exceeding 70 m.p.h. It is evident that Mr Ackford had a lucky escape. As for visibility there is an issue as to whether the trailer had side lights visible to oncoming motorists. Mr Reed is adamant that there were none. The trailer was dark blue in colour and did not show up well in the dark. More pertinently there was a steady stream of traffic travelling north. These vehicles were displaying headlights and although their headlights were dipped they greatly obstructed Mr Reed's view ahead. I would be reasonably optimistic that Mr Reed will be held blameless for the accident.

6   Liability for the second collision follows in part liability for the first and in part an assessment of Mr Jones' speed and the Court's view on whether he was properly concentrating on the road ahead. The police evidence suggests that the scene of the junction had changed appreciably between the two collisions. By the time Mr Jones ploughed into the Rover a number of cars had stopped and serious attempts were being made to warn oncoming drivers of the hazards in the road ahead. I would anticipate the Court holding Mr Jones partly to blame for the second accident, together with Mr Telford who was responsible for the first accident.

7   *Apportionment of injury.* Mr Roulston has done his best for Mr Telford as first defendant, and there is some force in what he says. I consider that the photographs assist his argument. Nevertheless he spoilt his case in my view by seeking to blame Mr Reed's concussion primarily on the second collision. Unless Mr Telford will say that Mr Reed plainly remained conscious after the first collision, e.g. Mr Reed engaging in conversation with him, the evidence is against him. Given also that it is plain that Mr Reed struck the trailer at an appreciable speed it is hard if not impossible to attribute the bulk of the chest bruising to the second collision. The Court is likely to accept that Mr Reed's injuries might not have been quite so severe had there not been the second collision, but in terms of damages if a separate award is made it will in my view be of a very modest amount, and not more than 10% of the total sum assessed for Mr Reed's injuries.

8 *Provisional damages.* My Instructing Solicitor wishes to amend the Particulars of Claim to claim provisional damages. The most serious of Mr Reed's injuries involves the fracture to the right foot. Healing is complete and Mr Reed is left with a gross inconformity of the distal articular surface of the sub-taloid joint and the development of significant degenerative changes to the posterior facet of the sub-taloid joint. On some days the foot is reasonably pain-free. On others it goes into spasm. In his most recent report Mr Kenneth Brand FRCS states that there is a risk of significant further deterioration, and on the basis of this view it is arguable that there is an appropriate case for provisional damages. The difficulty however is that the medical response to further deterioration is a triple arthrodesis. This treatment is already advocated both by Mr Brand and Mr George who acts for Mr Telford's insurers. I note that Mr George puts the success rate of the operation at 75%.

9 In a majority of cases an arthrodesis does not make a great deal of difference to general damages. The Plaintiff loses mobility but at the same time is relieved from pain. In Mr Reed's case the impact on damages is more likely to come under Special Damages. Assuming that Mr George is wrong to say that Mr Reed will be able to drive heavy goods vehicles after an arthrodesis, and I am reasonably hopeful that this can be established, an arthrodesis will result in him having to give up his employment. He is now almost 52 years of age. It may be very difficult for him to obtain alternative employment.

10 In the circumstances I suggest that further amendments are made to the Particulars of Claim to cover provisional damages. Since the Particulars of Claim have been served, we will require the written consent of all the other parties or the permission of the court for such an amendment (see CPR, r. 17.1(2)). Part 22 requires the amendment to be verified by a Statement of Truth. If, as I assume, consent is not forthcoming, Instructing Solicitors should file an Application Notice in accordance with Part 23 using Practice Form N244 and attach a copy of the proposed amended Particulars of Claim. As Mr Brand's report has not yet been verified by a Statement of Truth, please send him a draft verification to be annexed to his report so that the report can stand as evidence in support of the application (r. 22.2).

11 The case has not yet been allocated to any track. Therefore the Court is likely to treat the hearing of the application as an opportunity to conduct a Case Management Conference. Please therefore have an Allocation Questionnaire duly completed ready to support allocation to the multi-track and Draft Directions which should if possible be agreed with the Defendant.

12 I shall of course happily assist with these matters if required. In any event Instructing Solicitors may wish me to see the proposed Allocation Questionnaire and Directions before sending them to the Defendants. The only comment I would make at this stage is that the Court is likely to prefer a timetable for Directions which is realistic to one which is too short and is either breached or requires further applications to be made for time extensions. The only safe course is to assume that no extensions will be granted, particularly if they might impinge on the trial window.

13 If I can assist further please do not hesitate to contact me.

JOHN LEAM

Mobile Chambers, Temple EC4
15th May 1999

10.2 Liability and Damages — Personal Injury

This is another opinion of much the same kind. Note the emphasis not just on liability, but how it can be established. This opinion is also an example of a case where not everything is straightforward or in the claimant's favour when it comes to damages.

IN THE PROPOSED CLAIM

BETWEEN

DAVID GATTON Claimant

and

JOHN DONALDSON Defendant

OPINION

---

1 I am asked to advise Mr Gatton as to his prospects of successfully recovering damages against the Defendant, in respect of personal injuries unfortunately suffered by him when he was run down by a car on 13th September 1997. I am obliged to Instructing Solicitors for their full instructions, and for enclosing the medical report of Mr Woodhead, dated 30th October 1998.

2 According to Mr Gatton, he was together with two friends, in the process of crossing the road at the junction of Boggle Road and Boggle Hill, Nuthatch, Kent, when the Defendant drove his car over a red light, and struck him. His friends were fortunate enough to be able to run to the other side of the road. It may well have been that Mr Gatton was affected by a moment of indecision as to whether to continue or retreat, but this is presently unclear.

3 The Defence is based on the Claimant's own negligence — it being alleged in the Defendant's Reply to the Letter of Claim that the Defendant was lawfully travelling through green traffic lights, and that the Claimant effectively drunkenly wandered into his path. It seems to be common ground that Mr Gatton had been drinking, although there is some discrepancy between his account to Instructing Solicitors (2/3 drinks), and his statement to the police 'I had had several drinks', although in each case he maintained that he was not drunk. Additionally, Mr Gatton told the police that the car was not in sight when he began to cross the road, and that he was already in the middle of the road when it arrived. However, according to his companions the other car was in sight, having stopped at the traffic lights. This discrepancy may be accounted for by the fact that Mr Gatton said that he had little recollection of the events, in view of his injuries (and hopefully it will not have been due to alcohol, as will almost certainly be alleged by the Defendant).

4 There appears to have been one additional witness, this being the driver of a Ford Escort who had pulled up at the traffic lights on the side from which the Claimant and his companions were crossing. It seems from correspondence that this person is a potential witness for the Defendant, although his insurers have been curiously reluctant to provide Instructing Solicitors with any further details. These would doubtless be supplied in the form of a witness statement after the issue of a claim, although it may be worth a further letter being written asking for details of the witness with a 'Calderbank' endorsement as to costs in the event of any being thrown away by non-disclosure. Remind the Defendant of the terms of para. 1.2 of the 'Pre-Action Protocol for Personal Injury Claims' requiring better and earlier exchange of information, and also the passage in para. 2.4 which provides that:

'The spirit, if not the letter of the protocol, should still be followed for multi-track type claims. In accordance with the sense of the civil justice reforms, the court will expect to see the spirit of reasonable pre-action behaviour applied in all cases, regardless of a special protocol.'

5 The question of liability is likely to have to be resolved by the Court on the evidence, in view of the Defendant's reluctance to negotiate reasonably. It is certainly true that the Defendant appears not to have informed his insurers of the accident, but this is not necessarily a compelling indication of liability. However, it is interesting to note

that the Ford Escort was apparently stationary at the traffic lights, although the Defendant (approaching from the opposite direction) claims that they were green. At the moment however, there is clearly a considerable conflict of evidence, and Mr Gatton must arrange for his potential witnesses to contact Instructing Solicitors so that a full proof can be taken for trial. A plan of the area will also, of course, be helpful.

6   In so far as the claim for general damages is concerned much will depend on the degree and extent to which Mr Gatton may be permanently affected by the injury to his foot. The first matter of concern, is that the fracture to his ankle was not diagnosed by the casualty department of the hospital, but only came to light two weeks later. Although I do not consider that this fact taken in isolation, will affect the direct liability of the Defendant (if proved), significantly or at all, I am concerned as to whether it may be relevant to the formation of the deep vein thrombosis that appears to be the cause of the majority of Mr Gatton's present problems. If there is any such possibility, a further Defendant in this respect would be the local area health authority.

7   Over 7 months have elapsed since the medical report, and I consider that it would be appropriate for a supplement to be obtained, to deal not merely with the question raised in the last paragraph, but also with the present or future capability of Mr Gatton to carry on the type of work for which he has been trained. I do not presently think it appropriate to advise on the quantum of general damages that may be awarded until an up to date prognosis has been obtained.

8   In so far as special damages are concerned, the position is fraught with conjecture. At the time of the accident Mr Gatton was still a student, but had already applied for a job with Fragile Pottery Company, which was a business run by a Mr M Smith. There seems to have been some competition for the job, but Mr Gatton was accepted one week after the accident. Mr Smith states that the job was permanent, subject to one month's trial, however he was unable to keep the position open, and the employment was thus lost. Mr Gatton is of the view that he could ultimately have become a partner with Mr Smith, or may have been able to start his own business. As it happens, he did attempt this in 1998, but the business was unsuccessful, and had to close down. The problem is that these matters are all highly speculative, and the Court will not be able to discount the possibility that things would not have worked out as expected. I am reasonably confident that the Court will not be too concerned about the trial period, but some evidence from Mr Smith as to Mr Gatton's potential would be helpful if it could be obtained. It would also be interesting to note what happened with the employee who took the job in place of Mr Gatton. Is the business still going? Is he still in the job? Has he been promoted, and if so to what?

9   I am also concerned as to the degree and extent to which Mr Gatton is incapable of work due to the accident. It seems clear that he is unable to use a manually operated pottery wheel, and this was apparently the cause not merely of his being unable to take up the job with Mr Smith, but also his inability to obtain any other employment. Nevertheless, it seems that he felt sufficiently capable in 1998 of attempting to set up his own business, and it also seems that he is now able to use an electrically operated wheel. In order to claim future loss of earnings (or loss of earning capacity under the *Smith* v *Manchester* provisions), it will be necessary to show that Mr Gatton will have a continuing disability such as will make him either unfit for any type of work, or unable to achieve the earnings that would otherwise have been the case but for the accident. This will have to be supported by medical evidence. Additionally, I am concerned to know if electrically operated wheels are reasonably common and/or available in the trade, and if so, why Mr Gatton did not seek to use one when he set up his own business. How many operations use electric wheels? Are there any jobs available using such wheels, for persons such as Mr Gatton? Is there any other form of occupation that he has attempted to pursue (apart from part-time teaching), and if so what? All these matters are highly pertinent to the quantum of the claim, and must please be answered as soon as possible. Nevertheless, I am of the view that a claim for loss of opportunity to set up his own business should not be pursued, as I consider that the Court will hold it, in the circumstances, to be too remote, even without considering the question of the electric wheel.

10   I regret that I can be no more precise at the moment, but will naturally be pleased to advise further upon receipt of the information requested above. In the meantime, I hope that Mr Gatton continues to make progress towards a recovery.

ANDREW BRIGHT

8 Grosvenor Buildings, Temple EC4
2nd May 1999

10.3   Liability — Insufficient Information

The writer of this opinion finds it impossible to reach a conclusion on the basis of the information provided. Note however that the opinion still advises as far as it can on the basis of the information to hand, and gives a clear indication of what further information is required and how it could affect liability.

RE: JOHN EDWARDS

ADVICE ON LIABILITY

1   On the 7th March 1998 Mr Edwards suffered personal injury when he collided with the corner of an open window. He was in the process of leaving his place of work by taking a route to the car park along a pathway. The pathway bordered the offices of a company called Reality Publishing Limited. It seems that a window was open to the maximum extent and neither Mr Edwards, nor a colleague to whom he was talking as they walked, observed the danger in time. I am now asked to advise on liability.

2   The accident occurred at about 4.45 in the afternoon. Mr Edwards states that although it was not quite dusk, the light was beginning to fade and the weather was overcast. The window was open to its maximum extent and encroached some two feet into the path which was five foot wide. I have photographs which show the scene of the accident though obviously they were taken in much better light than at the time of the accident. Following early notification of the potential claim under para. 2.6 of 'Pre-Action Protocol for Personal Injury Claims'. Liability has been denied by insurers acting on behalf of the freeholders of the building and also by solicitors acting for Reality Publishing Limited who appear to be lessees and occupiers of the offices where the offending window is located.

3   I am instructed that Mr Edwards is a partner in a firm of Chartered Accountants who have their offices at 35/37 Coral Street London NW4. The offices of Reality Publishing Ltd are at the same address. I gather that the two organisations use different parts of the one building, perhaps in conjunction with a number of other organisations. Therefore the windows used in the two sets of offices were almost certainly the same. Despite the fact that Mr Edwards states he has not personally opened windows in his office that overlook any path or walkway, Mr Edwards is likely have been familiar with the windows and the manner in which they opened, at least from the inside. I do not know how long Mr Edwards's firm had been at the address. The photographs indicate that the building is relatively modern and it may be that no substantial period had elapsed between the time when his firm moved in and the date of the accident. However, even if this were correct it would appear that emphasis would have to be laid on the degree that this particular window was opened rather than surprise that there was a window which could be opened at all.

4   At first sight this would seem to be a case involving consideration of the Occupier's Liability Acts. However it may be that liability will rest under the principle of common law negligence. I doubt that Mr Edwards could be construed as a visitor to premises occupied by Reality Publishing Limited. It would surprise me if any lease that the company held gave control over the path or walkway which ran past the windows of the offices. Assuming that all occupants of the building had a right to use the path in question control over the path may rest with the freeholders and, in my view, it would

be difficult to argue that the 'owners' or occupiers of the path were responsible for what happened. It is more probable that the potential liability of Reality Publishing Limited should be considered on the basis of opening a window so that it protruded over someone else's land, which would be beyond the scope of the Occupier's Liability Acts.

5   Unfortunately I am unable to advise on the basis of the information that I have at present. There are a number of aspects about which I would require further instructions. I need to know:

(a)   Whether there are other ways of proceeding to the car park from where Mr Edwards's office is and if so how much longer a route they represent. A plan of the whole building and its car park area would be very helpful.

(b)   Which window Mr Edwards collided with. It may be important to know how far along the path Mr Edwards had gone before the injury happened. The distance of travel, at the very least, affects the length of opportunity to observe the protruding window edge.

(c)   How many people could be expected to use the particular path during the course of the day and at what times.

(d)   Lighting up time for the date of the accident.

(e)   Whether the lamps that are situated above a number of the windows depicted in the photographs were illuminated at the relevant time and if not why not. I would also like some idea as to the type and quality of light that these lamps produce.

(f)   How many times Mr Edwards had made the journey to the car park via the path before and whether he had noticed windows open to a full or maximum extent during such journeys.

6   It would be advisable to have the benefit of a statement from Mr Edwards's colleague, Mr Morris, at the earliest opportunity. His corroboration as to the quality of light at the material point and the difficulty he had of seeing the window edge may be helpful for the purposes of negotiation as well as for the purposes of my advice.

7   I should mention that I am a little puzzled why a window of this size should be open to its maximum extent at 4.45 p.m. at the beginning of March. One would have expected the temperature outdoors to be too low to contemplate such a course of action. Has Mr Edwards any information or explanation? I am thinking either of a breakdown of the heating thermostat in the building so that the temperature indoors was much too hot, or a very unseasonal outside temperature on that particular day, or perhaps that cleaners were in the office and were engaged in cleaning the windows.

8   On receipt of the above information I will be able to advise properly on the question of liability and if appropriate contributory negligence. I do note, however, at this stage, that simple steps such as advocated by the local authority of fixing stays together with coloured corners to the windows would have prevented this injury. I am at a loss to know why the windows were not designed with those safeguards from the outset. However it seems to me that a potential claim against the designers would be more costly, more time consuming and less likely to succeed than one aimed at those responsible for opening the window in question. I would advise therefore that liability against the latter be examined exhaustively before any decisions are made as to the former.

9   Finally, I would remind those instructing me of the requirement under para. 3.1 of the Pre-Action Protocol to send to the proposed defendant two copies of a Letter of Claim **immediately** sufficient information is available to substantiate a realistic claim and before issues of quantum are addressed in detail. I shall be happy to settle such a letter if required. The following is a checklist of the information required for the purposes of such a letter:

- claimant's name, date of birth, address (and phone), National Insurance number;
- employer's name and address;
- date and place of accident (Photographs? Police or HSO Report?);
- the circumstances of the accident (Witnesses? Statements!!);
- the allegations of negligence/breach (Expert required?);
- the claimant's injuries (Expert medical evidence required?);
- the claimant's occupation and any time off work? (Pay slips, etc.?);
- the identity of the likely Defendant(s) and their insurers;
- relevant documents held by the Claimant and the Defendant(s) (Copies!);
- letter of authority to obtain medical records. (Plus, see Annex B to the Protocol for Clinical Disputes for the form to be used when obtaining medical records in medical negligence and personal injury claims.)

10   I hope that assists and I shall be happy to assist further in due course.

MARIA COLES

Lincoln House Chambers
18th August 1999

10.4   Unfavourable Advice

As often as not a barrister has to give a client advice that is unfavourable, and this opinion provides an example of how this can be done clearly yet sympathetically. Note also that the writer deals with both the main issues, even though, if the advice on the first issue is correct, the second does not even arise.

IN THE MATTER OF LEGAL FUTURES
AND IN THE MATTER OF HERBERT BUTLER & CO.

ADVICE

1   Instructing Solicitors act for Legal Futures, an unlimited company which trades as an employment agency specialising in legal placements. I am asked to advise on a possible claim for commission arising out of the employment by Herbert Butler & Co. ('Herbert Butler'), a firm of solicitors, of a solicitor called Paul Doyle.

2   The factual history, to the extent that it has been disclosed, is uncomplicated and, in the interests of brevity, I do not propose to set out any narrative here. There is, however, one point on the facts which must be made. Herbert Butler have refused to state whether details concerning Mr Doyle forwarded by Legal Futures reached them before the arrival of similar material sent by Legal Placings. This reticence strongly suggests an affirmative answer, but the question is incapable of being resolved definitively until after the disclosure of all relevant documents. Legal Futures rightly accept that if they were not the first to deliver the information they cannot succeed in a claim for commission. This advice assumes that the details from Legal Futures arrived first.

3   My instructions raise, essentially, two questions:

    (i)   Did Legal Futures introduce Mr Doyle to Herbert Butler?

    (ii)   If the answer to question (i) is 'yes', was the action of Legal Futures the effective cause of the engagement of Mr Doyle by Herbert Butler?

I will deal with these issues in turn.

Question (i)

4   In correspondence Mr M R Harvey, a director of Legal Futures, has argued his case with courtesy and clarity. There is, however, a premise underlying his argument which

is, in my view, open to considerable doubt. That premise is the assumption that delivery of an anonymous curriculum vitae constitutes, by itself, an introduction for the purposes of the agreement between Legal Futures and their clients.

5 The relevant contractual terms are contained in the Legal Futures Terms of Business, which included the following provisions:

> 1. The interviewing of an applicant introduced by us constitutes acceptance of these Terms of Business and an agreement by the client to pay our fee should an engagement of the applicant in any capacity occur.

> 'Introduced' in these Terms of Business includes supplying to a client the details of an applicant who the client is not aware is currently seeking employment. . . .

> 4. No fees are charged unless an applicant introduced by us is engaged, as provided in these Terms, . . .

> 6. If a client employs an applicant introduced by us, our fee is . . .

6 It is implicit in clause 1 that an introduction may be effected by sending details of a potential employee to a client. This accords with principle and justice. A court would require highly compelling grounds for holding that, where an agent made an applicant known to his client and provided his client with the means of making contact with the applicant, with the result that the client interviewed and ultimately engaged the applicant, the agent should nonetheless be denied his commission. So, for example, it would be no answer to a claim for commission in such a case for the client to complain that the agent had not been present at, or even arranged, the interview.

7 The difficulty with the present case is that the material sent by Legal Futures was not sufficient to make Mr Doyle known to the clients. Delivery of an anonymous curriculum vitae may stimulate interest on the part of the client. No doubt in the ordinary course of events an interested client may be expected to communicate his interest to the agent. And any such communication would ordinarily result in the agent bringing the client and the applicant together or giving the client the information necessary to enable him to make contact with the applicant direct. On this analysis there is a three-stage process: first, delivery of the anonymous curriculum vitae to the client; second, communication of the client's interest to the agent; third, further steps by the agent to bring the applicant and the client together. It is only when the third stage is completed that an introduction can be said to have taken place. I regret that, in my view, it cannot be argued that Legal Futures went beyond the first stage.

8 For the reasons given above, I have come to the conclusion that it is unlikely that a court would be persuaded to find that there was an introduction of Mr Doyle by Legal Futures to Herbert Butler within the meaning of the agreement. Put another way, I do not think that an anonymous curriculum vitae falls within the words 'the details of an applicant' in clause 1 of the Terms of Business. I would therefore answer question (i) in the negative.

Question (ii)

9 If my view on question (i) is correct, no right to commission in favour of Legal Futures can arise. In case I am mistaken on question (i) however, it is necessary to deal with question (ii). The issue is whether, even if the delivery of anonymous particulars did amount to an introduction, that act by Legal Futures was the effective cause of Mr Doyle being engaged by Herbert Butler.

10 The law in this area is dominated by property agency cases. These demonstrate that no hard and fast rule can be laid down for determining the question of effective cause: it is an issue of fact in every case. Two points in particular need to be made. First, an 'introduction' in which the name and address of the person being introduced to the client are not divulged may well not be held to operate as the effective cause of

the ultimate transaction between the client and the party so introduced: see *Coles* v *Enoch* [1939] 3 All ER 327. Secondly, where two agents claim commission, the first introduction in time is not by any means decisive: see *John D Wood & Co* v *Dantata* [1987] 2 EGLR 23.

11   In my opinion, it is distinctly unlikely that a court would hold that the introduction by Legal Futures (if, as I strongly doubt, there was such an introduction at all) was the effective cause of the engagement of Mr Doyle. The evidence is that Legal Placings played the principal part. It was they who made Mr Doyle known to Herbert Butler, and it was they who did what had to be done to bring them together.

Conclusions

12   A claim for commission could only succeed if both questions set out in paragraph 3 were decided in favour of Legal Futures. For reasons which I have attempted to state shortly above, I consider that the merits of both questions are weighted quite heavily against Legal Futures. In these circumstances, I do not recommend any further action for the recovery of commission in this case.

13   In expressing this conclusion, I would not wish Mr Harvey to think that I am unsympathetic. Legal Futures have every reason to feel hard done by, and the behaviour of Mr Doyle in particular has been shabby to say the least. Regrettably, however, it is not uncommon that a good moral case is unsustainable in law.

ELIZABETH KNOWLES

2 Boswell Buildings
Temple
London EC4

9th July 1999

10.5   Advice on Merits, Evidence and Further Conduct

Not all opinions are written before an action is commenced, or in the early stages. This opinion is written at an advanced stage of proceedings, and so must necessarily deal not only with the merits, but also with evidence and the conduct of the action.

QUINN v B & I INVESTMENTS

ADVICE

1   Instructing Solicitors represent Mr Mark Quinn, the Claimant in proceedings against B & I Investments, a firm for which he worked between March and October 1997. I am asked to advise on the merits, and on evidence and further conduct.

The merits

2   I agree with Instructing Solicitors that the agreement under which Mr Quinn worked was curious. I think it most unlikely that a court would be persuaded that he was self-employed, notwithstanding the 'label' which the parties both agreed to attach to his status. In all probability, he was, in law, an employee. I am glad to say that this appears to have little bearing on the legal merits of the case.

3   The terms on which Mr Quinn was engaged were agreed orally and evidenced in a letter sent by Clive Nice, a partner in the Defendants' firm, to the Claimant dated 16th February 1997. That letter states, 'You will benefit from a minimum twelve months contract'.

4   There is no dispute that the Claimant left the Defendants on 5th October 1997. The main issue is whether there was a termination of the agreement by consent or whether

there was a unilateral termination by the defendants. Ultimately, this is an issue of fact which could go one way or the other. That said, Mr Nice's credibility is not helped by the discrepancies between the general reference dated 15th October 1997 and the reply to question 3 of the questionnaire of Special Money Services Limited dated 29th November 1997. Nor will it be easy for Mr Nice (if his case really is that there was a termination by agreement) to give a convincing explanation for his failure to respond to, and take strong issue with, the Claimant's letter dated 25th October 1997, in which he complains of having been summarily dismissed. In these circumstances, I am reasonably confident that the question of how the termination happened will be decided in the Claimant's favour.

5   If it is shown that the agreement was terminated summarily by Mr Nice, the Defendants will be driven to rely on their second line of defence, which consists of the allegation that the contract only required one month's notice to terminate. This is a curious contention to set up side by side with an admission of paragraph 1 of the Particulars of Claim, in which it is averred that the agreement expressly provided for a minimum term of 12 months commencing in March 1997. I consider that the Defendants' fall-back argument, which is based on an alleged implied term plainly in irreconcilable conflict with an admitted express term, is wrong and unsustainable.

6   For the reasons summarised above, I regard the Claimant's case as a strong one. I would, however, caution Mr Quinn against running away with the idea that his claim is invincible: there is no such thing as an invincible claim.

7   I am not asked to deal specifically with quantum at this stage and in any event, as I will explain below, a number of important facts remain to be established before a reasonably precise assessment can be attempted. Furthermore, I have not yet grasped the reasoning which underlies the holiday pay claim as pleaded, or the total of £13,166.44. I would therefore say no more for the present than that, if liability is established, an award of damages of well over £10,000 should follow.

8   In my view, this is in every way a proper case to be brought to trial.

Evidence and further conduct

9   A draft witness statement in the Claimant's name should be prepared. This should set out the full history in chronological order, and should deal with the issues raised in the statements of case. Those issues, of course, include the question of loss. The statement should disclose how many days' holiday had been taken by 5th October 1997, and how the special damage claim under paragraph 3(b) of the Particulars of Claim is calculated. It should also address the quantification of loss under paragraph 3(c). What was the make, model and year of manufacture of the car provided? What was the monthly value of the free petrol used for private travel? Was the Claimant allowed to use the mobile telephone for personal calls? If so, what was the monthly value of the personal calls made? And what was the average monthly value to the Claimant (in the way of free meals, drinks, theatre tickets, etc.) of the entertainment expenses allowance? Although the Defence does not allege that the Claimant failed to mitigate any loss which he may prove, the witness statement should, for completeness, also contain an account of the steps which Mr Quinn took to obtain work and the work which he did obtain up to 10th March 1998, specifying as precisely as possible starting and finishing dates and rates of remuneration.

10   Short statements in the names of Mr Parker and Mr Lane, based on their letters both dated 25th October 1998, should be prepared. In the case of Mr Parker, the statement should specify that the Claimant started working for him on 4th March 1998, so that there was precisely one full working week within the twelve months period expiring on 10th March 1998. The statements, duly signed and dated, should be served on the Defendants' solicitors, who should be invited formally to agree their contents. If no such agreement is forthcoming, Civil Evidence Act notices should be served.

11   On my understanding (which should be firmly corrected if it is mistaken) that there is no other person who can give any valuable evidence as to the terms of the ageement between the parties, the circumstances in which the agreement was terminated or the Claimant's mitigation of his loss thereafter, I see no reason why any witness other than the Claimant and, possibly, Mr Parker and Mr Lane, should be called.

12   Assuming that the Defendants will be relying on the evidence of Mr Nice only, I agree that the case should be listed for hearing with a time estimate of half a day. It would, however, be wise to press the solicitors on the other side for an answer to the letter of 12th November 1998 before a final decision is taken on the question of the time estimate.

13   The Claimant should be asked to provide Instructing Solicitors with all documents in his possession relating to the contract between the parties and his efforts to find work after the termination. Those representing the Defendants should also be asked for their comments on the contents of a trial bundle. Key documents would appear to be the Defendant's letters dated 16th February and 2nd March 1997, the references dated 15th October and 28th November 1997, and the Claimant's letter dated 25th October 1997.

14   If Instructing Solicitors so wish, I will be more than happy to advise further on documentation and final preparations for trial when the various steps advocated above have been taken.

ELIZABETH KNOWLES

2 Boswell Buildings
Temple
London EC4

2nd March 1999

10.6   A Short Advice

There is no rule that says an opinion must be long. If it does not need to be, keep it short. Here is an example of a short advice on a single specific issue. Note also how the writer makes it clear, tactfully, that it is a fairly simple point which the instructing solicitor could probably have looked up for himself or herself.

DISTRICT BANK v PRINCE

ADVICE

1   This case concerns a cheque in the sum of £2,000 drawn by M. Prince trading as Windsor Coffee Shop on the Royal Bank of Gloucester. The cheque was drawn in favour of the payee, C. S. Lloyd. Mr Lloyd presented the cheque for payment at the Summertown, Oxford branch of the District Bank and Mr Lloyd was credited with the sum in his account.

2   Unfortunately District Bank have been unable to receive payment or effectively reimbursement from the Royal Bank of Gloucester since the latter received instructions from the drawer countermanding payment. The cheque was marked 'Refer to drawer' by the Royal Bank of Gloucester when payment was refused. Mr Lloyd has drawn on his account in all innocence because of the credit that was made to his account on the strength of the uncleared cheque and District Bank now wish to proceed against M. Prince on the cheque. I am asked to advise whether a cause of action exists between District Bank and the drawer of the cheque.

3   It is clear that there is no contract between District Bank and M. Prince and there can be no cause of action based on contract. A cheque, however, is a form of negotiable

instrument and privity of contract has little application. The essential feature of negotiable instruments is that they are readily transferable from holder to holder and the rights conferred by the instrument are transferred at one and the same time. Thus in general terms the original payee of a cheque can bring an action to enforce it but similarly a person or holder that the payee has endorsed the cheque over to would be able to pursue the drawer of the cheque. Any number of endorsements can be made but the eventual holder is the person entitled to the proceeds of the cheque: hence the 'negotiability' of the negotiable instrument. Authority for the propositions outlined so far are contained in sections 31(1), (3), 32(1), (6), 34(1), (2) and 38 of the Bills of Exchange Act 1882.

4   The major difference in this case from the everyday situation of the payee endorsing the cheque over to a third party by signing the cheque on the reverse side and therefore passing title to the cheque to the new holder, is the likelihood that Mr Lloyd did not endorse the cheque at all. He probably simply passed the cheque over to the the bank's counter clerk unendorsed. This situation is covered specifically by section 2 of the Cheques Act 1957. This deems that District Bank, provided they have provided some value to Mr Lloyd in exchange for delivery to them of the cheque, are in the same position as if Mr Lloyd had endorsed the cheque in such a way as any holder had title to it, i.e. endorsed it in blank. The effect of this section was considered in *Midland Bank v Harris* [1963] 2 All ER 685. In *Westminster Bank v Zang* [1966] 2 WLR 110 the House of Lords considered what was meant by value in order to trigger the effect of the section. Both cases make it clear that a bank which pays the holder of a cheque before it has cleared has the rights which the holder had before he or she presented the cheque to the bank for payment.

5   Thus once section 2 of the Cheques Act 1957 is activated District Bank should acquire rights to sue the original drawer by tracing back through sections 34(1), 31(2), 29(1) and 38(1) and (2) of the Bills of Exchange Act 1882.

6   If my Instructing Solicitor is unclear about any aspect of this Advice, please feel free to contact me.

MARIA COLES

Lincoln House Chambers
30th October 1999

10.7   A Problem-Solving Opinion

In this case, advice to the client simply as to their legal position will not be of much use. Accordingly the writer goes on to suggest some practical means whereby the client's problems might be resolved.

IN THE MATTER OF A BOUNDARY DISPUTE INVOLVING JORDAN SCHOOL

ADVICE

1   In this matter I am asked to advise Jordan School in connection with a dispute that has arisen between it and some of its neighbours over the school's boundaries.

2   The school's boundaries are marked (insofar as they are material to this dispute) by a ditch which runs around the edge of the playing field. The school maintains that the ditch is part of its land and that it has accepted the responsibility for cleaning and maintaining it. I have seen the plan attached to the school's lease and frankly feel that it is to too small a scale to be of any assistance in determining the precise location of the boundary. This is a view shared by Mr Candle, a chartered surveyor of Marchwood Property Services, who has inspected the property. The owner of 4, The Spinney, one of the adjoining properties, a Mrs Major, has relied upon Land Registry maps in support of her assertion that the ditch is within her land. I agree with those instructing

me that the documents produced by Mrs Major are also unclear on the precise boundary.

3   In the absence of clear cartographical evidence about the boundary, it is difficult to see what rules relating to the determination of boundary disputes will be of assistance in resolving this matter. There is a well-known presumption that if there is a hedge alongside a ditch, the boundary is presumed to be on the farside of the hedge from the ditch (see e.g. *Vowles* v *Miller* (1810) 3 Taunt 137). Even if there is no hedge, the existence of a bank on which soil extracted from the ditch remains may suffice in place of the hedge. I rather gather from correspondence that there is no hedge or even bank here, so that presumption is not operative here. Probably the best evidence of title is the school's apparently undisputed ownership of the ditch up until the late 1980s. Mr Candle has suggested that it may be necessary to measure Mrs Major's property to establish exactly where her rear boundary is by reference to the front boundary. I think it likely that in view of the ambiguity of all the other evidence a court would find that the school is the owner of the ditch.

4   The school has I understand been at the same premises for over 60 years and throughout that time until the late 1980s no-one had challenged its ownership of the ditch. I am not entirely sure of the history of the school's occupation of the land. The present lease, granted in 1986, was in favour of Olive Knight. The normal principles about the acquisition of a title by adverse possession apply to ditches as they do to any other land (*Marshall* v *Taylor* [1895] 1 Ch 641). Whatever the original boundary, I think the school will have acquired a title in that way by now. By reason of section 15 of the Limitation Act 1980 the purported owner of property is prevented from bringing an action more than 12 years after the right to bring that action accrued. That date here would be when the school, regardless of whoever was its then owner, went into possession. This was clearly more than 12 years ago. The fact that it is a predecessor in title rather than Mrs Major who was in possession for most of the period is irrelevant. Accordingly I think the school will almost inevitably have acquired a title by adverse possession regardless of whether or not it was the original owner.

5   Matters appear to have come to a head between the school and Mrs Major recently. According to correspondence the school demolished a fence erected by her on the school side of the ditch. This was done in the light of Mrs Major's apparent acceptance that the ditch was not on her land. However Mrs Major's solicitors have asserted that this was an act of criminal damage and have even hinted that the school might be prosecuted for it. I do not think any credence whatsoever can be attached to this or any other threat made in respect of the removal of the fence.

6   Those instructing me have stated that the school is concerned that it may be liable to the lessor for damage to the reversion if the owners of 4, The Spinney acquire title by adverse possession. Although it is virtually inconceivable that such a title could be acquired I do not think that that would be the case even if Mrs Major did acquire such title against the school. Adverse possession would only be acquired against the school *qua* tenant. The doctrine of adverse possession does not allow the squatter to acquire a better title than that of the person against whom he has set up that possession (*Fairweather* v *St Marylebone Property Co. Ltd* [1963] AC 288).

7   If the school wishes to protect its position in relation to the ownership of the ditch it will be necessary to seek a declaration. Such proceedings should be commenced against any of the adjoining owners not prepared to recognise the school's title. If the school does wish to take the matter any further, I would therefore suggest that as the next step, a letter be sent to each of the owners of the houses in The Spinney that back onto the ditch, including Mrs Major. They should be asked whether they recognise the school's title and pointing out the possible costs consequences if they do not give such an acknowledgement making proceedings against them unnecessary. Such a letter might include a pro forma recognition to be signed by the owners. Assuming proceedings are commenced against Mrs Major, these should include a claim for damages for trespass. Such damages are likely to be nominal unless any actual expenditure was incurred in removing her fence.

8   I believe that I have said all that I usefully can at this stage but should those instructing me wish to discuss any aspect of this case further they should of course not hesitate to contact me.

WALTER HOPE

8 North Square, Gray's Inn, London WC1
22nd June 1999

10.8   Medical Negligence

This is an advice on the merits in a professional negligence case. In such cases the barrister's opinion has to be based almost entirely on the opinions of experts, rather than on his or her own professional judgment. It is a common fault in students' opinions for them to express a personal view on a matter in respect of which they are not experts. Note that the advice in this case depends on a very thorough analysis of the facts and (expert) evidence. This has led the writer, somewhat unusually, into quoting from the client's statement and the expert reports quite extensively.

IN THE BOGGLE COUNTY COURT   Claim No. ZG7 14778

BETWEEN

ALBERT GROUT   Claimant

and

BOGGLE & DISTRICT NHS TRUST   Defendant

_____

OPINION

_____

1   I am asked to advise Mr Grout as to the merits of his present action for damages for alleged negligent medical treatment arising from an operation that he underwent in June 1994. I am grateful to Instructing Solicitors for their very full instructions, and for the voluminous medical evidence also enclosed, in particular the medical reports of Mr Julian Pipe FRCS, consultant urologist, dated 24th October 1996 and subsequent letter dated 4th November 1997, the very full and detailed report of Arthur J.B. Bucket ChM FRCS, consultant urological surgeon, dated 20th March 1998, and letter of the same date, and the report of Mr W.F. Hose MC ChM FRCS, genito-urinary surgeon, dated 16th May 1998. I am also grateful to Mr Grout for his detailed annotations set out in the scheduled chronological analysis and summary of medical notes etc., which I have read thoroughly.

2   The sad history of this matter and the previous years of pain suffered by Mr Grout are set out in very great detail in the reports and records, and I do not therefore intend to repeat them here, save in outline. There is no doubt that since about 1986 Mr Grout has suffered pain in and around his testicles, and that in the following years various attempts to treat this by conservative methods had failed. His condition was diagnosed early on as epididymitis, being inflammation in the drainage portion of the testicle, and his symptoms were described as 'a classic picture of epididymitis' in the report of Mr Bucket (p. 3). Mr Bucket goes on to say (on p. 4) that:

The majority of patients with epididymitis have no obvious organic cause. In other words there is no frank infection to account for the symptoms.

In the case of Mr Grout tests for various possible causes were instituted and were negative. Mr Bucket considers that their normality was in keeping with the diagnosis.

The problem remained that Mr Grout continued to suffer from pain, and that nothing that was being done appeared to relieve this, or find the cause.

3   By the latter part of 1993, it became clear that conservative treatments were not working, nor were likely to be of any effect in the future. Consideration was then given to performing an epididymectomy. There is little doubt that such an operation is normally, and was at the time considered to be a last resort, as a bilateral epididymectomy would leave the patient sterile, there was a strong likelihood of post-operative pain, and the operation also has a significant failure rate. The operation is not commonplace, and it appears that its lack of success has caused it to become very much less popular today than it was a few years ago, although Mr Bucket and Mr Pipe consider it to be perfectly acceptable whereas Mr Hose (whose report is the most, indeed the only one, favourable to Mr Grout) considers that it is 'seldom a sensible one' to undertake and 'it very often fails to relieve the very symptoms for which it is done'.

4   Although a letter dated 7th November 1993 from Mr Steel (the consultant urological surgeon) indicates that in an outpatient review on 26th October 1993 the matter of an epididymectomy was discussed with Mr Grout and that he explained 'all the details of that operation quite clearly to him and he has accepted', it is clear that at the time the operation was intended to be confined to the right epididymus. When the operation was ultimately performed it was a bilateral epididymectomy which proved to have no effect on the pain. Indeed, as a consequence of the operation, Mr Grout suffered from additional pain as described in the reports. The questions on which I am asked to advise are:

(1)   whether the operation was necessary or advisable in the first place;

(2)   whether it was necessary or advisable for the operation to be bilateral rather than confined to the right epididymus;

(3)   whether Mr Grout was given sufficient indication of the nature and consequences of the operation (including its limited prospects of success) prior to consenting to it;

(4)   whether Mr Grout appreciated that the operation was to be bilateral rather than confined to the right epididymus;

(5)   whether Mr Grout received appropriate and sufficient after-care.

I will deal with each of these in turn.

Was the operation necessary or advisable?

5   On reading the various reports, it seems clear that this was a 'last ditch' operation 'designed to remove not the cause of the pain but its outward manifestation, namely the epididymus' (Mr Bucket, p. 8). Mr Hose considers that:

. . . since the epididymes were both normal on histological examination one has to question whether the operation that was done was, in fact, of any use at all. It is my opinion that the operation of epididymectomy is seldom a sensible one and it very often fails to relieve the very symptoms for which it is done.

Nevertheless he does not, in my view, categorically state that a decision to recommend or perform the operation was negligent, and his rationale for questioning the necessity of the procedure overlooks, in my respectful view, the fact that the operation is performed to remove the *effect* of the pain rather than the cause. Mr Pipe considers that Mr Grout had 'had several episodes of documented epididymitis and the decision to remove the epididymes was a reasonable one' (final page), Mr Bucket is of the view that 'the operation was reasonably indicated . . .' (at p. 21), and I therefore consider it unlikely that the Court would consider that a decision to recommend or perform the operation was itself negligent.

Should the operation have been bilateral?

6   As I have said, it is clear that originally it was intended that the operation should be confined to the right epididymus. Mr Grout states that at no time did he realise that the operation was to be bilateral, and that when he was asked to sign the consent form on the day of the operation, the word 'bilateral' was obscured by the thumb of Mr Guy, who presented it to him. However a letter dated 11th April 1994 from Mr Popper (Senior Registrar) refers to Mr Grout having complained of discomfort on the left side as well, although less marked, in the course of an out patient appointment on 3rd April, and says that consideration would be given to a bilateral operation if the symptoms are still troublesome on both sides. Further it seems clear from the records that the admission was for a bilateral operation — i.e. the decision to perform a bilateral operation was taken prior to the surgery itself. The notes at pp. 13–14 of the hospital records (referred to at p. 9 of Mr Bucket's report) also appear to suggest that the matter was reviewed both by the admitting House Officer and by Mr Guy, and a bilateral operation proposed. None of the three experts who have reported on Mr Grout's behalf states that an operation on the right epididymus rather than a bilateral operation should have been carried out, and I therefore do not consider that there are grounds for alleging the decision to perform a bilateral operation was of itself negligent.

Was Mr Grout given sufficient indication of the nature and consequences of the operation (including its limited prospects of success) prior to consenting to it?

7   It is here that a fundamental conflict of evidence arises, which cannot be entirely resolved by expert evidence. In his report at p. 9, Mr Bucket states:

> A patient being offered an epididymectomy should therefore understand that the operation is a 'last ditch' attempt to control symptoms. It is not required for any other reason and in particular not required to treat any health or even life-threatening disease of the genitalia. Its short-term (i.e. bruising infection in the scrotum) and long-term (i.e. persistent pain and embarrassment of testicular circulation) complications should be known before surgery. In effect a patient undergoing an epididymectomy for persistent/recurrent epididymitis must understand that despite the operation and the occurrence of any complications he may still have pain of a similar nature in the post-operative period despite the absence of his epididymus.

Additionally of course, there is the not inconsiderable disadvantage that a bilateral operation must lead to sterility. It is thus quite clear that a patient should not undergo an epididymectomy unless and until full explanation has been given to him.

8   Mr Grout is emphatic that such an explanation was not so given. He states that at first Mr Popper told him that he would be able to lead a completely normal life and that the operation would not in any way affect his sex life (Statement 6th February 1996, p. 3) but concedes that when he saw Mr Steel on 26th October 1993 the assurance was repeated, but he was told that he might not be able to have children (*ibid* p. 4). The relevant medical notes appear at p. 12 of the medical bundle, and seem to relate to a right epididymectomy — 'details of operation explained clearly'. In his undated statement, Mr Grout says of that meeting: 'I was categorically told there would be no operation on my left testicle'.

9   Both Mr Pipe and Mr Bucket are of the view that a right epididymectomy would not significantly affect his fertility, and therefore conclude that the fact Mr Grout subsequently enquired about sperm storage was evidence that the full operation had been discussed and agreed with him. Mr Hose does not deal with this point. If this is right, it does with respect appear strange that Mr Steel would have discussed the question of sterility with Mr Grout in the context of a right epididymectomy, rather than in that of the full bilateral operation. However, the fact that Mr Grout states that he was 'categorically told' there would be no bilateral operation may in my opinion lead the Court to infer that the consequences of such an operation being carried out were made known to him at the time.

10   Mr Grout states that as a result of what he had been warned, he decided that he would want the safeguard of sperm storage before going into hospital for what he considered to be a right epididymectomy (notwithstanding that the admission was clearly for the bilateral operation). He continues (Statement 6 February 1996, p. 5):

I explained [to Mr Gosling] that as there was a risk I would not be able to have children after this operation I would like to consider retaining some sperm now in case I ever decided to remarry. Mr Gosling explained he did not think that this could be done at the Royal Boggle Hospital and certainly was not sure whether it could even be done on the NHS and he advised that in all probability it would have to be done privately. He urged me to make up my mind quickly because he was coming to see me for the purpose of a pre-operative assessment and he would need me to sign the consent form for the surgery that day if it was to go ahead the following morning. Mr Gosling gave me about 15 or 20 minutes to make up my mind before signing the consent form or being discharged if I was to have this test done [sic]. I felt somewhat under pressure not least because I could not afford to pay for the sperm retention to be done privately, so having thought about the matter I signed the consent form to undergo the operation the following day.

In his undated statement, Mr Grout makes it clear that at no time did he appreciate that they were intending to operate on both testicles. In particular he says:

Just before the operation itself I was seen by Mr Gosling and given 15 minutes to make up my mind by Mr Gosling whether to proceed with the operation or not. Mr Gosling returned with a form. I had not been given an opportunity to read the form and when the form was thrust under my nose Mr Gosling's hand covered the top part which I now know had written 'Bilateral epididymectomy'. Mr Gosling said words to the effect of 'sign here'.

11   The pre-operative notes of Mr Gosling state however:

He has been told that 'open-ended' sperm storage is not available on the NHS, and at 55 he's not really worried about his fertility.

There is thus a fundamental conflict of evidence as to what actually took place between Mr Gosling and Mr Grout, and if the latter is right it is clear that the medical notes have not accurately recorded the very important circumstances surrounding his consent to the operation.

12   Mr Hose states in his report that

. . . the mistake seems to have come between the suggesting by Mr Popper in April 1994 that the left epididymus could be examined and the decision to remove it at the time of operation in June 1994. Insufficient time seems to have been taken to explain this fully pre-operatively to Mr Grout and he clearly feels that he was rushed into this decision.

This, of course, presupposes that Mr Grout's evidence will be preferred to that of Mr Gosling and Mr Steel. If the circumstances were as described by Mr Grout, then I have little doubt that the Court would hold that he had not been given sufficient information and that an actionable breach of duty therefore arose.

13   Unfortunately however, I consider that there will be real evidential difficulty in making out Mr Grout's case, parficularly if, as I suspect will be the case, Mr Steel and Mr Gosling maintain that the position was fully explained to him. There is as I have already said, evidence that a right epididymectomy would not cause any real danger of sterility, that examination of the left epididymus was proposed in the event of continuing difficulty, that the operation was clearly scheduled to be bilateral, that the question of sterility was discussed, and that Mr Grout signed the consent form. Additionally of course, the medical records indicate that Mr Grout was not concerned as to his fertility. Against that, Mr Grout says that the question of a bilateral operation

was never mooted with him, and that he was pressured into signing the consent form, which had the word 'bilateral' obscured. I must confess that, looking at the form (p. 21 of the medical bundle), it is difficult to see how the word 'bilateral' could have been obscured when it was signed, and I fear that as the case will be decided on the balance of probabilities, the Court may feel that the evidential weight is against Mr Grout.

14   Did Mr Grout appreciate that the operation was to be bilateral rather than confined to the right epididymus?

I think that I have dealt with this question above, and again regret that in my opinion, the balance of evidence will lead the Court to decide that the nature and extent of the operation had been fully explained to Mr Grout.

15   Did Mr Grout receive appropriate and sufficient after-care?

There is, in my opinion, no doubt that this operation carried with it the likelihood of unpleasant short-term after effects even if it was successful in stopping the pre-operative pain. This appears to have been borne out in Mr Grout's case, with the additional drawback that the procedure was not successful in any event. Having carefully read all three of the independent medical reports on Mr Grout, I cannot see any evidence that any of them considers that the after-care fell below acceptable standards. Even Mr Hose, who considered that there had been a serious fall below accepted standards in the final approach to the operation, does not appear to be of the view that post-operative care was lacking in any manner, and thus I cannot, regret-fully, advise that there is any prospect of a claim under this head succeeding.

16   I fully appreciate that Mr Grout will be extremely disappointed by the contents of this Opinion. He has suffered considerable pain for many years, and has undergone an operation which essentially has only added to his misfortunes. I also accept that Mr Hose (alone of the experts) considers that there was a serious breach of accepted standards prior to the operation. Nevertheless his view is predicated on the assumption that Mr Grout's version of events would prevail over that of the potential Defendants, and for the reasons outlined above, I regret that I do not consider that this will be the case. Additionally, although Mr Hose clearly implies that the operation was performed when there may have been insufficient physical evidence to suggest that the epi-didymus on either side was diseased, this in my respectful opinion fails to take account of the fact that the operation was performed in order to relieve the effect of the symptoms, rather than the cause. In summary therefore, I very much regret that I see little prospect of the proposed action succeeding, and must advise accordingly. I will naturally be pleased to advise further if required.

ANDREW BRIGHT

8 Grosvenor Buildings, Temple EC4
26th April 1999

10.9   Opinion Based on the Law

This short opinion, though not complex, raises almost no issues of fact. The answer to the question asked by the clients is to be found almost entirely in the law. This opinion is therefore an example of how to make use of legal reasoning to give the required advice.

RE PASTORS COTTAGE, BRIGHTON, EAST SUSSEX

OPINION

1   I am asked to advise Mr and Mrs Lemmon in respect of their occupation of Pastors Cottage, Brighton in East Sussex, where they have lived since they moved in immed-iately after they were married in July 1972.

2   Initially, Mr and Mrs Lemmon did not pay rent on the property as Mr Lemmon worked on the adjoining farm, the owner of which, a Mr Spinster, also owned the cottage. Unfortunately however, Mr Lemmon was made redundant in May 1973 and it appears that although Mr Spinster requested him to vacate the property for an 'incoming tenant', Mr and Mrs Lemmon were, in the event, allowed to remain in the property upon payment of rent. The sum required was £2.50 per week which was increased to £5 per week on or about 19 December 1973, this date being the first entry in Mr and Mrs Lemmon's rent book.

3   Mr Spinster unfortunately died sometime in 1975, and the Lemmons then paid their rent to his personal representatives until, on 1st November 1975, they were served with a Notice to Quit as the property was apparently going to be sold. Notwithstanding that, it appears that the Lemmons did not vacate the property even though there seem to have been some discussions about leaving between Mr Lemmon and solicitors for the subsequent landlords.

4   The property changed hands again in about September 1977 and Mr Lemmon paid the rent to the new landlords until 23rd May 1980, when he was informed that the cottage had been sold and the new owners would be taking over the following week. He was not told the identity of the new owners. Since that time he has continued to occupy and look after the cottage with Mrs Lemmon but there has been no request for rent and they have not paid any. They did attempt to ascertain the identity of the owners but such efforts have been unsuccessful.

5   Mr and Mrs Lemmon have therefore occupied the property on a rent-free basis for about 17 years. Section 15(1) of the Limitation Act 1980 provides that no action can be brought to recover land after the expiry of 12 years from the date on which the right of action accrued, and section 17 provides that the title of the owners is extinguished upon the expiry of that period.

6   In *Treloar* v *Nute* [1976] 1 WLR 1295 Sir John Pennycuick, having reviewed what are now sections 15(1) and 17 of the 1980 Act, stated (at p. 1300):

> The law, as we understand it, is that if a squatter takes possession of land belonging to another and remains in possession for 12 years to the exclusion of the owner, that represents adverse possession and accordingly at the end of the 12 years the owner's title is extinguished.

What is necessary, for the extinction of the owner's title therefore, is for there to have been uninterrupted adverse possession of the property for a period of 12 years from the date that the owners were entitled to its recovery.

7   The date from which the 12 years is to run is governed by Schedule 1 to the 1980 Act and depends, *inter alia*, upon the nature of the lease under which the Lemmons occupied the cottage. There does not appear to be any written agreement to rent the cottage (the existence of a rent book being insufficient to create a lease in writing: *Moses* v *Lovegrove* [1952] 2 QB 533) and accordingly the tenancy has, in my view, been an oral weekly tenancy.

8   As such, by virtue of Schedule 1, paragraph 5 of the 1980 Act, the tenancy is deemed, for the purposes of the Act, to be determined at the expiration of the first week and the right of action of the owner to recover possession of the property accrues at the date of that deemed determination. However, paragraph 5(2) goes on to provide that if rent is received after such determination (which, of course, in this case it was) the right of action is deemed to have accrued on the date of the <u>last</u> receipt of rent. That date in this case was 23rd May 1980 and accordingly the period of limitation seems to have expired.

9   There seems little or no dispute that the Lemmons have been in possession for that period without interruption. What seems to concern the Portsmouth District Land Registry is their suggestion that time has not run against the owners because the

Lemmons have not been in *adverse* possession as required by Schedule 1 paragraph 8(1) of the 1980 Act. In my opinion this concern does not take into account the fact that the tenancy is deemed to be determined by the operation of Schedule 1 paragraph 5(2).

10   The letter from the Land Registry of 1st November 1993, setting out their concern about the Lemmons' application to be registered, referred those instructing me to a passage in *Ruoff and Roper on Registered Conveyancing* which states that mere non-payment of rent cannot amount to adverse possession for the purposes of the Act. This assertion is, in my view, accurate in respect of tenancies for a term of years, as the tenancy continues to operate notwithstanding the tenant's default, and in such circumstances it is the tenant who occupies the property, and he is therefore estopped from denying the landlord's title (*Industrial Properties (Barton Hill) Ltd* v *Associated Electrical Industries* [1977] QB 580). Accordingly his possession cannot be adverse to the landlord's title.

11   In my view the position is different in the case of a periodic tenancy, as this is deemed to be determined under Schedule 1, paragraph 5(2). In *Moses* v *Lovegrove* [1952] 2 QB 533 the defendant in an action for the recovery of a property was a weekly tenant until 1938 after which time he had not paid any rent. The county court judge held that the owner's title had been extinguished by virtue of the Limitation Act. The Court of Appeal upheld that finding, Romer LJ stating (at p. 543):

> The point is that after the expiration of one week from the date of the last payment of rent, the defendant is deemed to have had no contractual right to possess and therefore to have been a trespasser or squatter.

Further examples can be found in the cases of *Hayward* v *Chaloner* [1968] 1 QB 107 and *Jessamine Investment* v *Schwartz* [1978] 1 QB 264.

12   Thus, in respect of a periodic tenancy, the non-payment of rent is, in my opinion, sufficient to constitute adverse possession because the tenancy is determined as a result and the occupier becomes a trespasser or squatter. Accordingly it is my view that for a period of 17 years Mr and Mrs Lemmon have had possession of the property which has been, and continues to be, adverse to the owner and in such circumstances are entitled to be registered as proprietors of the cottage under section 75 of the Land Registration Act 1925.

13   As a result, I suggest that a further application to the Portsmouth District Land Registry should be made setting out the position in respect of the periodic tenancy under which Mr and Mrs Lemmon occupied the cottage until it was determined by operation of the Act, and hopefully the position will be reconsidered, and they will be invested with the title. I will naturally be pleased to advise further if required.

ANDREW BRIGHT

8 Grosvenor Buildings, Temple EC4
6th June 1997

10.10 Opinion following Legal Research

This opinion raises issues of law and the writer has had to do some legal research. Note how the opinion nevertheless addresses the issues rather than the law, and applies the law to the facts, thereby avoiding an academic approach.

IN THE MATTER OF THE CASTERBRIDGE SHOPPING COMPLEX

OPINION

1   I am asked to advise Tess Ltd ('Tess') in this matter. Tess are the tenants of the above premises ('the Complex') and hold under a lease ('the Lease') dated 26th May 1993 from

D'Urberville Ltd ('D'Urberville'). Tess contend that D'Urberville are in breach of covenant in that they are not managing the Complex properly, so that vandalism is becoming rampant. This is reducing Tess's profits substantially, despite the heavy service charges which include a large amount supposedly for security. The vandalism creates a climate of fear. Many traders have left giving as their reason lack of security. Shoppers too stay away. One problem is that D'Urberville seem not to be exerting themselves overmuch to try and resolve these problems. Another is lack of evidence to prosecute offenders. I am asked to advise Tess whether there has been a breach of covenant and whether they can have the Lease determined. I am not at present asked to advise on remedies.

A breach of covenant?

2   Tess contend that D'Urberville are in breach of Clause 6 of the Lease. This reads as follows:

> **6**   To administer the Complex according to principles of good estate management.

Clause 6

3   Tess must prove that D'Urberville's failure to take any or any effective steps to prevent the losses which Tess are presently suffering through vandalism contravenes the 'principles of good estate management'.

4   I have scoured the practice books and cannot find any authority on the meaning of 'good estate management'. That being so, in my opinion it must be a question of fact to be determined by expert evidence. This means that we need a suitably qualified expert to give an opinion on whether taking steps to avoid this type of trouble falls within the ambit of good estate management. We need a firm of surveyors who specialise in estate management. If Tess can obtain a report from such a firm, I shall be happy to advise further.

The covenant for quiet enjoyment

5   The Lease contains (Clause 9) an express covenant for quiet enjoyment, which is in fairly standard form. Tess contend that this has been broken.

6   The express convenant, even though it is followed by the words 'or by any other person or persons whomsoever' (which is not so in the instant case) does not extend to the unlawful acts of third parties having no title: e.g. *King* v *Liverpool City Council* [1986] 1 WLR 890 (CA) (damage by vandals). Where the covenant is general against everyone, the alleged breach must show an interruption or disturbance by some person having *lawful* title: *Lucy* v *Leviston* (1673) Freem. 103. Here the covenant is expressly limited to 'any *lawful* interruption or disturbance from or by the Lessor or any person or persons *lawfully* claiming under or in trust for it'. (My italics.)

7   In my opinion therefore, Tess cannot sue for breach of the covenant for quiet enjoyment here.

Rescinding the lease

8   Ideally Tess would like to rescind the Lease. This I can quite understand after what they have suffered. One can rescind a lease for mistake or misrepresentation: *Solle* v *Butcher* [1950] 1 KB 671 (mistake); and *Sowler* v *Potter* [1940] KB 271 (where a tenant with a previous material conviction took a lease under a different name from that under which she had been convicted. The lease was held void for mistake). I should perhaps point out that these older cases must now be read in the light of section 1 of the Misrepresentation Act 1967, which permits rescission even after the contract has been completed (here by the granting of the Lease). This, however, does not apply to a breach of condition, only to a pre-contractual misrepresentation made to induce the contract in the first place.

9   In my opinion there is no evidence here of any misrepresentation or mistake at the time the contract was entered into. The question then becomes, can one rescind a lease for a breach of a condition? If so, the question becomes, is the trouble here sufficient to constitute a breach of condition, or is it only enough to create a breach of warranty?

10   I have found two cases on this topic, neither of which is directly in point on the facts of the instant case. In *Johnstone* v *Milling* (1886) 16 QBD 460 a lease for 21 years was determinable by the tenant after the first four years on six months' notice. The landlord covenanted to rebuild the premises after the first four years on six months' notice from the tenant requiring him to do so. Within the first four years the landlord often told the tenant that he could not procure the money to rebuild. The tenant therefore gave the requisite notice determining the lease. The tenant remained in possession hoping the landlord would rebuild, but when this did not happen the tenant claimed damages. It was held as follows: (1) The covenant to rebuild was never actually broken, because the lease had ended before the time for its performance arrived. (2) Therefore the tenant could not recover damages unless there had been an anticipatory breach by the landlord within *Hochster* v *De la Tour* (1853) 2 E & B 678. (3) In the circumstances of this case, the landlord's acts did not amount to repudiation, because he did not indicate that he would not rebuild *whether or not* he had the money (*per* Lord Esher MR at p. 468). (4) Even if he did, there was no breach of contract unless the tenant elected to treat those acts as ending the contract. (5) Here the tenant had not so elected. *Quaere* whether *Hochster* v *De la Tour* applies to a lease or a contract containing various stipulations, where the whole contract cannot be treated as ended on the wrongful repudiation of one stipulation by the promisor.

11   In *Surplice* v *Farnsworth* (1844) 7 M & G 576 the Defendants were yearly tenants to the Plaintiff of certain malt-offices at £25 payable half yearly. They took possession at Michaelmas 1838 and quit in March 1843, because the premises were not in a fit state of repair for malting. It was held (*per* Tindal CJ; Coltman and Cresswell JJ agreeing) that where the landlord covenants to do repairs under a lease, there is no implied condition that the tenant can quit if the repairs are not done.

12   *Prima facie* these two cases are directly against us. Here Tess wishes to rescind the Lease for the breach of two covenants contained in the Lease neither of which goes to the whole consideration. Equally there is no express term in the Lease allowing them to do so. Can these two cases be distinguished? In my opinion the only way we might achieve this without an express stipulation in our favour in the Lease would be to show that it was expressly contemplated by Tess and D'Urberville, when the Lease was granted, that the problems Tess are now facing would not happen. It might be possible to argue that certain dicta of Lord Esher MR and Cotton LJ in *Johnstone* v *Milling*, though they clearly state that one cannot rescind a lease for breach of covenant, leave the way open for an action for rescission for breach of condition. They also appear to contemplate that a lease *could* be rescinded for breach of condition (if, but only if, the breach were sufficiently serious) on the basis that it is a contract. The difficulties which I see with this argument are firstly that the actual decision in *Johnstone* v *Milling* went the other way, secondly that *Surplice* v *Farnsworth* is even more strongly against us. In particular it says that one cannot rescind a lease for breach of covenant unless there is an express term allowing one to do so. Thirdly I have been unable to find any authority in which a lease was actually rescinded in circumstances which were akin to the instant case. Indeed even if I were able to devise a stronger argument for distinguishing these cases, I would still have to advise Tess that they would probably have to fight a test case right up to the House of Lords in order to establish this point, with all the uncertainties and risks as to costs which that would entail.

13   I must therefore advise Tess that in my opinion that they cannot rescind the Lease on the present facts.

Frustration

14   Another way in which Tess could rid themselves of the Lease would be if they could argue successfully that it has been frustrated by the actions of the vandals. The

doctrine of frustration can apply to an executed lease, but in practice it will rarely occur: *National Carriers v Panaplina (Northern) Ltd* [1981] 2 WLR 45 (HL). In this case the only access road to the demised premises was closed by the local authority for an expected period of about 20 months while a Victorian warehouse in a dangerous condition was demolished. Lords Hailsham, Simon and Roskill said: Frustration occurs when the nature of the outstanding rights and obligations is so significantly changed by some supervening event from what the parties could reasonably have contemplated at the time of its execution that it would be unjust to hold them to its performance. Here there was no triable issue as to frustration, having regard to the likely length of the lease after the interruption in relation to the original term.

15   In my opinion there are two insurmountable hurdles if trying to argue frustration in the instant case. Firstly, in my opinion the instant case is a less serious contender on its facts for the application of the doctrine than the *Panalpina* case. Secondly, and in the light of that, there is the comment by the House of Lords that in practice it will rarely apply to leases.

Final points

16   I should perhaps just mention two things. Firstly, Tess may be able to obtain specific performance or damages from D'Urberville. Secondly, the legislation makes provision for challenging service charges which are excessive. If Tess wish to consider either of these possibilities, I shall be happy to advise further.

Conclusion

17   My conclusions are as follows:

(a)   To prove a breach of Clause 6, we require expert evidence from a surveyor specialising in the field of estate management, that D'Urberville are not adhering to the principles of 'good estate management'. On receipt of such a report I shall be happy to advise further.

(b)   In my opinion Tess cannot sue under the covenant for quiet enjoyment, because the trouble is not being caused by the landlord or someone claiming *lawfully* under or through them.

(c)   In my opinion, Tess cannot rescind the Lease on the present facts.

(d)   In my opinion Tess cannot extricate themselves from the Lease by invoking the doctrine of frustration.

(e)   Therefore any remedy lies in damages, specific performance or challenging the service charges.

T. V. BEDE

Lincoln Court
Lincoln's Inn
London

1st September 1999

10.11   Opinion in a Complex Case

The case here is quite involved (and uses pre-Woolf terminology, as proceeding were issued prior to April 1999). It raises several issues of fact, evidential difficulties, points of law and tactical considerations. Not surprisingly the opinion is therefore quite long and thorough. Note once again how the overall purpose behind the opinion is a practical one, though, and how the law is researched and relied upon simply to help the writer give advice to his clients on the facts of the case and the steps they should take.

<u>IN THE THRING COUNTY COURT</u>   Case No. TH3 06166

BETWEEN

FRIENDLY MORTGAGES PLC
(FORMERLY UGLY MORTGAGES PLC)   <u>Plaintiff</u>

and

YOUSOF HASSAN (Male)   <u>1st Defendant</u>

and

MARGARET HASSAN (Female)   <u>2nd Defendant</u>

OPINION

---

1 I am asked to advise the Plaintiff Company in respect of the rather complicated situation that has arisen over their advance of £55,000 to the Defendants secured by way of mortgage on their property at 1 Phoebus Road, Thring, London SE9. I am grateful to Instructing Solicitors for their full and cogent instructions, and will endeavour to set out the history of the matter as follows:

2 Mr and Mrs Hassan were married in November 1982. Mr Hassan was born in the Turkish part of Cyprus in November 1960 and on 10th March 1985 the Home Office removed any restrictions on the period for which he might remain in the UK. There appears to be evidence that the majority of his time during his marriage has been spent in this country, in that the home was originally purchased on 13th May 1984, he obtained a British driving licence in February 1985 and appears to have worked here as well. Thus, he was married in this country at the age of 22 and is now 38. This may be of importance when considering the degree and extent to which he spoke English at all relevant periods.

3 There appears to be no dispute that Mr Hassan, together with his wife, signed the original papers whereby the property was charged to the Woolwich Building Society on 13th May 1984, for an amount which is presently unknown. For reasons which will become apparent, it would be helpful if this sum could be ascertained. On 25th August 1987 what appears to have been a further charge in favour of Barclays Bank PLC was taken out. The original mortgage was redeemed from a mortgage advance from Western Trust & Savings Ltd on 6th March 1989, the Barclays charge being postponed in priority to that charge. The Barclays charge was in turn redeemed from a mortgage advance by Cedar Holdings Ltd on 2nd July 1989, in the sum of £1,118.37. Thus in mid-1989 there were two charges on the property, from Western Trust, and Cedar Holdings. A further charge was taken out by Barclays on 24th December 1989, but this was redeemed, and does not come into the present equation.

4 Both the above charges were redeemed from a mortgage advance from the Plaintiffs (then known as UGLY Mortgages PLC) on 22nd August 1992. Repayments fell into arrears, and in April 1993 proceedings were taken against the Defendants by the Plaintiffs, which culminated in a Court order dated 3rd August 1993 for possession, neither Defendant making an appearance at the hearing. The arrears were then fully discharged by a cheque from Mrs Hassan. The account went into arrears again shortly afterwards, and despite various negotiations, the present proceedings were issued in April 1995. The case was then adjourned on a number of occasions due to extensive negotiations, but although correspondence was naturally addressed to both parties,

117

oral communication always took place with Mrs Hassan, as it appears that the Plaintiffs understood that Mr Hassan did not in fact speak English very well.

5   On 7th August 1996, Mr Hassan filed a Defence in the course of which he denied that he had ever applied for or entered into a legal charge with the Plaintiffs, and that his signature had either been obtained by the deception of his estranged wife, or (somewhat inconsistently one might think) had been forged. On 2nd December 1996 Mrs Hassan filed a Defence in which she admitted the Plaintiff's right to possession of the premises, denied deception and forgery, and claimed that her husband had full knowledge of the transaction and signed the mortgage deed. I understand that Mr Hassan also claims that his signature had been forged on all charges created after the charge to the Woolwich, and has commenced Third Party proceedings against Mr Fothergill, the solicitor who allegedly witnessed his signature on the mortgage deed, which proceedings specifically do not allege that Mr Fothergill was instructed by him. In a rather interesting Defence to Third Party Notice, Mr Fothergill does not deal with whether or not he was instructed by either Defendant and, curiously, does not admit to witnessing Mr Hassan's signature on the Plaintiff's legal charge. It is perhaps not without significance however, that in a letter to Messrs Howe and Whenne, solicitors for Cedar Holdings, dated 30th June 1992, Mr Fothergill confirmed that his firm was

> acting for Mr and Mrs Hassan in connection with a remortgage of their property number 1 Phoebus Road, Thring, London SE9 with a view to re-paying the loan from your client company

and that there was then some considerable correspondence with his firm on this matter. Instructing Solicitors have naturally sought the opinion of a handwriting expert on the question of alleged forgery, but unfortunately his report is inconclusive, and if anything will be more helpful to Mr Hassan than to the Plaintiffs.

6   The position is thus complex, and I have been asked to advise on a number of matters of law and evidence, and generally. Although there will naturally be an amount of overlap, I will deal with the various matters discretely.

Res judicata

7   I have considered whether it could be alleged that Mr Hassan is in some way estopped from denying that he is the mortgagor of his interest in the property to the Plaintiffs, by virtue of his having a judgment against him in the proceedings taken in 1993, and/or that the matter is *res judicata*. I regret that I do consider that such an argument would be successful, in that no attendance was made on the summons, and judgment was effectively given in default of a defence. It would technically be possible for Mr Hassan to seek to set aside the original judgment against him, although he is clearly well out of time, and as the question of his signature to the mortgage deed was not specifically considered by the Court, I feel that there may be more appropriate ways of approaching the present case.

Knowledge

8   There is, of course, very considerable suspicion that Mr Hassan knew full well of the various transactions that had been taking place with regard to the property, and that the present Defence is a complete sham. Instructing Solicitors have investigated the situation with regard to one of the alleged witnesses to Mr Hassan's signature on previous documents, but with a cynicism doubtless born of considerable and bitter experience, have concluded that it is unlikely that the witness can be traced, or would in any event be willing to attend Court. I fully concur with Instructing Solicitors' view that it will be necessary to seek disclosure of files relating to the previous transactions, as the issue is obviously vital. I do however, note that there is no evidence of any direct contact with Mr Hassan in the past, and that all correspondence appears to have originated from his wife. As I have already said, the handwriting report is more likely to favour Mr Hassan than the Plaintiffs, as it is clear that the signatures are not his normal one and bear only a superficial similarity to his specimen. The conclusion would thus have to be that if they were genuine, Mr Hassan had formed the intention

at the time to raise the present argument, and altered his regular signature so that he could later allege that they were forgeries. I fear that the Court may find this difficult to accept.

9   Notwithstanding this, it would be helpful if all possible evidence was obtained as to Mr Hassan's capacity to speak and understand English. I note that the Conciliator's Report of Mr Bowsprit for Cedar Holdings dated 26th May 1991 evidences that he attended the premises, and that both Mr and Mrs Hassan were present, but Mr Hassan was entertaining guests, and he therefore dealt with his wife. In the light of her defence, it may be interesting to see the degree and extent, if any, to which her solicitors would be prepared for her to cooperate in the case against her estranged husband, and what evidence, if any, she would be able to disclose.

10   It does appear however, that Mr Hassan accepts that he signed the application for the mortgage with the Plaintiffs, but did not understand what he was signing, only believing that it was something to do with 'Canada'. Even if this somewhat unlikely account is accepted by the Court, such an argument will not, in my view negate the effect of what he did: see *Barclays Bank PLC v Schwartz* (1995) *The Times*, 2 August 1995. In that case the Court of Appeal held that illiteracy and unfamiliarity with the English language did not by themselves provide a defence to an action in contract, even if the other party was aware of their existence. Millett LJ stated that there was a difference between the above disabilities and those of mental incapacity or drunkenness, in that the former might not only deprive the sufferer of understanding the transaction, but also deprive him of the awareness that he did not understand it. A man who was unfamiliar with English was aware of that fact. If he signed a document which he did not understand he had only himself to blame, and was in no better a position than the man who signed a document which he did not read because he was too busy.

11   Additionally, Mr Hassan may have some difficulty in convincing the Court that he remained entirely unaware at all material times as to the various difficulties pertaining to his inability to repay the mortgage, particularly when he was apparently either unemployed or very short of work for a considerable time, and must surely have been aware of the mounting debt. To put some pressure on Mr Hassan, I have drafted some Interrogatories, but do not consider that a Request for Further and Better Particulars of the Defence will do anything but further delay the trial of this matter, and add to the overall expense. The Interrogatories themselves may not advance the issues much further, in that the cases of the respective parties are clear, but may of course expose further weaknesses in the Defence.

Success on the facts

12   I am not overly optimistic as to the prospect of success on the facts, notwithstanding the almost overwhelming suspicion that Mr Hassan knew full well what was going on, although I certainly would not advise conceding the issue. The main difficulty that may occur is that of Mr Fothergill. It may be of course, that he will contend that he did witness a signature, and believed at the time that it was that of Mr Hassan. If this is or is found to be the case, an overwhelming suspicion will fall on Mrs Hassan, and her husband's case will be considerably enhanced. The same may be true if Mr Fothergill concedes that he did not actually witness the signature at all, but witnessed a document which had already been signed. His pleaded case is somewhat ambiguous on this point. On the other hand, if Mr Fothergill (who appears to have acted for both Defendants for some time) states that he knew Mr Hassan and that he signed the document, I suspect that the Court will accept his evidence in preference to that of Mr Hassan. However, if that was the case, it is not unfortunately borne out by the manner in which the Third Party Defence has been pleaded.

The Third Party Defence

13   I have been asked to comment on the Defence to the Third Party Notice, in which Mr Fothergill contends that, in any event, Mr Hassan has suffered no loss and damage.

The grounds of this are twofold. First, it is contended that if Mr Hassan did sign the document, he is duly and properly indebted to the Plaintiffs, and that any failure to witness the signature will have caused no loss. In such an event, I consider that the Court would have little difficulty in accepting this, unless some form of *non est factum* is then contended by Mr Hassan, which might be difficult in the circumstances. Secondly, Mr Fothergill alleges that as the purpose of the loan was to pay off an indebtedness to Cedar Holdings and Western Trust, and that such indebtedness both exceeded that to the Plaintiffs and was paid off, no loss has been suffered as a result of any negligence. Such an argument would, in my view, be unassailable save and to such extent as it may be held that the previous indebtedness did not exist by virtue of fraud. In *Target Holdings Ltd v Redferns* [1995] 3 All ER 785, the House of Lords extended the principle and held that solicitors who acted in breach of trust were not liable to compensate the beneficiary for losses which the beneficiary would, in any event, have suffered if there had been no such breach. If however, the previous securities were themselves invalid through fraud, the position will be far less certain, as will be discussed later below.

Did Mr Fothergill owe any duty to the Plaintiffs?

14   It is in my view arguable that Mr Fothergill owed a duty not merely to his own clients, but also to the Plaintiffs to ensure that he validly witnessed the signature on the mortgage deed. It is in my opinion strongly arguable that the witnessing of a signature constitutes a representation to the other side that the document has been signed by the person purporting to sign it, and that a duty therefore lies to the other side to ensure that all proper care is taken in the circumstances. I base my view on the following. It is clearly inappropriate for a solicitor to sign that he has witnessed a signature when the document has already been signed before it is brought into his presence. To hold otherwise would be to make a nonsense of the act of witness. If therefore Mr Fothergill put his signature to a document that had already been signed in his absence, I am of the view that the Court would hold that he would be in breach of a duty to those persons who would foreseeably be relying on him for the purposes for which the signature was witnessed. If therefore, it is necessary for a person actually to sign before the witness, the purpose of such presence must, in my opinion, be to witness not merely that the document had been signed (which would not require physical presence for the reasons above), but also that, insofar as it was practical to do so, that it was being signed by the person who purported to sign it. Of course, if a deception was practised on the solicitor, he may not be in breach of his duty. However, the manner in which the Third Party Defence has been drafted suggests that there was some obvious material irregularity in the procedure, and I would therefore advise that proceedings be extended to allege breach of duty against Mr Fothergill as well. I will be happy to draft the appropriate claim upon receipt of instructions to that effect.

Are the Plaintiffs entitled to 'stand in the shoes' of Cedar Holdings, and/or any other party, under the principle of subrogation?

15   The ease with which this question can be answered will depend very much upon whether the previous charges were valid. If it can be shown that the charge to Cedar Holdings and Western Trust was valid insofar as Mr Hassan is concerned, then I have little doubt that the Court will hold that the purpose of the loan was for the express purpose of discharging the previous mortgage(s) and substituting the Plaintiffs for the mortgagees thereof, and that indeed there was a clear negative intention that it should not be used for any other purpose: see *Boscawen & Others v Bajwa; Abbey National PLC v Boscawen & Others* (ChD) 27th May 1994 (unreported), applying the principles laid down in *Orakpo v Manson Investments* [1978] AC 95. These principles have now been revised slightly in view of the demise of the Bankruptcy Act 1927 (on which that case was predicated), which has removed the requirement for an express term of the contract to the effect that it was the common intention of the parties that the money borrowed was to be used to pay the holders of existing charges, to be incorporated in a written memorandum. In *Roberts v National Guardian Mortgage Corporation* (CA) 8th November 1993 (unreported), the lenders brought an action to enforce what appeared to be a legal charge on a property in Porthcawl, executed by a husband and wife. It was

accepted however, that the husband had no knowledge of the charge, and that his signature had been forged on the documentation by his wife. The lenders claimed rights of subrogation on the footing that they were entitled to stand in the shoes of a previous second mortgagee of the property, whose charge was paid off and discharged out of the advance made to the borrowers. The borrowers claimed that the purpose of the loan was for the purpose of consolidation of debts, and that although there was power to discharge the previous mortgage, it was not the express intention of the loan for that purpose to be achieved. Insofar as the wife was concerned, the court had no hesitation in applying the principle stated in *Ghana Commercial Bank* v *Chandiram* [1960] AC 732 to hold that it was the common intention of the wife and the lenders that a previous charge would be discharged out of the new advance, and that the lenders were entitled to claim subrogation to the previous chargees. Although it was alleged that they should have taken greater precautions, and if they had done so they would not have had a legal charge which was a forgery palmed off on them before they parted with their money, they suffered from that in that, by subrogation, they could only recover what was due under the valid prior charge, and not any more that they may have advanced. Roch LJ stated in his judgment that he adopted the test laid down by Lord Salmon in the *Orakpo* case, where he stated 'The test as to whether the courts will apply the doctrine of subrogation to the facts of any particular case is entirely empirical. It is, I think, impossible to formulate any narrower principle than that the doctrine will be applied only when the courts are satisfied that reason and justice demand that it should be.' In any event, in the present case, the Plaintiffs would have a valid equitable charge over all the estate that Mrs Hassan could convey, namely her equitable interest in the trust for sale affecting the property, see Law of Property Act 1925, s. 63 and *Williams and Glynn* v *Boland* [1981] AC 487, approved in *First National Securities Ltd* v *Hegerty* [1985] QB 850.

16 Insofar as the husband was concerned the Court held that the position was different, in that he did not know that there was any advance being made by the lenders. It is perhaps worth quoting the judgment of Dillon LJ at some length on this point, as it is, in my view, highly relevant to the question of whether it is possible to 'trace' the subrogation through to the original and conceded legal debt:

> But so far as he is concerned, the position is covered in my judgment, by the two decisions at first instance of *Butler* v *Rice* [1910] 2 Ch 277 decided by Warrington J and *Chetwynd* v *Allen* [1899] 1 Ch 353 decided by Romer J. These found, on the position which is referred to as a 'well-known equitable doctrine', that if a stranger pays off a mortgage on an estate he presumably does not intend to discharge that mortgage but to keep it alive for his own benefit.

Warrington J considers the questions that have to be dealt with:

> Is it material that the owner of the property, the mortgagor, had not requested the person who paid the money to make the payment?

> And is the Plaintiff's right affected by further differences between the proposals for the new charge, which was ineffective, and the terms of the previous charge which was paid off?

Warrington J continues:

> Here there was an existing charge, and the only question is whether it has been paid off or kept alive. On such a question as that it appears the concurrence of the mortgagor is immaterial. Her position is not affected. The only alteration in her position is that instead of owing the money to A she will in future owe it to B.

He refers then to *Chetwynd* v *Allen* and expresses the view that the judgment there is consistent with the view he has expressed.

> As I see it, Mr Roberts cannot claim to have achieved the windfall that the debt he owed to [the mortgagees], which was charged on the property, has been discharged

so that . . . he has no responsibility for the monies paid out by the Plaintiffs to discharge the debt to [the mortgagees].

Nolan LJ stated in his judgment:

Therefore it seems to me, it helps Mr Roberts not at all to maintain, as indeed was the case, that he was unaware of his wife's transactions with the Plaintiffs and took no part in it.

The governing principle is that he should not suffer as a result, in the sense of being worse placed before than he was afterwards as regards the obligations contracted by him and by his wife under the previous and valid mortgage. But his situation in that respect has been safeguarded in the present case. No more is claimed from him than was claimable under the earlier mortgage.

17   It is, in my view, arguable that the above principle can be extended to apply to the present case. Even if all the previous charges were invalid save for the first, it is possible to allege that, to the extent that he was indebted to the Woolwich Building Society under the original charge, Mr Hassan is still liable to the Plaintiffs, in that he would otherwise have gained a windfall by taking advantage of the fact that a debt for which he is liable has been paid off by the Plaintiffs. Put another way, each succeeding purported chargee adopts the rights of subrogation of the previous, with regard to the original debt. The difference in the present case is, of course, that it is the amount of the original debt only, for which Mr Hassan would continue to be liable, and not the latest in the chain. However, I nevertheless consider that he would be liable for accumulated interest thereon if it was originally chargeable, as the debt would still be outstanding (provided the term had not expired). This point was expressly dealt with by the Court of Appeal in *Western Trust & Savings Ltd* v *Rock*, 26th February 1993 (unreported), where the right to subrogation was admitted, but the dispute was as to whether the Defendant was liable for interest on the original sum charged. Balcombe LJ held that the rights of the original mortgagee to which the Plaintiff was subrogated, included a right to compound interest, and that right was also included in the subrogation.

18   Thus, in the present case, I would advise that an action should be brought against Mr Fothergill (whether by inclusion in the present proceedings, or possibly more efficiently by separate action, and consolidation; and the case should be pursued on the facts against Mr Hassan, with the alternative claim for subrogation in the event of it being held that he did not sign the present charge. I consider that a Reply should be filed to allege the right to subrogation, although leave for this may have to be obtained, in view of the fact that Pleadings are presumably closed. I will draft the appropriate document upon receipt of instructions.

19   I have considered the question of a split trial, but respectfully concur with Instructing Solicitors that this should be resisted. The issues are largely concomitant, and the question of credibility is paramount. I do not, with respect, see that much, if any, saving of time will be achieved by a split trial.

20   I hope that I have covered the relevant issues in this difficult case, but I will naturally be pleased to advise further if required.

ANDREW BRIGHT

8 Grosvenor Buildings, Temple EC4
3rd November 1998

ELEVEN

ADVISING FOR THE PURPOSES OF LEGAL AID

11.1 Introduction

In late 1999 the well publicised Access to Justice Bill should be enacted. It will, amongst other things, fundamentally alter the way in which civil litigation is funded in this jurisdiction. The Legal Aid Fund for civil cases currently costs the taxpayer £800 million a year. It is intended to cut this bill drastically by replacing the current funding arrangements with a new scheme. The Act will provide the framework for the provision of legal services (information, advice, assistance and representation) through a Community Legal Service and the provision of funding through a Community Legal Service Fund. This fund will replace legal aid in civil and family cases. It will not be available to assist many litigants previously eligible for legal aid. In effect, legal aid will not be available in the following cases:

- negligence claims for damages for property damage or personal injuries (save in clinical negligence cases and public interest cases);

- defamation;

- company/partnership proceedings;

- trust cases (other than those involving joint ownership or occupation of domestic property);

- boundary disputes.

The fund's availability is to be limited in various other cases. The funding of these types of cases will therefore be through other means, the most important of which are: private means, conditional fee arrangements and insurance contracts.

However, over the next few years many legal aid funded cases, started before the Access to Justice Bill was passed, will remain live. Consequently, you will still often be instructed to advise as to whether legal aid should be extended or allowed to continue in a certain case.

Legal aid certificates almost invariably contain restrictions both as to the nature of the work that can be done under them (for example, limited to the obtaining of counsel's opinion on merits and quantum and thereafter the settling (but not the service) of proceedings); and as to the amount of costs that can be incurred before a further extension is required. Furthermore, you are under a duty to keep the Legal Aid Board informed as to circumstances which should or may influence the continuation of an existing legal aid certificate *even if these circumstances are adverse to the interest of your client!* This includes (but is not limited to) advising the Legal Aid Board of (and of the reasonableness of) any offer made by the other side to settle the claim, and any circumstances which may significantly adversely affect the prospects of success on which you have previously advised.

Generally speaking, the format and structure of an advice on legal aid should not differ from that of an 'ordinary' advice on merits or on evidence. It is necessary however, to have regard to the provisions of the Legal Aid Act 1988, and the annual *Legal Aid Handbook*. A knowledge of the General Council of the Bar's *Legal Aid Guidelines* (although these are not mandatory) should however, be sufficient for most purposes, and these are summarised below.

11.2 Advising for the Purposes of Legal Aid

11.2.1 THE STATUTORY TEST

Provided that an applicant is financially eligible, he or she must still show:

(a) That he or she has reasonable grounds for taking, defending or being a party to the proceedings; and

(b) That it is not unreasonable that he or she should be granted representation in the particular circumstances of the case.

Test (a) above is said to have been satisfied if, assuming the facts alleged are proved, there is a case which has *reasonable prospects of success in law* and, assuming the applicant had the means to pay the likely costs, *he or she would be advised to take or defend the proceedings privately.*

Test (b) above may not be fulfilled if, for example, the case is *not likely to be cost effective*, where the application reveals *some illegal motive or conduct by the applicant*, where *compensation could be obtained from the Criminal Injuries Compensation Authority*, or where *rights could be exercised either in a different court where costs would be lower, or other sources of funding such as insurance are available to the applicant.*

The above list is not exhaustive, but gives a good general indication of the criteria that have to be applied when advising whether or not a case is suitable for legal aid.

11.2.2 CONTENTS OF BARRISTER'S OPINION ON MERITS

Your written opinion on merits should:

(1) show that both the legal merits and the reasonableness tests have been specifically and separately addressed before a conclusion is reached;

(2) set out any conflict as to facts concisely so as to enable the Legal Aid Board to assess the relative strengths of rival factual versions;

(3) express a clear opinion as to whether the applicant's version is likely to be accepted by the court and why;

(4) summarise any issues of law sufficiently to enable the Legal Aid Board to come to a view about them without going outside the opinion;

(5) express a clear view as to whether the legal case has a reasonable prospect of being accepted by the court, and why;

(6) draw attention to any lack of material or other matters which could now or in the future materially affect your assessment of the outcome of the case and consider the need for a conference;

(7) quantify at least the bracket within which damages are likely to be awarded (where damages are claimed);

(8) confirm that you are of the view that the proceedings are cost-effective — i.e. that the costs are likely to be justified by the potential benefit to the applicant (bearing in mind the Legal Aid statutory charge);

(9) suggest any limitation or condition that should be placed on the certificate (subject to further advice), in order to protect the interests of the Legal Aid Fund.

11.2.3 PROSPECTS OF SUCCESS

In estimating the prospects of success, it is not now sufficient merely to give a generalised view that the case is fit for legal aid. The prospects of a successful outcome should be given by reference to the following categories:

A Very good (80%)

B Good (60–80%)

C Reasonable (50–60%)

D Less than evens

E Impossible to say.

In the event that your assessment falls within categories D or E, further explanation should be given if you are nevertheless of the view that the Board should still consider that legal aid be granted.

11.2.4 THE MEANS TEST

When considering whether a client would be advised to take or defend the proceedings privately had he or she the means, such a client should be assumed to be of moderate but not excessive means. Such a client should therefore be taken as being able to meet the likely costs, albeit with some difficulty, or as something of a sacrifice.

11.2.5 COSTS

It is also necessary, where appropriate, to advise your solicitors to provide the Legal Aid Board with an estimate of the likely costs should the matter proceed to a fully contested hearing.

11.3 Sample Opinion on the Extension of Legal Aid

IN THE PROPOSED ACTION

BETWEEN:

MARY PETERS <u>Claimant</u>

and

FIELD RIDING CLUB <u>Defendant</u>

—————————

OPINION

—————————

1 <u>FACTS</u>

On 22nd April 1998 Mary Peters was offered a part-time vacation job at Field Riding Club, Hen Road, Worcestershire. The job commenced on 14th July. On 21st July 1998

Miss Peters was carrying out some work on a spectators' stand by a dressage arena. I am instructed that she was working under the direct instruction and supervision of Michael Dell who was the Riding Club's assistant manager.

2   She and Mr Dell were trying to loosen a bolt on the underside of the spectators' stand as some sections needed to be replaced. I am instructed that a 'grinder' was normally used for this job, which I assume is a power driven tool. Apparently the grinder could not be found on this occasion and the job was being done manually.

3   A ratchet was placed on top of the bolt and a scaffolding pole placed at the end of the ratchet in order to create leverage. Mr Dell was using the ratchet and pole to loosen the bolt. Miss Peters was holding the other end of the bolt using a spanner in order to prevent it moving and creating the necessary resistance to the loosening action.

4   Suddenly the ratchet slipped off the bolt and this in turn caused the spanner to jump out of Miss Peters' hand, land on her fingers and cause injury.

5   <u>LIABILITY</u>

There is no doubt that Miss Peters was employed by the Riding Club. As employers they owed her a duty to provide a safe system of work and safe supervision and competent fellow employees. The duty to provide suitable equipment would also arise pursuant to the Provision and Use of Work Equipment Regulations 1992.

6   In my view liability could be established against the club provided that the following matters were established:

(a)   that a grinder or other mechanical device should have been used to carry out this job rather than it being done by hand;

(b)   if a grinder had been used, either Miss Peters would not have had to hold the underside of the bolt, or if she did, it would have been unlikely that the spanner would have been caused to jump;

(c)   that Michael Dell was instructing and/or supervising Miss Peters and that either the grinder was not available or the decision not to use it was made by Michael Dell.

7   It does seem to me that carrying out this operation manually was rather dangerous, although I find it a little difficult to understand how the spanner came out of Miss Peters' hand when she was gripping it firmly.

8   I am instructed that Miss Peters clearly states that she was under the supervision of Mr Dell. She also says that she was told by Mr Dell, before they started the job, that a grinder was normally used for loosening bolts in these circumstances.

9   My initial view therefore is that this claim has a good prospect of success (60–80% category B). In view of the merits and the quantum (which is in excess of £7,000 as discussed below) it is reasonable for legal aid to be extended to allow for proceedings to be issued. I am also of the view that following the issue of proceedings, an expert report should be obtained from an engineer experienced in health and safety matters. It is reasonable for legal aid to be further extended if necessary to allow for this.

10   <u>QUANTUM</u>

(This opinion would continue with a discussion and valuation of quantum in the usual way.)

Chambers address   SUSAN REES

11.4 Sample Opinion on Payment into Court

IN THE SUFFOLK COUNTY COURT   Claim No. S5223344

BETWEEN:

SARAH TOWNS   Claimant

and

HENOR GARAGE LIMITED   Defendants

ADVICE ON PART 36 PAYMENT

---

1   On 6th August 1999 the Defendants made a Part 36 Payment into Court of £3,000. Liability is not in dispute in this case. I am now asked to consider the likely quantum of the claim and to consider whether the Part 36 Payment into Court should be accepted or not.

2   Mrs Towns should understand that a Payment into Court is a powerful weapon in the hands of a Defendant in this type of case. If she were to reject the Payment into Court and, after a trial was awarded a sum which was the same or lower than the amount paid into court, she would have to bear both parties' costs from the date of Payment into Court. In this type of case, where she will receive substantial damages in any event, were she to fail to beat the Payment into Court, those costs would be taken out of the damages she did recover.

GENERAL DAMAGES

3   I last advised on quantum in this case in November last year, when I suggested that general damages were likely to be in the region of £6,000 subject to up to date medical evidence. The evidence of Mr Dan Smith, as provided in his report of 11th May 1999, describes ongoing symptoms in three areas:

(a)   at the level of the cervical spine, tenderness over the trapezius muscle;

(b)   at the level of the thoracic spine, tenderness in the interscapular area (from T4 to T7);

(c)   at the level of the lumbar spine, tenderness over the lumbo-sacral supraspinous ligament sprain and over the right sacro-iliac joint.

4   Of these the pain at lumbar level is not expected to persist in the long term. That is consistent with a diagnosis of ligamentous sprain. But Mr Smith considers that the trapezius pain and interscapular pain are likely to be permanent in some degree. A possible reason for this might be the fact that Mrs Towns' right leg is half an inch shorter than her left. Limb length discrepancy commonly leads to tilting of the pelvis, which in turn can have secondary effects if the discrepancy is not corrected. In his letter of 3rd March 1999, a copy of which I have now seen, Mr Smith makes a speculative connection between the discrepancy and the perpetuation of Mrs Towns' symptoms. In his second report, however, he seems to be more doubtful of the relationship, indicating that building up the shoe would not make a lot of difference.

5   It would assist if Mr Smith could explain why he thinks the cervical and thoracic pain is likely to be permanent, since the Defendant's expert clearly takes the view that Mrs Towns' symptoms ought to have resolved themselves within a few months of the accident. If Mr Smith does attribute the perpetuation of pain to the limb length discrepancy, he needs to explain why building up the shoe is unlikely to make much

difference. The fact that Mrs Towns might be unexpectedly vulnerable because of her shorter right leg does not of itself make any difference to the quantum, because of the application of the 'egg-shell skull' principle. On the other hand, the possibility that the pain could be substantially controlled by the wearing of a stacked shoe might well make a difference, because Mrs Towns is obliged to act reasonably in mitigating her loss.

6 The effects of Mrs Towns' injuries are described in her undated letter. They are rather more serious than had been apparent when I last advised. What she describes, in short, is daily pain and restrictions of movement which significantly impair her day-to-day functioning.

7 Assuming that these symptoms are consistent with and attributable to the injuries suffered in the accident, general damages are in my view likely to be in the region of £8,000 to £10,000. That puts this case in category (B)(b)(ii) for the purposes of the JSB Guidelines (4th edn.). It may be necessary to review this figure in the light of any further comments from Mr Smith.

8   SPECIAL DAMAGES

Osteopathy fees

9 There is a dispute as to the need for Mrs Towns to undergo this treatment. The important issue is whether it is reasonable for her to incur (and to go on incurring) the cost of osteopathic treatment; and that really depends on whether it is doing her any good. Mr Smith needs to be asked whether treatment is clinically justified, and if so for how long and with what frequency. His opinion will form the basis of the claim, and until then I cannot advise specifically on quantum under this head. However, since he has indicated that some of the pain symptoms are likely to be permanent whatever treatment is applied, it will probably be difficult to justify the full cost of osteopathic treatment indefinitely.

Travelling expenses

10 The bulk of this head of claim relates to the cost of attending the osteopath. Whether the claim is recoverable therefore depends, again, on Mr Smith's opinion as to the clinical justification for seeking this treatment.

Clothing and personal effects

11 It is not clear from the Schedule annexed to the Particulars of Claim whether this item is being claimed, and if so in what sum. In principle, of course, such costs are recoverable.

12 If Mr Smith advises that a stacked heel should be worn to control or reduce the back pain then the cost of buying shoes should be added to the Schedule.

13 No claim for loss of earnings is pleaded or suggested.

Evidence

14 As I have said, my Instructing Solicitors will need to go back to Mr Smith for his further comments on various matters, namely:

(a) whether the symptoms described in Mrs Towns' undated letter (a copy of which he will not have seen) are consistent with the injuries sustained in the accident;

(b) what is the explanation for the persistence of her symptoms and, in particular, whether there is any causal link between the continuation of pain and the limb discrepancy;

(c) if there is such a link, whether wearing a stacked heel would improve the condition; whether the cost of osteopathy treatment to date is clinically justified, and if so to what extent;

(d) whether the cost of osteopathy treatment in the future is clinically justified, and if so for how long and at what frequency.

15   Once I have that further evidence, I will be able to advise on the appropriate likely level of damages. My feeling at this stage is that damages overall are unlikely to exceed £14,000, even if all the medical issues are decided in Mrs Towns' favour, and that the offer ought realistically to be pitched some where below that figure. However, the current Payment into Court of £3,000 is below the realistic level of general damages and Mrs Towns is not yet at a substantial risk of failing to beat the current offer. In these circumstances my advice is that legal aid should be continued to allow for the further investigations set out above, at which point I will be happy to advise again as to the level at which to make a Part 36 offer. Should the Defendants increase the Payment into Court this will of course require urgent reconsideration.

16   If I can assist further in the meantime, my Instructing Solicitors should not hesitate to contact me in writing or by telephone.

Chambers address   JUSTIN GOOD

11.5   Advice on Offer of Settlement

IN THE CAMFORD COUNTY COURT   Claim No. S 60000

BETWEEN

PHILIP ADRIAN SMITH   <u>Claimant</u>

and

SHARON LOUISE JONES   <u>Defendant</u>

ADVICE ON PAYMENT INTO COURT

---

1   I am instructed to advise on behalf of Mr Philip Adrian Smith in respect of the likely quantum of damages he can expect to receive following his involvement in a road traffic accident on the 19th January 1995.

2   Liability is not in dispute. By means of a Notice of Payment into Court dated the 29th September 1998, the Defendant has paid into Court the sum of £32,000 in relation to Mr Smith's claim. This sum is to be taken together with interim payments of £967.49 paid on 1st April 1996, £2,500 paid on 1st August 1996, £2,640 paid on 1st September 1996 and £6,000 paid on 1st October 1996, making a total offer in full and final settlement of the claim of £44,107.49.

3   I am now asked to consider the likely quantum of the claim generally, and to specifically consider whether or not the Payment into Court should be accepted.

4   Mr Smith must understand that a Payment into Court is a powerful weapon in the hands of a defendant in this type of case. It represents a formalised offer of settlement. A Claimant has 21 days from receiving the Notice of Payment into Court to accept the payment without penalty: see CCR 1981, O. 11, r. 3(1), and r. 36.11 of the Civil Procedure Rules.

5   If Mr Smith was to decide not to accept the Payment into Court, and after a trial, he was awarded a sum, including interest, which was the same as or lower than the

sum which had been paid into Court, he would have to bear both parties costs from the date of payment in. In this type of case, where he will undoubtedly receive a considerable sum of damages in any event, were he to fail to beat the Payment into Court, the costs would be taken out of the damages he did recover. Since the costs of trial are likely to run into some thousands of pounds, it can be seen that this is a formidable weapon indeed and a development in his case which is deserving of very careful scrutiny at this stage.

General damages

6   It will be recalled that I saw Mr Smith in conference in my Chambers back in June 1997. At that time I gave certain advice concerning the likely quantum of the claim, although I did express the view it would be necessary to obtain further medical evidence before the question of the probable quantum of General Damages could be fully addressed.

7   Accordingly further medical evidence has been obtained. In order to assist me in my task of assessing General Damages at this time, namely those damages which are designed to compensate an injured party for their past and continuing pain and suffering and loss of amenity, I have been provided with the following medical reports:

(a)   Mr A.B.C. Brown, M Chir., FRCS, Consulting Neurosurgeon, dated 1st September 1995, 18th September 1996, 25th March 1997, 1st February 1998 and 29th September 1998;

(b)   Mr John D.E. Small, FRCS, Consultant Orthopaedic Surgeon, dated 31st March 1998, 2nd June 1998 and 11th September 1998;

(c)   Mr James M. Large, BA, MB, FRCS, FRCSI, Consultant Orthopaedic Surgeon, dated 11th July 1998.

8   I do not propose to rehearse the content of these various reports here. It has to be acknowledged straightaway that the medical evidence obtained on behalf of Mr Smith from Mr Small creates some considerable problems for him. It highlights, perhaps with rather more emphasis than they deserve, the past history of symptoms with regard to his lumbar spine. Mr Small advises that because of this past history with regard to his lumbar spine, Mr Smith:

. . . would have had symptoms at some stage in any event, regardless of the accident. What I think the accident did was to bring forward in time maybe four or five years, the onset of these more severe symptoms. He was investigated for back pain in 1987, and although he was told that there was no problem, it was clear that he was having some symptoms, even if they only lasted a day or so, and therefore he would have come to further problems in any event. I would however expect the degeneration to be gradual in onset, rather than the immediate and sudden impact that occurred in his every day activities as a result of the accident.

9   The Defendant has arranged for Mr Smith to be examined by Mr Large. I have considered his report carefully, particularly because Mr Small has reported that Mr Large 'agrees entirely with me as far as he goes'. Somewhat unusually, I am bound to say I found Mr Large's report of rather greater assistance to Mr Smith, as he did not emphasise to the same degree the pre-existing problems identified by Mr Small.

10   Accordingly for the purposes of this Advice, I am going to rely heavily upon the report of Mr Large, as I consider it serves Mr Smith's purpose rather better than Mr Small's report. Mr Large confirms that when he examined Mr Smith in July 1998, some three years and six months after the accident, he was still complaining of mid-dorsal pain which radiated up towards the back of his left shoulder and occasionally down the left arm and into the dorsum of the hand. Mr Smith remains constantly aware of this dorsal pain which varies a good deal in intensity and affects him in a great many ways both at work and in his activities of daily living.

11   For the purposes of this Advice, I accept Mr Large's expert opinion evidence that Mr Smith now suffers from chronic dorsal pain from the compression fractures of D4 and D7 which he sustained and that this chronic dorsal pain is likely to continue. Whilst there may be some further improvements, it is doubted that Mr Smith will ever be totally symptom free for any length of time.

12   The difficulty which Mr Smith has however is that the report from Mr Small is now in evidence and the Defendant could and undoubtedly would rely upon it at trial, without needing to call Mr Small to give evidence to the Judge. The Defendant will be able to do this by virtue of CPR, r. 35.11. In short, r. 35.11 allows for a party to any cause to put in evidence any expert report disclosed to him by any other party. Here the report from Mr Small was disclosed and accordingly the Defendant will be able to rely upon this Rule allowing a party to put in evidence an expert's report disclosed by another party.

13   Mr Smith will understand that when Counsel advises on the likely quantum of General Damages, he does not engage in an exact science. Counsel has available for his consideration a wealth of material enabling him to consider comparable cases, together with his own experience of similar cases handled. However, no two cases are ever precisely the same, and for this reason it can be misleading to place too much reliance on any one other similar case.

14   Mr Smith will recollect that during the course of the conference, I told him of the existence of *The Judicial Studies Board Guidelines*, now in their third edition. These Guidelines are published by a working party of the Judicial Studies Board, and are now regularly used by Judges up and down the country in arriving at an appropriate bracket of General Damages in these types of cases. However, it is to be stressed they are only guidelines, and are not to be slavishly followed.

15   In their treatment of back injuries, the latest edition of the Guidelines asserts that subject to injuries involving paralysis (e.g. quadriplegia, which are dealt with elsewhere within the Guidelines) relatively few back injuries command awards of General Damages above £20,000. Those that do depend upon special features.

16   The Guidelines identify a bracket of General Damages between £5,500 to £12,500 as being appropriate for moderate back injuries. The Guidelines maintain that a wide variety of injuries qualify for inclusion within this bracket. The precise figure depends upon the severity of the original injury and/or the existence of some permanent or chronic disability.

17   I consider Mr Smith's injuries to be deserving of compensation in a higher bracket. I do not consider his injuries would fall to be compensated within the bracket of £17,500 to £28,000, which is reserved for serious back injury cases, involving disc lesions or fractures of discs or vertebral bodies where, despite treatment, there remained continuing pain and discomfort, impaired agility and sexual function, depression, personality change, alcoholism, unemployability and the risk of arthritis. Instead, I consider the next bracket down to be appropriate, which ranges between £12,500 to £17,500. The Guidelines indicate that this bracket is appropriate for cases involving permanent residual disability albeit of less severity than in the higher bracket. I would be reasonably confident that the claim would fall to be compensated within this bracket. The Guidelines do go on to say this bracket is appropriate for a large number of different types of injury, for example, a crush fracture of the lumbar vertebrae with 40% risk of osteo-arthritis and constant pain and discomfort and impaired sexual function, or traumatic spondylolisthesis with continuing pain and 70% likelihood of spinal fusion, or a prolapsed intervertebral disc with substantial acceleration of back degeneration.

18   It can be seen from this that the upper parameters of this bracket are reserved for cases in which there are very serious long-term consequences. By using the Guidelines in conjunction with comparable reported cases, I can advise with similar confidence that this particular case will fall to be compensated towards the bottom end of this bracket.

19   I have also derived assistance from, amongst others, the following reported cases: *Acers v London Borough of Southwark* (1990) *Butterworths Personal Injury Litigation Service* 1X 1612; *Hyland v George* (1993) *Butterworths Personal Injury Litigation Service* 1X 1614; *Hennigan v Jackson* (1990) *Butterworths Personal Injury Litigation Service* 1X 1633; *Betts v London Regional Transport* (1991) *Butterworths Personal Injury Litigation Service* 1X 1694; *Hunter v Trugenal Laboratories* (1979) *Kemp and Kemp* E3–025/4; *Blamire v South Cumbria Health Authority* (1992) *Kemp and Kemp* E3–019/1.

20   Doing the best I can, and particularly bearing in mind the unhelpful nature of certain aspects of Mr Small's evidence, I consider the highest award of General Damages Mr Smith could reasonably expect to receive should this matter proceed through to trial would be in the region of £12,500 to £14,000.

<u>Other heads of loss</u>

21   Mr Smith will of course be entitled to further heads of loss, representing both his past pecuniary losses and the future losses which a Court feels it reasonable for him to be awarded.

22   I should make it clear that whilst I have seen Mr Smith's Amended Schedule of Loss, and the Counter Schedule of Loss served in response by the Defendant, I have seen none of the documentation which supports the various losses being claimed by Mr Smith. I have had the opportunity of considering both the original List of Documents served on Mr Smith's behalf in this action dated 18th April 1998, together with a Supplemental List of Documents which presently remains undated. From my perusal of these lists of documents, it is clear that there is a reasonable amount of supportive documentation for some of the heads of claim, although without seeing the documentation myself, it is of course difficult to assess just how strong we are on any one particular head of loss.

23   The Counter Schedule of Loss served on behalf of the Defendant accepts that in respect of the insurance excess, the transfer of his number plate, clothing damaged in the accident, medical treatment and associated expenses, and travelling and parking expenses, Mr Smith will be entitled to an award of damages of £1,277.25, as compared to the £1,353.33 being claimed on his behalf. The only difference between the parties on these various heads of loss is mileage allowance to be made for travel by car. Mr Smith's Schedule claims 35.7p per mile, whereas the Defendant's Counter Schedule only allows 25p per mile. My recent experience in Court suggests the Defendant's contention is far more likely to be accepted, and given there is so little difference in any event (only £76.08), clearly this is not worth litigating over. Accordingly I propose accepting the Defendant's assessment for the first five items identified on Mr Smith's Schedule in the total sum of £1,277.25.

24   Mr Smith has been fortuitous in the stance taken in the Defendant's Counter Schedule to admit his claim for past loss of earnings in the sum of £6,000. It seems as if there was little documentation in support of this head of loss, and I recall that at the time of the conference, when pressed on this prospective head of loss, Mr Smith maintained he did not want to proceed with claiming it because of the evidential difficulties he would face in proving it.

25   Nevertheless the Defendant is offering the sum being claimed for past loss of earnings of £6,000. This should be recognised by Mr Smith as being a good result for him in the absence of supporting evidence. I say this not least because in the first report from Mr Brown, which followed his examination of Mr Smith on the 26th May 1995, some four months after the accident, Mr Brown reported that Mr Smith had 'returned to his normal work and normal hours'.

26   For the purposes of this Advice, I propose making allowance in full for the claim for £1,174 in respect of removing a pool and re-turfing over the area. Unless Mr Smith is in a position to evidence this however, given the stance being taken by the Defendant

to not admit this particular item of loss, he will not recover the expense. The same goes for any other items of loss they have not agreed in the Counter Schedule and which they are calling for him to prove at trial.

27   The claims for the past cost of general maintenance work at his home, together with DIY costs, would also need to be proved with supporting documentation. Without sight of the documentation itself, once again I am simply unable to assess how strong Mr Smith is in respect of these heads of loss. For the purposes of this assessment of his claim, I propose allowing £500 in respect of past general maintenance and a further £500 in respect of past DIY costs.

28   In respect of the claim for administrative expenses, clearly Mr Smith will not recover the £150 being claimed. I consider the offer being made by the Defendant in the sum of £50 to be more than reasonable, and this is the figure I propose allowing on this head of loss.

29   Whilst Mr Small supports the claim being made for the extra cost of automatic transmission as something which would be advisable and advantageous for him, it is by no means certain that the Court would agree. This is the type of head of loss which despite strong medical evidence can however still be refused by the Trial Judge as not being something which is reasonably claimed in all the circumstances of the particular case. Of course the pre-existing problems identified by Mr Small with the spine might very well cause the Judge to not award such a head of loss. Furthermore, I note with interest the reference within Mr Smith's witness statement to him recently purchasing a Morgan Sports Car (see paragraph 29). I would be interested to learn whether or not this was an automatic car? Is there evidence in support of this purchase and the fact that it was an automatic car, if indeed it was? Mr Smith would undoubtedly be asked these questions at trial and accordingly they need to be considered now. In the meantime, I propose making no allowance for the extra cost of automatic transmission.

30   Taking the various heads of loss I have identified above, this serves to produce a total for past losses of £9,501.25.

31   All of these losses have been incurred close to the time of the accident, and I respectfully agree with my Instructing Solicitor that accordingly it is right to claim interest on the Special Damages at the full special account rate. I have calculated this would amount to 30.01% running from the date of the accident in January 1995 to the 29th September 1998. Accordingly, on a sum of £9,501.25, a sum of £2,851.32 interest should be awarded. This produces a total for Special Damages inclusive of interest of £12,352.57.

32   With regard to future losses, once again, much will turn on the weight given by the Trial Judge to the evidence of Mr Small as to the nature of the pre-existing problems in the lumbar spine and what their effect would have been in any event. The Defendant's case on this is made clear in the Counter Schedule, and they of course rely upon the evidence of Mr Small in this regard. It remains their case that Mr Smith would have had problems with his back in any event regardless of the accident, and the accident has done no more than accelerate his problems by a period of 4 to 5 years. Accordingly, whereas Mr Smith's Schedule of Loss claims for future losses using a multiplier of 17, the Defendant contends for a future loss multiplier not in excess of $1\frac{1}{4}$. Mr Smith will understand only too well the big difference this will make as to how his future losses will be quantified.

33   For the purposes of this assessment, I propose putting to one side the pessimistic opinion of Mr Small. I am only able to do so on the basis Mr Smith would not in fact rely upon his evidence at trial, and leave it to the Defendant to put his evidence in, which would not be agreed. Instead, Mr Smith could, and should, utilise the evidence of Mr Large as his own evidence, by agreeing the same in advance of trial.

34   Mr Smith is now 35 years of age. If one considers Table 1 of The Ogden Tables, which sets out the appropriate multipliers for pecuniary loss for life, utilising the 3%

discount rate, for a male aged 35 at trial, it can be seen the appropriate multiplier calculated with allowance for population mortality would be 22.2. From this figure one must make the further judicial discount referred to in the cases, which given the pre-existing problems in the back, I consider has to be reasonably significant in this case. I propose making a further discount of 25% which I feel is certainly the minimum further judicial discount that would be made at trial. Accordingly the best multiplier I consider Mr Smith will achieve at trial, if the Judge were to be persuaded to not follow the evidence of his own medical expert, would be 16.65, which I consider it right to round down to the figure of 16.

35   The Defendant accepts the claim being made for prescriptions in the sum of £33 per annum but disputes the multiplier. Using a multiplier of 16 produces a claim for the future cost of prescriptions in the sum of £528.00.

36   The claim being raised for the cost of travelling to request and collect prescriptions will not be allowed in full. I am bound to express some surprise that the Counter Schedule makes any allowance for this head of claim at all. The Counter Schedule proposes an allowance of £4.50 in respect of this annual loss and I propose adopting this figure, making a further claim of £72.00.

37   I regret to say that on all of the medical evidence presently available, I consider it unlikely the Court would allow anything in respect of the future costs of physiotherapy and surgery. Whilst a sum of £1,000 has been claimed in the Schedule, I cannot see that all of the evidence taken together makes this a head of loss which is likely to be recovered.

38   The claim for £400.00 in respect of the orthopaedic bed is not disputed and accordingly I allow it in full.

39   Similarly I allow the cost in full of £230.00 in respect of erecting a fence and the shaping of flower beds. Clearly this is work the Claimant would have done himself if he was fit enough to do so.

40   The Claimant claims in his Schedule for the cost of gardening in the sum of £1,064.13 per annum. Whilst this may well be supported by estimates, simply because there is an estimate in existence, it does not mean that the sum will be allowed in full by the Trial Judge. Photographs would need to be obtained of the garden showing just how much work is entailed. Given the size of the prospective head of loss, consideration would also need to be given to proving the actual number of hours work required in the garden by the calling of the appropriate evidence from an independent witness. In the absence of this type of evidence, and for the purposes of assessing the Payment into Court, I consider it prudent to adopt the figure of £500 per annum set out within the Counter Schedule. Utilising the multiplier of 16 produces a claim for the future cost of gardening of £8,000.

41   In respect of DIY costs, I similarly propose adopting the figure set out in the Counter Schedule of £750.00 per annum. A multiplier of 16 produces a claim for the future cost of DIY in the sum of £12,000.

42   For the reasons I have already given, I consider it would be unwise to allow anything in respect of the future cost of automatic transmission. I say again that whilst this might be a head of loss which we could pursue at trial, for the purposes of assessing a Payment into Court, where there is a real risk that such a head of loss might not be awarded at all, Counsel has to 'play safe' and disregard the potential item of loss.

43   If one adds together these various heads of future loss which I have made allowance for, this serves to produce a claim for future losses of £21,230. If one adds this figure to the figure of £12,352.57 in respect of past pecuniary loss and interest thereon, this serves to produce a total sum of £33,582.57.

44   The sum of money which has been offered in full and final settlement of this claim is £44,107.49. If one deducts from this figure the sum of £33,582.57, this leaves a sum of £10,524.92. The question therefore arises as to whether or not this is a reasonable sum to compensate Mr Smith in respect of his General Damages for pain and suffering and loss of amenity?

45   Given my assessment that the likely quantum of General Damages, on a 'best case' scenario, would be somewhere in the region of £12,500 to £14,000, given the risk as to costs Mr Smith will be under should he decide not to accept the Payment into Court, I cannot advise that the sum of £10,524.92 in respect of General Damages is so unreasonable that it should not be accepted. Whilst I have given my own assessment of what I consider the appropriate award would be in this case, it is perfectly conceivable that a Trial Judge would award somewhat less than £10,000, particularly if he was to accept some of the unhelpful evidence provided in this case by Mr Small.

Summary

46   Accordingly I advise that this Payment into Court should be accepted. The benefit Mr Smith might achieve by refusing the present offer and seeking to achieve a higher award cannot be justified when consideration is given to the costs risk he would be exposed to.

47   In so advising, I have considered the question of whether or not a separate award for future handicap upon the open labour market is likely to be made. For the purposes of assessing the Payment into Court, I consider it right to disregard such a head of loss, as it is certainly possible a Judge would refuse to make any such award in light of Mr Small's evidence as to the long-term prognosis in any event.

48   I regret not being able to proffer more optimistic advice, but Mr Smith will I am sure understand the difficulties his claim now faces in light of the medical expert opinion evidence from Mr Small. In all the circumstances, I consider the offer being made of £40,107.49 to be a reasonable one which should be accepted. I strongly suspect there would be no further offer made, and should Mr Smith choose to reject this offer, he will have to strictly prove his case and all the proposed losses which remain in issue at trial.

49   I was greatly assisted in this case by the helpful witness statements from Mr Smith and his wife. Taking all the medical evidence into account and these helpful witness statements, even on a best case scenario, I would be surprised if Mr Smith was able to achieve an overall award of damages in excess of say £45,000. This is why I advise that the potential benefit to be achieved by pressing on cannot be justified when one considers the considerable costs he would have to bear should he fail to beat the Payment into Court.

50   I hope this Advice is of assistance. Should any matters arise, please do not hesitate to contact me in Chambers in order to discuss them further.

IVOR HOPE

Beef Chambers
Beef Building
TEMPLE
London EC6Y 8LA

15th May 1999

TWELVE

ADVICE ON QUANTUM

In this chapter there are three opinions by three different barristers, illustrating the various approaches that may be taken to giving advice on quantum in a personal injury case. You should read this chapter in conjunction with **Chapter 11** of the **Remedies Manual**.

12.1 First Example

<u>RE EMMA BENSKIN</u>

<u>ADVICE ON QUANTUM</u>

1 On the 9th February 1997 Miss Emma Benskin was involved in a road traffic accident and injured when she swerved to avoid an oncoming vehicle which had strayed on to her side of the road and collided with a wall. The driver of the other vehicle did not stop and has never been identified and a claim is therefore being pursued against the MIB under the terms of the Untraced Driver Agreement. I am asked to advise on the value of Miss Benskin's claim.

2 Miss Benskin was born on the 10th January 1969. She is therefore now just 30 years of age. She sustained the following injuries:

(a) a blow to her head leading to concussion and the other serious consequences to which I refer below;

(b) a whiplash injury to her neck.

After the accident Miss Benskin was admitted as an in-patient for investigations and observation to St. Peter's Hospital Chelmsford. She remained in hospital until the 13th February 1997 and was then discharged home wearing a surgical collar.

3 The full extent of the injuries sustained by Miss Benskin in the accident has only really become apparent since she left hospital. The whiplash injury to her neck has left her with some restrictions on movement, particularly to the right and some discomfort, both of which are expected to be permanent. The restriction on movement makes for particular difficulty whenever Miss Benskin is driving. Her neck is stiff, particularly in the mornings.

4 X-rays taken of Miss Benskin's skull revealed no fracture but the symptoms she has experienced since the accident are suggestive of a fracture having been sustained. She was rendered unconscious in the accident. When she did regain consciousness at the hospital she experienced a severe pain behind her right ear. The fact that she sustained a nasty blow at this point was confirmed by the appearance of a large bruise. The day after the accident she experienced a sense of fullness and pressure in her right ear accompanied by pain which radiated into the right side of her face. These problems persist to the present day. She is also troubled by spells of dizziness and the hearing in her right ear has been adversely affected in two ways. First her ability to hear has

been somewhat reduced and, secondly, disturbance within the ear has been such as to render some noises very distressing and painful for her. Sounds which cause this problem are ordinary everyday sounds such as a telephone ringing, traffic noise and ordinary kitchen noises. Miss Benskin also finds that the noises made by children have the same effect. While there is the prospect of the pain decreasing, the other problems are likely to be permanent.

5   On any view the accident has had serious consequences for Miss Benskin and a most helpful insight into some of the everyday problems faced by her has been provided by her sister with whom she lives. She often comes home from work drawn, tired and in pain and whereas she was lively before the accident, her personality has changed for the worse. There is understandably some concern about how she will manage with children given the effects that shouting and other every day noise have on her.

6   In my view the whiplash injury sustained by Miss Benskin comes towards the upper end of the bracket suggested for category (e) of the Neck Injuries section of the *Judicial Studies Board Guidelines* (3rd edn):

> Whiplash or wrenching-type injury and disc lesion of the more severe type, if they result in cervical spondylosis, serious limitation of movement, permanent or recurring pain, stiffness or discomfort, the potential need for further surgery or increased vulnerability to trauma: £6,000 to £11,000.

Further assistance may be gained on this aspect of the case from three decisions noted in *Current Law*. First, in *Ward v Booth* [1988] CLY 1093 a man aged 30 who suffered slight permanent loss of neck movement to one side and ongoing neck discomfort which prevented him playing squash and obliged him to seek some help with some aspects of his work was awarded £5,500 in respect of pain, suffering and loss of amenity in the middle of 1988. This award would be worth about £8,360 today. Secondly, in *Thomas v Fury* [1990] CLY 1618 a woman aged 42 who experienced permanently restricted movement and ongoing considerable discomfort was awarded £6,500 (worth about £8,580 today). Thirdly, in *Corthorn v Foster* [1990] CLY 1620 a man aged 39 who also had permanently restricted movement and occasional discomfort was awarded £5,000 (worth about £6,600 today). My impression is that the whiplash injury sustained by Miss Benskin has not been as serious as that in the case of *Thomas* but on the other hand she is more than ten years younger than the Plaintiff in that case and will therefore have to suffer her symptoms that much longer. On balance, were the claim restricted to the whiplash injury, I would expect an award within the bracket of £7,500 to £8,000.

7   However, Miss Benskin also has the hearing problems which are more serious than just a relatively mild degree of one-sided hearing loss, the facial pain and dizziness to which I have referred. For *Judicial Studies Board Guideline* purposes the hearing loss may be classified as 'moderate': (see section 4(B)(d)(ii), the bracket for which is £6,500 to £13,000. It has to be borne in mind that there is the prospect of the pain subsiding and the probability is that the dizziness will improve. The hearing problems are, however, likely to be permanent and in these circumstances I consider that taking all of the injuries including the whiplash injury together, the pain, suffering and loss of amenity aspect of the claim warrants an award in the region of £14,000.

8   At the time of sustaining injury Miss Benskin worked as an assistant in a child care centre but she is a qualified nurse with a speciality in pediatrics and has since resumed nursing work. Bearing in mind the general shortages of skilled nurses in the country I anticipate that her employment will be regarded as secure but it is not impossible that she will be unable to go on with this work for reasons other than her employers determining her employment. Her inability to work comfortably in what to her will seem a noisy environment may well serve to limit her choice of alternative jobs and in these circumstances it is arguable that she is entitled to an award of damages for loss of employment prospects (the '*Smith v Manchester Corporation*' award). If such an award is made, it will be modest because of the considerable security attaching to

her present work and the range of nursing work available. Nevertheless, for the purposes of negotiation with insurers I advise that a *Smith* award should be sought and that a reasonable target would be the sum of £4,000.

9   Insofar as Miss Benskin has suffered any losses or expenses as a result of the accident these should be included in the claim but I anticipate that she has sustained no loss of earnings as yet and her expenditure is probably limited to the pain killing medications she has purchased.

10   Finally, I would remind those instructing me of the requirement under para. 3.1 of the Pre-Action Protocol for Personal Injury Claims to send to the proposed defendant two copies of a Letter of Claim **immediately** sufficient information is available to substantiate a realistic claim and before issues of quantum are addressed in detail. I shall be happy to settle such a letter if required. The following is a checklist of the information required for the purposes of such a letter:

* claimant's name, date of birth, address (and phone), National Insurance number;
* employer's name and address;
* date and place of accident (Photographs? Police or HSO Report?);
* the circumstances of the accident (Witnesses? Statements!!);
* the allegations of negligence/breach (Expert required?);
* the Claimant's injuries (Expert medical evidence required?);
* the Claimant's occupation and any time off work (Pay slips, etc.?);
* the identity of the likely defendant(s) and their insurers;
* relevant documents held by the claimant and the defendant(s) (Copies!);
* letter of authority to obtain medical records. (Plus, see Annex B to the Protocol for Clinical Disputes for the form to be used when obtaining medical records in medical negligence and personal injury claims.)

11   I hope that assists and I shall be happy to assist further in due course.

CHARLES ATKIN

1 Morrison Buildings
Temple EC4

23rd May 1999

12.2   Second Example

RE MR FREDERICK JOHN ACTON

OPINION

1   I am asked to advise Mr Acton as to the quantum of damages that he can expect to be awarded by the Court in respect of personal injuries unfortunately suffered by him in a road accident on 12th July 1997. Liability will not, I suspect, be in dispute, and I therefore confine this Opinion to quantum only.

2   The accident occurred when a car emerged from a side road into the path of three motorcycles, of which Mr Acton was riding one. As a result, he was unable to avoid running into the car and was thrown headlong into the road. I am obliged to Instructing Solicitors for enclosing the medical report of Mr J. Dalston FRCS dated 9th March 1999, which sets out the injuries suffered by Mr Acton, and the treatment and prognosis.

3   In essence, Mr Acton sustained bruising on the inner side of his left arm and left thigh and lower leg, all of which resolved within a period of about two months. By far the most serious injury however was a partial dislocation of the joint between the collar bone and the left shoulder blade. As a result he was unable to return to his work as a

garage owner/mechanic for three months, and even today experiences pain around the left shoulder when lifting anything heavy overhead. He also suffers regular aching, and is unable to lean comfortably on his left arm, or lie comfortably on his left side for long periods. It is doubtful if this will improve substantially in the future, and there is a real, although less than 50%, prospect that he will require a minor operation in the future. There is an almost certain prospect of osteoarthritis with the passage of time. I am unaware whether Mr Acton is right or left handed, but shall presume the former.

In *Chatham v Hinton Poultry* [1992] CLY 1741 a 25 year old man suffered a severe wrench injury to his right shoulder, involving soft tissue injury. He experienced considerable pain for three weeks and significant discomfort for three months thereafter, but overall made a very good recovery. He was expected to make a full recovery over the next 12 months, but during that time had to avoid heavy lifting. General damages of £2,000 (probably about £2,320 today) were awarded.

The injuries in the present case are clearly greater than in the above report, and thus the award of general damages should, in my opinion, be higher.

5   In *Bedford v Ackworth Working Men's Club* [1992] CLY 1736 a 59 year old housewife suffered a fracture to the top right of her shoulder. This was painful for six weeks, and she was discharged from out patient care three months after the accident. She still experienced discomfort at the extreme range of movement after 18 months, but a full recovery took place within two years of the accident. General damages of £3,500 were awarded (probably about £4,060 today).

I still consider the reported injuries to be less serious than those sustained by Mr Acton. Although the actual physical damage may have been slightly more severe in the reported case, Mr Acton will unfortunately suffer a permanent disability together with degenerative changes and a risk of further operative treatment. This must be reflected in the damages.

6   In *Davison v The Post Office* [1992] CLY 1676 a 46 year old lady sustained a whiplash injury to her neck, a traumatic capsulitis of the right shoulder creating restriction of movement of internal rotation, and dislocation of her left little toe. (The latter injury cleared up in six weeks.) She recovered from the whiplash injury within two years, but there was continuing loss of movement and some minor discomfort continuing in relation to the shoulder injury, which was considered to be permanent, and would result in minor restriction and discomfort. General damages of £6,000 were awarded (about £6,960 today).

I feel that it is likely that the award in the above case would not have been assessed solely on the most important injury (i.e. to the shoulder), and that the total figure is thus slightly higher than could be attributed to the shoulder injury on its own. Nevertheless, in my opinion it provides a useful guideline as to the level of damages which Mr Acton can expect.

7   In *Re Laverick* [1992] CLY 1674 a 40 year old nursing assistant sustained a rotator cuff lesion to her right shoulder. She did not have to perform any lifting duties in her work, but six months later she was transferred to a ward where she did, and suffered a relapse. At the date of the hearing, three years later, her right arm elevation was restricted by 10 degrees and she was suffering from a dull ache in her shoulder. These residual symptoms were unlikely to resolve completely, although she was expected to return to full-time work within three months of the hearing. General damages of £7,500 were awarded [about £8,700 today].

In *Nicholson v Hallamshire Construction* [1992] CLY 1672 a 61 year old man suffered a violent wrenching injury to his right shoulder with dislocation. A manipulation under general anaesthetic was performed followed by 36 sessions of physiotherapy. A second manipulation under general anaesthetic was performed 11 months after the first. The diagnosis was of traction lesion of the right shoulder, producing post-traumatic pericapsulitis of the shoulder. He was left with severe limitation of movement, although he was able to continue work to retirement age. General damages of £9,500 were awarded [about £11,020 today].

I consider this case to be somewhat more severe than the injuries suffered by Mr Acton.

8   In my opinion the likely award of general damages that Mr Acton can expect will be in the region of £6,800 to £7,800. I regret the somewhat large 'spread', but much will depend on the degree to which the Court considers that future degeneration and operative treatment will be likely. I consider that the median figure of £7,300 is not unrealistic.

9   Additionally however, Mr Acton considers that his business has suffered as a result of his being unable to play as full a role in it as would otherwise be the case. This will be difficult to prove, and expert evidence will be required. This will necessitate an examination of the accounts, of the jobs performed by Mr Acton (both presently and in the future), and an assessment of the extent if any to which any decline in profits can be reasonably attributable to the injury rather than market or other forces. I regret that I cannot advise any further on this point until such evidence is available.

I can suggest the names of suitable experts if that would assist. I would remind those instructing me of the need to obtain the services of a jointly instructed expert if possible and of the procedure for instructing experts set out in paras 3.14–3.20 of the Pre-Action Protocol for Personal Injury Claims. Please also bear in mind the requirement to send two copies of a detailed Letter of Claim **immediately** sufficient information is available to substantiate a realistic claim. I shall be happy to assist in the drafting of a suitable letter if required.

10   In the meantime, I hope Mr Acton continues to make good progress, and I will naturally be pleased to advise further if required.

ANDREW BRIGHT

8 Grosvenor Buildings, Temple EC4
1st May 1999

12.3   Conflicting Medical Evidence

In this case, there is a major divergence of views between each side's expert. This advice will give you some idea as to how you might advise on quantum in such circumstances.

IN THE CENTRAL LONDON COUNTY COURT

BETWEEN

THOMAS WHITBY   Claimant

and

YELLOWSTONE HEALTH AUTHORITY   Defendant

_____

ADVICE
_____

1   In this matter I am asked to advise generally. As liability does not seem to be in dispute and as I have already advised fully on that topic, on 3rd April 1998, I shall deal only with quantum and procedural matters.

2   As far as quantum is concerned the main difference between the parties is that their respective experts have taken vastly differing views of the extent to which Mr Whitby's

present condition can be attributed to the accident. In essence Mr Poll FRCS, who was instructed by Mr Whitby believes that the accident had the effect of aggravating a pre-existing condition, which might not have manifested itself to anything like the same extent had it not been for the accident. Mr Anns FRCS, instructed by the Defendant, however believes that all effects of the accident had been neutralised within a few months of it taking place, when Mr Whitby temporarily resumed playing squash.

3   Although this is a pre-April 1999 claim, under the Transitional Arrangements (Part 51 and Practice Direction) the general scheme of the CPR is that they should be applied to all defended cases 'so far as practicable'. The Court is therefore likely to try to use its case management powers to resolve the dispute between the experts if possible. Directions for trial will have to be sought in this claim so an application will have to be made to the Court under Part 23. Since liability does not appear to be in dispute, it would be appropriate to apply for summary judgment with damages to be assessed under Part 24. The Claim is likely to be allocated to the fast track so instructing solicitors should prepare an Allocation Questionnaire and draft Directions for the Court's consideration. These will all be dealt with at the same hearing (r. 1.4(i)). In accordance with the Practice Direction to Part 28 at para. 3.7(4), the Court's primary aim will always be to have a single joint expert if possible. However, it is too late for that in this case as the costs of both parties' experts have already been incurred. However, at the very least the Court will insist upon a without prejudice meeting between the experts in order to try to resolve or narrow the areas of disagreement.

4   This advice will therefore proceed on the assumption that this case will go to trial with the two current experts giving evidence and that they are unable to resolve their disagreement at such a without prejudice meeting. It is rarely easy to be able to say on the basis of reports alone which of two conflicting medical opinions a court is likely to prefer. However it does seem to me that here there are slight indications why Mr Poll's might be regarded as more convincing. It appears to me that Mr Poll, but not Mr Anns, has had the benefit of seeing the x-rays of Mr Whitby's back. Assuming this is correct, it is likely to mean Mr Poll's report carries marginally more weight. That however is not of great significance, because if the matter went to trial, the Defendant's expert would be given an opportunity to examine those x-rays and it is unlikely he would alter his view in the light of them. I am also a little puzzled by the significance Mr Anns attaches to the fact that a subsequent episode of Mr Whitby's suffering was brought on by his turning over in bed. It was highly unlikely that turning over could be the underlying cause of the episode, though it could have exacerbated latent symptoms that had been brought about by a more traumatic occurrence such as this accident. If this is a main plank of Mr Anns's reasoning it might be possible to attack him effectively in cross-examination. The DSS regard Mr Whitby as 10% disabled as a consequence of this accident, although he is appealing, hoping for a higher percentage to be assessed. I do not think that much importance can be attached to that matter for the purpose of these proceedings.

5   On the basis of Mr Poll's views I think a pain suffering and loss of amenity figure of about £10,000 is appropriate. I found the following case particularly helpful in coming to my conclusion:

   Butler v *Guildford BC* 24th April 1990 His Honour Judge Lawiston, *Kemp & Kemp* E3-021/2, where a 46 year old man was awarded a sum now equivalent to £10,500. He had had a pre-existing condition aggravated and suffered disability and discomfort very similar to Mr Whitby's in consequence. The restriction of movement in the back was only half of the normal, which made the injury marginally more serious than Mr Whitby's.

6   On the other hand if Mr Anns's view is to be preferred, a sum in the region of £2,000 is appropriate. In coming to that opinion I was assisted by the following case (which I suspect the insurers may have referred to):

   Davies v *Massey Ferguson Perkins* 30th January 1986 Evans J, reported at *Kemp & Kemp* E3–040, where a 50 year old man was awarded a sum now equivalent to

£2,000. He had suffered a twisting injury to the lumbar spine, which was found not to have exacerbated a pre-existing condition. He was in a diminishing degree of pain for around six months after which the symptoms were attributed to the pre-existing condition.

7   I do not have any specific instructions on special damages but I note that they seem to have been agreed at £500, which figure is presumably not dependent on any particular medical view being preferred. I also assume for the present at least Mr Whitby's earning capacity is not impaired as a consequence of the injuries. Having discussed the matter on the telephone, I understand those instructing me will prepare a schedule for inclusion in the Particulars of Claim.

8   This is a case where damages might be awarded on the *Smith v Manchester* principle. Mr Whitby would not be able to carry out anything other than a narrow range of nursing duties if he lost his present job. Because of his age and the nature of his qualification and experience I do not think he could expect a particularly great amount on this basis, perhaps £3,000. Any award on this basis would be dependent on a court accepting Mr Poll's views rather than Mr Anns's.

9   I note that the insurers have offered the sum of £2,250 in full and final settlement. Taking into account special damages and interest this is an entirely reasonable sum if and only if Mr Anns's view prevails. If Mr Poll's view prevails a figure of around £13,000 general damages plus special damages and interest is likely to be awarded. For the moment it would obviously be inappropriate to settle the matter on the basis of Mr Anns's view.

However, the Defendant has not paid any sum into court yet so the Claimant is not at any serious risk on costs. It may be possible to increase the pressure upon the Defendant to make a more realistic offer by making a Claimant's Offer to Settle under Part 36. In order to be effective the sum offered must obviously be significantly better than the Claimant's 'worst case' (£2,250) but sufficiently below the Claimant's 'best case' (£13,500) to be both a temptation and a real risk to the Defendants that they might fail to beat it and therefore have to pay indemnity costs and enhanced interest. I would suggest an offer of £9,500 be made in the circumstances.

10   Liability does not appear to be in dispute. Accordingly if Mr Whitby would be assisted by an interim payment at this stage of proceedings, I see no reason why the Defendant's insurers should not be approached with a view to securing such a voluntary payment at this stage.

11   As stated above, if such a payment was not made voluntarily, I would have to advise against making an application to the Court to obtain an order for an interim payment to be made. One of the conditions a Claimant must satisfy in order for an application for an interim payment to be ordered by the Court is that he must show that he would recover a 'substantial sum of money' if the case went to trial: see CPR, r. 25.7. Given the dispute between the medical experts here, I fear that any District Judge would be very reluctant to award Mr Whitby an interim payment, if there is the possibility of general damages of as little as £2,000 being awarded. The Court would not wish to leave Mr Whitby vulnerable to the possibility of an order for repayment of any sums received by way of an interim payment being made against him in the event of the trial judge preferring the expert opinion evidence of Mr Anns.

12   I believe that I have said all that I usefully can at this stage but should those instructing me wish to discuss any aspect of this case further they should of course not hesitate to contact me.

WALTER HOPE

6 Eldon Square, Lincoln's Inn, London WC2
11th May 1999

THIRTEEN

ADVICE ON EVIDENCE IN A CIVIL CASE

13.1 An Approach to Writing a Civil Advice on Evidence

13.1.1 WHAT IS THE PURPOSE OF A CIVIL ADVICE ON EVIDENCE?

The purpose of the advice on evidence in a civil case is to tell the solicitor what further things need to be done in order to ensure that the case is in proper order for the trial.

13.1.2 WHAT SHOULD AN ADVICE ON EVIDENCE CONTAIN?

A good advice on evidence should tell the instructing solicitor, clearly and succinctly, precisely what needs to be done in order to prepare the case for trial. It will provide the solicitor with a plan of campaign, both for dealing with all outstanding preliminary matters and for assembling and presenting the evidence which counsel will tender to the court on the client's behalf at trial.

The contents of an advice on evidence will vary from case to case. There are no rules which govern what must and what must not be said. What is required is a practical advice, suited to the particular case and to the particular solicitor to whom it is addressed.

However, almost every advice on evidence will contain at least the following:

(a) A list of the matters in issue in the claim, stating on whom the burden of proving each issue lies. The purpose of this is to help the solicitor in the preparation of the case, by identifying the relevance of the items of evidence which must be got ready. It also serves to identify the matters upon which it is *essential* that evidence is tendered on the client's behalf in order to make out his or her case. Even in apparently simple cases, claims may be lost for want of some certificate or other formal piece of proof.

(b) A list of the things which need to be done to get the case ready for trial. The preparation of this list will usually involve:

   (i) a review of the statements of case, disclosure and other preliminary matters dealt with so far;

   (ii) a consideration of what other preliminary steps in the claim might usefully be taken to advance one's own case or to attack one's opponent's case prior to trial (such as applications for further information, specific disclosure etc.);

   (iii) a consideration of what further practical steps (such as making further enquiries, commissioning reports by experts etc.) should be taken to obtain evidence for the trial.

(c) A list of the evidence to be tendered at trial, giving the names of the witnesses who will be required to attend court to give evidence, a list of the documents which will be required to be produced etc.

(d) A list of the things that need to be done in order that evidence may be tendered to the court at the right time and in the proper manner (e.g., exchanging witness statements, serving any necessary notices under the Civil Evidence Act, preparing the trial bundles etc.).

13.1.3 ARE THERE ANY FORMAL REQUIREMENTS?

There are no formal requirements: but, as a matter of the practice, a barrister's advice on evidence is almost always set out in the following way:

(a) The advice is headed with the names of the parties.

(b) Underneath that, the words 'Advice on Evidence' appear in block capitals between tramlines.

(c) The advice itself is written in short numbered paragraphs, in clear grammatical English.

(d) At the end, the advice is signed by the barrister in the bottom right-hand corner (usually above his or her typed name) and the barrister's chambers address and the date of the advice are stated in the bottom left-hand comer.

13.1.4 HOW SHOULD I SET ABOUT WRITING AN ADVICE ON EVIDENCE?

Every barrister has his or her own way of approaching this task, which is one of the most important parts of the work of a junior barrister.

Just as success at trial so much depends upon the care with which the case is got up beforehand, the writing of a successful advice on evidence depends upon careful analysis and preparation. As with all a barrister's written work, the golden rule is: Think before you write. Once the thinking and analysis has been done, the actual writing will be straightforward.

An important part of this analysis is the barrister's ability, using his or her experience and knowledge of the rules of civil procedure and evidence, to run the case through in the mind, from the very first words of the case to the last. The barrister must imagine what is likely to happen at each stage during the trial, anticipate what may go wrong, fill in any blanks and ensure that everything that needs to be done to be prepared for each point in the trial is noted and put in hand.

13.1.5 WHEN SHOULD THE BARRISTER BE ASKED TO WRITE HIS OR HER ADVICE ON EVIDENCE?

The ideal time for counsel to be asked to advise on evidence will usually be after disclosure and before the exchange of witness statements. However, the appropriate time will vary from case to case and in fact timing is entirely in the hands of the instructing solicitor. It is a part of the barrister's practical skill to be able to tailor the advice given to the time at which he or she is asked to advise. If asked to advise only days before trial is due to begin, there is little point in advising lengthy further investigations unless it is practical to obtain an adjournment of the trial date! Since April 1999 the courts have been very reluctant to grant adjournments, particularly if the reason for applying is a failure to prepare in good time.

13.1.6 A STEP-BY-STEP APPROACH

In order to ensure that they do not leave out any important matters, many barristers adopt a step-by-step approach to writing their advices on evidence. By following the same scheme as a checklist on each occasion they can ensure that they have considered all of the relevant points.

One such step-by-step approach goes like this:

13.1.6.1 Step 1: Read the brief

(a) *Ensure that you have been sent the materials that you need to write your advice* The first step in writing any advice is to read your instructions: and the first stage in reading your instructions is to look at the list of contents with which your instructions will usually begin and to check that you have, in fact, got all the enclosures which the solicitor says have been sent down to you.

The second stage is to ensure that the solicitor has sent down to you all of the things that you need in order to be able to write your advice. You should normally expect to have been sent:

(i) copies of all the statements of case and interim orders that have been made,

(ii) copies of the lists of documents that have been exchanged and of the documents referred to in those lists,

(iii) copies of any experts' reports that have already been obtained or disclosed, and

(iv) proofs of evidence from at least the principal potential witnesses on your side.

It is often helpful for you also to see the material parts of the correspondence between your instructing solicitor and your client and of the correspondence between your instructing solicitor and the solicitor on the other side.

If any of these items are missing, you should telephone your solicitors and ask them to send you the missing items. It is important that you read your instructions as soon as possible after you receive them, so that no time is wasted in getting together the materials that you need in order to be able to write your advice.

(b) *Extract the relevant information from the materials you have been sent* Before you can start your analysis, you must master the contents of your instructions and ensure that you have an overall 'feel' of the case.

Each barrister must work out his or her own system for 'gutting' a set of papers, flagging important documents and highlighting relevant passages. If you have not already done so, now may be a good time to make a chronology and a list of the *dramatis personae* in the case.

A useful tip is also to make a list, as you read through your papers, of any obvious points, inconsistencies, omissions etc. that you notice as you go along. By writing these down as you first think of them, you save yourself from forgetting them when it comes to writing your advice.

13.1.6.2 Step 2: Examine the statements of case

(a) *Check your own statements of case* You should examine your own statements of case in the light of the proofs of evidence and documents that you have been sent, to see whether they actually put forward the case which you will wish to, and be able to, put forward at the trial.

Statements of case are still important. Although the court will usually grant permission to amend where any injustice to the other side can be compensated by a suitable award of costs, there are still some cases which are won and lost on points arising from problems with the way statements of case are formulated: see, e.g., *Ketteman v Hansel Properties Ltd* [1987] AC 189 and *Practice Direction 3*. In any event, the statements of case are usually the first documents which the judge considers. It is desirable that they should present your case as well and convincingly as possible.

Also, you will use the statements of case in the next step in the preparation of your advice on evidence to find out what the issues in the case are. If some material allegation is missing from your statements of case, it will also be missing from the list of issues.

The purpose of this check is to satisfy yourself that your statements of case are *sufficient in law and accurate in fact.*

(i)   *The law*   If you did not settle the statement of case, you will want to ensure that the view of the law taken by whoever drafted the document is the view which you consider ought to be put forward on your client's behalf at trial.

Even if the statements of case are your own drafts, you should reconsider them at this stage. The law may have changed or been clarified by decisions of the courts, or your own view of the law may have changed since you prepared your drafts.

(ii)   *The facts*   You are likely to have more factual information about your case than was available when the statements of case were settled. You will have seen the other side's statement of case. If there have been any interim applications (e.g., for summary judgment) there may be witness statements or other written evidence telling the story from different points of view. Disclosure will have made available the other side's documents. You may have additional proofs and further documents from your own side.

You should check that your case as set out in your statements of case is (1) the best case which your evidence will support and (2) a case which can be supported by your evidence at trial.

(Note the provisions of the *Code of Conduct*, paragraph 606, and of the *Written Standards*, paragraph 5.8.)

(iii)   *Amendment*   If you want to change the way that your case is put — for example, because you can tell at this stage that there is likely to be a discrepancy between what is said in your statements of case and the evidence that you are going to call at trial — now is the opportunity to seek to amend.

But remember: any change in the way that you put your case on the facts may undermine the credibility of your evidence: and all amendments have costs consequences, some more serious than others. *Necessary* amendments have to be made: but the possible advantages of merely *desirable* amendments should be weighed against their possible disadvantages. You must use your judgment.

If you consider it is necessary or desirable for your statements of case to be amended, then settle draft amendments and make a note to advise your solicitor that these amendments need to be made, and how to go about it. Make a note to warn the solicitor of any serious risks or costs consequences involved in the course which you propose.

(b)   *Look at the other side's statements of case*   The purpose of this examination is threefold. First of all, to find out what the other side's case is going to be. Secondly, to see whether the other side's case is sufficient in law and accurate in fact, so as to identify any strengths or weaknesses. Thirdly, to see whether the other side's statements of case tell you enough about their version of events.

If the other side's statements of case do not provide sufficient details, or allow them too much latitude at trial, draft a request for any further information to which you consider that you are entitled and make a note to advise your solicitor to administer that request, and how to get the further information in the event that the other side does not supply it voluntarily.

13.1.6.3   Step 3: List the issues

Once you are satisfied that the statements of case are adequate, then use them to prepare a list of issues.

By following each allegation in the particulars of claim through the defence and the reply, and each allegation in a counterclaim through the defence to counterclaim etc., you should be able to isolate from the statements of case what matters are in issue in the claim.

This gives you a list of the matters to which evidence will have to be directed at trial. By analysing on which side the burden of proof on each of these issues lies, you will be able to tell the issues upon which your side *must* adduce evidence if it is to make out its case.

Many barristers prepare their list of issues in the form of a table. The left-hand column gives a reference number, the next column states the issue, the next columns (one each for statement of claim, defence, reply etc.) identify the paragraphs in the statements of case which give rise to that issue, and the column after that states on whom the burden of proof on that issue is placed.

Other columns in the same table can be used later on in preparing to write your advice on evidence to identify the issues upon which particular witnesses are able to give, or might be able to give, useful evidence, to list the documentary evidence available on each issue etc.

13.1.6.4   Step 4: Consider what evidence is available to you on each issue

Your consideration of the evidence should be a two-stage process: (a) What is available? and (b) What should we tender? At each stage, it is often useful to run through the various types of evidence, taking each separately, in order to reach your decision.

There are some things which one need not prove. For example, there are some matters of which the courts will be prepared to take judicial notice. Also, some issues may have had a special direction made under CPR Parts 32 to 34, as to the mode of proof. It is useful to note these issues on your table of issues.

(a)   *Oral evidence*   Go through the proofs of evidence that are with your papers. Mark on your table (perhaps with a tick) the issues upon which each witness's proof shows that they can give useful evidence. Where it seems possible from the circumstances that the witness would be able to give useful evidence on an issue, but their proof does not deal with it, mark that (perhaps with a question mark) on your table as well.

When you have completed this exercise, your table will be able to show you how many witnesses can give evidence on each issue. It will show up any issues upon which you have no (or not enough) oral evidence available to you. It will also highlight the issues on which you should ask your solicitor to take further proofs from the witnesses you intend to call, so that you know the outline of *all* of the evidence that they will give at trial.

It is also useful at this stage to mark on the table any special considerations affecting the witnesses — for example, that it may be difficult to get them to trial (e.g., because they are ill or old, overseas or likely to prove reluctant etc.). In this way you can identify whether any special steps need to be taken to ensure that their evidence is available to the court if, at the next stage, you decide it would be desirable for their evidence to be tendered.

(b) *Expert evidence*   You should consider on what issues (if any) it is necessary or would be helpful for you to be able to tender expert evidence. You should then consider what expert evidence has so far been obtained by your instructing solicitor. Does the expert have the right expertise? Will he or she be a good expert witness? Does it need to be expanded or revised? Is the expert's opinion helpful? Should a further or a different expert be asked to prepare a report?

You should also consider whether:

(i)   there should be a joint instruction of the expert(s);
(ii)   experts should be called at trial or whether it will be sufficient to rely on their reports;
(iii) there should be any discussions between rival experts; and
(iv)   written questions should be put to the experts to clarify their reports.

(c) *Documentary evidence*   Consider the disclosure given by your client and that of your opponents.

Has your client disclosed all the documents which ought to have been disclosed? If there is a possibility that documents have not been disclosed, make a note to advise your instructing solicitor to ensure that your client gives that further disclosure.

Have the other side given full disclosure of documents? If not, then consider whether you should make an application for specific disclosure. If so, make a note to advise how this should be done. If necessary, draft the application and supporting written evidence.

Consider whether you wish to challenge the authenticity of any document included in the other side's list of documents. If so, make a note to advise your solicitors (i) to give notice under CPR, r. 32.19(2) (if they have not already done so), and (ii) of the evidence — for example from a professional examiner of questioned documents — which will be needed to make or support that challenge. Add this issue to your list of issues.

Finally, consider which of the documents before you are relevant to which issues, so that you know the strength of the documentary evidence available on each of these issues.

(d) *Hearsay evidence*   This category overlaps with the previous category. Consider whether there is hearsay evidence available to you which is relevant to any of the issues, and whether a hearsay notice needs to be served under CPR Part 33.

13.1.6.5   Step 5: Selection of evidence

(a) *Oral evidence*   Decide who should be called to give oral evidence. Do not omit to call any witness whose evidence is the only evidence that you have on an issue on which the burden of proof is on you. However, do not necessarily call all the witnesses available to you on every point.

Consider whether witness summonses should be served on any of your witnesses. Consider whether any special steps need to be taken to ensure that the evidence of any of the witnesses you wish to call is available to the court — for example, adjourning the trial until a witness who is abroad is back to give evidence.

If one of the witnesses whom you wish to call to give oral evidence is elderly or very ill, consider the desirability of ensuring that a signed statement or a deposition is taken from them, so that in the event of their death that statement or deposition can be tendered in evidence.

(b) *Exchange of statements*   Having chosen which witnesses you would wish to call to give oral evidence, check that your side are able to comply with the direction for the exchange of witnesses' statements. The order will have been made either in the directions made at the track allocation stage or at the case management conference. Consider what more needs to be done in order to convert the proofs which are with your papers into statements which are suitable for exchange. You may need to settle the witness statements yourself at this stage. Make a note to give the necessary advice to your solicitor.

(Note the provisions of the *Code of Conduct*, paragraph 606, and of the *Written Standards*, paragraph 5.8.) Detailed requirements for witness statements are set out in *Practice Direction 32*. These include requirements that witness statements must:

(i)   be expressed in the first person;

(ii)   give the full name and residential/business address of the maker;

(iii)   state the occupation of the witness;

(iv)   state if the witness is a party to the proceedings or has a connection with any party (e.g. is an employee/relative);

(v)   be in chronological sequence, divided into consecutively numbered paragraphs;

(vi)   include a statement of truth;

(vii)   be signed by the witness;

(viii) be dated.

The CPR, r. 32.5(2) provides that unless the court orders otherwise, exchanged witness statements will stand as the witnesses' evidence-in-chief. Rule 32.5(3) and (4) go on to say that witnesses will only be allowed to amplify their statements or to deal with new matters arising since service of witness statements if there is a 'good reason' for doing so. Consequently, you must ensure your witness statements contain all the evidence which your witnesses can be expected to give and which would be asked of them in examination-in-chief. Further, the statements must accord with the oath/affirmation to tell the truth, the whole truth and nothing but the truth.

(c) *Expert evidence*   Decide whether expert evidence should be called, and if so what expert(s) should give evidence on your client's behalf.

If you wish to adduce expert evidence, consider what orders have been made or need to be applied for under CPR Part 35 and make a note to advise your solicitor accordingly.

Consider the form and content of the reports from your experts which you will disclose to the other side. Consider what more needs to be done in order to convert the reports which are with your papers into reports which are suitable for exchange, and in particular whether the reports comply with *Practice Direction 35*.

Consider how far the expert evidence can be agreed.

(d) *Documentary evidence* Consider what documentary evidence should be put before the court, and the form in which that documentary evidence should be presented.

(Do not automatically advise that *all* disclosed documents should be included in the trial bundles.)

Advise on the preparation of the bundles for use at the trial. These need to be lodged between three and seven days before the trial. Consider reminding your solicitor of the contents of *Practice Direction 39* and in particular of the requirements that:

(i) the documents must be included in identical files, arranged in chronological order, beginning with the earliest, paged consecutively at centre bottom, and fully and easily legible; and

(ii) there must be one single additional bundle containing the principal documents to which the parties will refer where the trial bundles are voluminous.

(e) *Hearsay evidence* Consider whether any of the evidence which you wish to adduce is hearsay. If so, consider what notices need to be served pursuant to the Civil Evidence Act 1995 and make a note to advise accordingly.

Consider any notices served by the other side, to see whether you should serve a counter notice.

Consider how to deal with any issue raised by any counter notice which has been served by either side.

13.1.6.6 Step 6: Final considerations

Bring together in a final note all of the other preparatory matters that you have considered.

Consider how best you can advance your own case or attack your opponent's case. Is there anything more that you need to do to the statements of case, or by way of further information or specific disclosure? Are there any more investigations that need to be made by your instructing solicitor, or an enquiry agent, or accountants, or other experts? Should you apply for security for costs (or additional security)?

Is your case ready for each stage of the proceedings up to and during the trial? Are your witness statements and expert reports ready for exchange? Have all necessary notices been prepared and served! Does your solicitor know what needs to go in the trial bundles? Are your witnesses ready, willing and able to appear at the trial? Should you serve witness summonses on any of the other side's witnesses?

Finally, consider whether your instructions have raised any particular matters for your advice. Are there any specific questions which your solicitor has asked? If so, you should give a specific answer.

13.1.6.7 Step 7: Writing

Finally, when all the thinking and analysis have been completed, write your advice. You will already have prepared lists of the things that you will want to say. For example, you will already have notes as to any amendments to the statements of case or further information which need to be requested or given (from step 2). Your list of issues is already ready (from step 3), as is your list of witnesses to give oral evidence (from step 5), etc.

After setting out the title of the action and the title of the advice, resist the temptation to begin your advice with a long introduction. The most you are likely to need is one or two prefatory sentences, something like:

In this action my client, Mrs Bloggs, claims damages against her former employers for personal injuries which she suffered in an accident at work. I am asked to advise on evidence.

Then, list the issues (so that you can refer to each issue by number at later stages in the advice) and set out step by step precisely what you advise your solicitor to do, in accordance with the notes that you have made as you have gone through your analysis.

Divide your advice into short numbered paragraphs.

When you get to the end, remember to sign it and to put the date and your chambers address at the bottom.

13.2   Sample Advice on Evidence

<u>KENTISH BOOKS LIMITED v SECURITY CAR PARKS PLC</u>

ADVICE ON EVIDENCE

1   The Claimant's claim in this matter that its Peugeot 205 GTI motor car was left in a car park in Darnley Street London WC2 managed by the Defendant on the 10th December 1996. It is suggested that the vehicle was stolen from the car park and that the Defendant's car park attendant on duty was negligent in allowing the thief or thieves to exit with the vehicle from the car park. A trial date has been fixed for hearing on the 30th April 2000 at the Westminster County Court. I am now asked to advise in respect of evidence for the forthcoming hearing.

<u>Oral Evidence</u>

2   There are a number of aspects on which the Defendant should call oral evidence. I suspect that Mr Enfield who was in charge of the car park at the relevant time would be the appropriate witness on most aspects. He may, however, not be able to deal with them all. My Instructing Solicitors should therefore check with the Defendant. The aspects I have in mind are as follows:

(1)   The system for entry and exiting the car park has to be explained. In essence the procedure averred to in paragraph 1(c) of the Defence has to be confirmed.

(2)   The presence of notices around and inside the car park setting out the Defendant's standard terms and conditions has to be dealt with. The positioning of the notices or signs is likely to be very important so precise location should be confirmed. Whoever is able to deal with this aspect should also produce a specimen ticket that a motorist is given on entry. I hope that this will confirm something to the effect that entry is subject to the Defendant's standard terms and conditions. Furthermore I presume that it will illustrate that no details of the particular vehicle for which it is issued appears on the ticket.

(3)   Could someone find out whether Security Car Parks plc or Mr Warren held a season or prepaid contract ticket for this particular car park at the relevant time or on any earlier occasion? I suspect it is unlikely but I am seeking to attribute knowledge of the Defendant's standard terms to the Claimant by a history of use of the car park in question.

(4)   I understand that this car park or the Defendant in general had only one other alleged car theft from premises it was managing in a seven-year period. This should be adduced at trial.

(5)   I have been given details of two ways in which a car theft can be committed that do not involve the absence of a valid ticket when the driver presents himself at

the exit barrier. The first is where one car is driven into the car park and the ticket obtained is then used to drive a stolen vehicle away. The other car is collected later without an appropriate ticket but with satisfactory proof of ownership provided. The second involves the use of a prepaid contract ticket which allows entry into and exit from the car park on multiple occasions. It would be helpful if a witness could give evidence of these possibilities. I presume that a third possibility would be if the true owner had obtained a ticket on entry and left it in the vehicle for the thief to use.

(6) I would like to know more about the video recorders that were supposedly in operation. Were they functioning at the time of the alleged theft? Did the police examine the tapes? Where were the cameras positioned?

(7) The witness evidence will have to be put into a form complying with *Practice Direction 32* before being exchanged with the other side.

3 Included in my papers is a short report from a security guard employed by Prevention & Detection Holdings Ltd. It records the number and frequency of security inspections of the car park on the relevant day. The requisite notice under the Civil Evidence Act 1995 should be given. Once served the report should be included in the trial bundle. Strictly speaking the Defendant does not need to rely on the truth of the contents of the documents. Evidence that a security firm were employed and the Defendant was under the impression that regular inspections were being made would suffice, but since the report is even stronger it should be used.

4 There is a suggestion in my papers from enquiry agents that the Claimant may have damaged the car in a road traffic accident. The hypothesis is that there would be a bogus claim that the car had been stolen and that the thieves were responsible for the damage. I feel that this is a very unlikely conclusion. The car seems to have been comprehensively insured subject only to a £100 excess. It also seems fair to assume from the time the police arrived at the scene in answer to a 999 call, as set out in the police report, that the theft was reported before that accident occurred. It is possible that the Claimant and the driver at the time of the accident were one and the same but it would greatly surprise me. In the circumstances it seems that to require Bus Inspector Buckley's attendance at court in the hope of identifying the man he saw walking away after the accident would be pointless. However if my Instructing Solicitors take the view that this avenue should be pursued the Inspector should be requested to come to court or a witness summons must be served. He could then be released if he is unable to give any assistance.

Potential police evidence

5 The onus in this case subject to one *caveat* is on the Claimant to prove that the car was left in the requisite car park, that it was stolen, and that the car park attendant was negligent. I expect the Claimant to give oral evidence in relation to the first two of these aspects. I would be surprised if their witness were able to give oral evidence of the third aspect, primarily because he would not have been present when the alleged theft was committed. The Claimant has pleaded a contract of bailment and if successful in that plea the onus regarding negligence is reversed. A bailee of goods who is unable to return them to the depositor has to show that the loss did not occur due to his or her negligence. Thus it is of special importance to decide whether there was a contract of bailment or simply a licence to occupy a car parking space. In my view the case law favours the Defendant.

6 The Particulars of Negligence in the Particulars of Claim together with the Further Information are quite precise and detailed. The question arises as to who can give oral evidence of such matters. In my view the only relevant person would be the car park attendant or the thief. If the Claimant serves a Civil Evidence Act notice indicating that it plans to use a written statement from the police officer who investigated the allegation of theft, it may be appropriate to seek an order under s. 3 of the Act for him to attend for cross-examination. Before taking a final decision on this, I would need to

see the witness statement which accompanies the notice to see if potential lines of cross-examination are revealed.

Documentary evidence

7   The DVLA search result should be included in the trial bundle together with a copy of the Defendant's standard terms and conditions. I have no doubt that the Claimant's solicitors will wish to include the police report relating to the traffic accident. There is no basis for opposing this, but there is nothing in that document which assists the Defendant. It is true that nothing by way of contents was taken from the car by the driver and his passenger at the time of the accident but items could have been removed earlier in the evening and I understand these personal items are not being pursued against the Defendant any longer in any event. Thus unless the Claimant wishes to include it it can be left out. I suspect also that various invoices disclosed will be sought to be included by the Claimant's solicitors.

8   My Instructing Solicitors have obtained a statement from PC Bull who supervises the property store at the police station where the theft was reported. This confirms that the car parking ticket was not retained by the police. This statement contradicts a handwritten addition to a letter dated the 11th April 1997 from my Instructing Solicitors to enquiry agents. I would like confirmation that the car park ticket was not given to the police. Consequently I advise that the Claimant be served with a notice to admit facts: namely (a) that the Claimant did not surrender possession of the car park ticket to the police and (b) the Claimant did not show the ticket to the investigating police officer. CPR, r. 32.18 permits service of such a notice up to 21 days before trial. Consideration of serving a witness summons on PC Bull can be deferred until after the Claimant's response is known.

9   There appears to be no need to utilise the Claimant's accounts. The Claimant operates as a publishing company and its assets are and were at all material times quite extensive. This adds further doubt to the enquiry agent's hypothesis of a fraud on an insurance company.

10   If there are any further matters or further developments that occur as a matter of urgency no doubt my Instructing Solicitors can contact me by telephone.

MARIA COLES

Lincoln House Chambers
11th November 1999

13.3   A More Complex Advice on Evidence

ALPINE SYSTEMS AG v MIDWEST BANK PLC

(1) CHARLES DICKENS AND HENRY JAMES (2) THOMAS HARDY
(3)   CHARLES DICKENS
(Part 20 Defendants)

ADVICE ON EVIDENCE

1   By this action Alpine Systems AG 'Alpine' claims SWF 65,105.70 and interest, said to be due from the Bank under the terms of an agreement which Alpine alleges is contained in a letter dated 6th August 1997 which the Bank wrote on behalf of a customer, Paulton Magna Armaments Limited ('PMA'), to Alpine. In the Part 20 claim, the Bank claims an indemnity against Alpine's claim from the three guarantors of PMA's indebtedness (who I will call the 'guarantors'). Trial is fixed for 21st May 2000. I am asked by the Bank to advise on evidence.

The statements of case

2   I have reconsidered the Bank's Defence in the main action and in the Part 20 claim, in the light of the further documents and information now available. I do not think that any amendments are required.

3   In its answer to the Bank's Request for Further Information under paragraph 3 of the Particulars of Claim, Alpine stated that it could not give further information until after disclosure. Disclosure has now taken place.

4   Similarly, the Guarantors' Further Information under paragraphs 4, 5 (Request 3) and 6 (Request 6) indicate that they cannot give proper information until after they have had access to PMA's records, which were then with the liquidator. Since the liquidation has now been completed, any necessary access could and should by now have taken place.

5   In the circumstances, we should renew our requests for the above information. Drafts of the necessary Requests accompany this Advice.

The issues

6   The real issues in this case can be stated very shortly. Did the Bank, by its letter dated 6th August 1997, take on a liability to Alpine to make payment if it received funds? If so, is the Bank entitled to an indemnity for that liability under the Guarantees, bearing in mind (a) the purpose for which those guarantees were taken, and (b) the terms of Mr Dickens' letter of 27th October 1997 and of the Bank's replies dated 31st October and 11th November 1997?

7   However, the issues set out in the statements of case are a little more complex. They are:

(a)   *On the Claim:*

Issue	PofC	Def
1. Is Alpine a company incorporated in Switzerland?	1	1
2. In August 1997:	2	2/3
(a) Did PMA owe Alpine SWF 65,105.70?		
(b) Was Alpine pressing for payment of that sum?		
(c) Was PMA supplying goods to Ruritania and anticipating payment of a substantial sum for those goods later in the year?		
(d) Did the Bank know any of (a)–(c)?		
3. Was any written agreement made between Alpine and the Bank, by the Bank's letter dated 6th August 1997 and Alpine's reply dated 14th August 1997? (Against the background, *inter alia*, of, the two similar letters written by the Bank on 6th September 1996, and what happened under those.)	3/4	4/5
4. Did the Bank on behalf of PMA receive sufficient money from Ruritania in October/November 1997 to pay Alpine?	5	6
5. Did PMA subsequently instruct the Bank to pay trade creditors in preference to Alpine? If yes,	5	7
(a) Was the Bank entitled to act on those instructions?		
(b) Did the Bank do so?		
6. Was the Bank's authority/duty to make payments to Alpine ended by the winding up of PMA?	5	7

Issue	Pt20 Def	Pt20 Rep

(b) *In the Part 20 proceedings:*

Issue	Pt20 Def	Pt20 Rep
1. What was PMA's business?	2	2
2. Did PMA enter into a contract with the Ruritanian Government in November 1995 for the supply of 10,000 medical kits, and need increased overdraft facilities for that? Did the Bank know of this?	3	3
3. Were the guarantees given specifically to obtain (in October 1995, June 1996 and March 1997) increased facilities for that purpose?	3/5	3/5
4. Did the Bank know of this and 'accept . . . the purpose and consideration for which the guarantees were given'?	6	1
5. Did the Bank on behalf of PMA receive sufficient money from Ruritania in October/November 1997 to extinguish its overdraft?	7	6
6. Did the Bank, *inter alia*, by its letters dated 31st October and 11th November 1997, treat the guarantees as having been discharged (except in the event of a fraudulent preference claim)?	8/9	7/8
7. As a result of (3) to (6), is the Bank estopped by convention or representation from asserting that its liability to Alpine is covered by the guarantees?	12	9
8. Did PMA request or authorise the Bank to incur personal liability to Alpine? If not, can the Bank in any event recover from PMA or its guarantors?	13	10

8 Two issues not set out in the Part 20 Defence, but which might be raised at trial, are:

9. Were the Bank's letters dated 31st October and 11th November 1997 effective as releases of the guarantees?

and

10. What was the effect of Mr Dickens' letter dated 27th October 1997, which purported to give notice of discontinuance prior to any demand being made?

Oral evidence

9 The Bank's principal witness will be Mr Donne. I should be very grateful if Mr Donne could be sent a full set of the relevant PM Cards and documents, statements of case (including further information) and affidavits to refresh his memory of events. Then a full proof should be taken from him, dealing specifically with the contents of each document and with each issue raised in the statements of case.

10 In particular, I am curious to know whether there is any substance whatsoever in the suggestion in the Part 20 Defence that Mr Donne and the guarantors by common consent treated the guarantees as covering (or assumed that they covered) only the Ruritanian contract indebtedness and no more. His letters dated 31st October and 11th November 1997 give a little support to this allegation. Similarly, I should like to know (a) why, having stated that he had irrevocable instructions to pay Alpine, he did not institute procedures to act on those instructions and did not, in the event, act on them; and (b) what happened to the payments from Indonesia etc., in respect of which he had previously written similar letters to Alpine. The distinction between Mr Forster's guarantee and the others will also need careful explanation.

11 Apart from Mr Donne, Mr Marvel also seems to have been involved with Mr Dickens' affairs (see, e.g. Mr Donne's letter dated 28th June 1996 referring to a

telephone conversation between Mr Marvel and Mr Dickens). Relevant PM card entries have the initials STC and WW. Mr Byron and Mr Shelley seem also to have written relevant letters. I should be grateful if proofs could be taken from them (after sight of the documents), and from anyone else that they or Mr Donne can identify as having been involved with PMA/Mr Dickens. We can decide whether or not to call them when we have had the opportunity to consider their proofs.

Documentary evidence

12 *Further disclosure* The correspondence with the liquidator is not privileged, is at least arguably relevant to the matters in issue in this action, and ought (as my instructions suggest) to be disclosed in a supplemental list. I cannot see any reference to PMA's bank statements in our List of Documents. Those for 1997 onwards (at least) might be relevant to the issues in this action, are not privileged, and should also be disclosed.

13 *Bundles for trial* I suggest that the trial bundles should consist of the following:

Bundle (A): Statements of case (together with further information); Statements of case in the Part 20 Proceedings (together with further information); Interim Orders; Summary judgment witness statements and exhibits.
Bundle (B): The guarantees; the relevant bank statements.
Bundle (C): Correspondence etc. (including the relevant PM cards), in chronological order.

14 I have flagged the pages in sections (8) (9) and (10) in my instructions which I consider should go into Bundle (C) with yellow sticky markers in the top right hand corners of the pages. Since the Claimant's solicitors will probably be the ones to prepare the bundles, we might tactfully remind them that each page of each bundle must be legible and should be numbered at centre bottom, in accordance with *Practice Direction 39*.

Notices

15 I do not think that it is necessary for us to serve notices on the Claimant or the guarantors at this stage. Part 20 claims seeking contributions would not be appropriate, and if Mr Donne is available to give oral evidence, a *Civil Evidence Act* notice will be unnecessary. The statements of case contain sufficient admissions to make the service of notices to admit unnecessary.

Security for costs

16 My Instructing Solicitor should check that the amount of our present security for costs is sufficient to cover the anticipated costs of a five-day trial. If it is not, we should ask (and if necessary apply) for more.

Settlement

17 There is no new material in the papers now before me to make me revise my view that the Bank is likely to be held liable to Alpine but entitled to an indemnity from the Guarantors. Three matters, however, suggest that a reasonable commercial settlement might be in the Bank's best interest.

18 First of all, there is the risk that the Bank may be the subject of critical judicial comment. For example, the judge might comment adversely on Mr Donne's actions in stating that he had irrevocable instructions but then not even protesting when those instructions were revoked and/or ignored. The judge might also criticise the Bank for not honouring its word to Alpine if, as I think is likely, he finds that the Bank is liable to them.

19   Secondly, this is a small claim, even allowing for interest and depreciation of sterling against the Swiss Franc. The costs are likely to be out of proportion to the amount at stake. Thirdly, there is the inevitable litigation risk, that the case will not in the event turn out as we now anticipate.

20   The Bank may be in a good position to 'broke' a without prejudice settlement between the Claimant and the guarantors. The inevitable discussions about bundles and other preparations for trial may provide a good opportunity to initiate settlement negotiations. Of course, the ideal settlement from the Bank's point of view would be for the guarantors to pay off the Claimant and pay the Bank's costs. However, some discount from this ideal position may have to be made to reflect the risks I have outlined and the irrecoverable costs of fighting this action through trial.

LEWIS ELLIOT

Gray's Inn Walks
Gray's Inn
London WC1R 5EA

8th November 1999

FOURTEEN

ADVICE ON EVIDENCE IN A CRIMINAL CASE

14.1 An Approach to Writing a Criminal Advice on Evidence

The golden rule in any advice on evidence is to ask yourself, 'How is this case to be proved?' If you are prosecuting, your job is to show how it is to be done. If you are defending, that task is still to identify the issues, to assess the strength of the prosecution case, and to recommend how the defendant may meet it. The advice is written in order to assist your instructing solicitors and is never seen by the other side. You are therefore free — indeed obliged — to be frank about your own case and very clear about what has to be done about it.

14.1.1 THE CHARGE

The advice should first set out the counts which are on the indictment, and point out their relationship to each other: for example, do they form a series of offences? Are there different ways of looking at the same set of facts? Are they alternatives, on which a jury can only be asked to convict on one? Prosecution counsel's role is different here from that of the defence. He or she is responsible for the indictment and sometimes may be asked to draft it. If you are so asked, your analysis of the evidence should include an explanation of why you have drafted the indictment as you have.

14.1.2 SUMMARISE THE EVIDENCE IN THE LIGHT OF CHARGES

This should be an analysis, not a mere recitation of the obvious. For clarity, concentrate on the narrative, showing how, at various stages, the witnesses — alone or corroborated — in effect tell the story and prove the case. Comment on the strengths and weaknesses and point out all discrepancies and how they might be resolved. Obviously, one must read everything in the brief with care.

14.1.3 FURTHER STATEMENTS MAY BE NECESSARY

If so, then indicate that, and set out what they must contain. This is not an invitation to suggest that the witnesses should think better of what they said before in order to harmonise their evidence with that of others. Further statements instead deal with gaps in the evidence or apparent inconsistencies. In practice, sometimes witnesses do say unexpected things of significance during their evidence, but you cannot count on them doing so, and the rule is that every matter which the Crown wishes to prove against a defendant must be reduced into statement form and served on the defence in good time.

14.1.4 NEVER EXPECT THE DEFENCE TO ADMIT ANYTHING

The Crown must prove each and every element of each and every charge, and often it is only when they are capable of such proof that the defence will make admissions in order to save court time. Set out each element of the charge and say how the evidence deals with it, bearing in mind that some things ('property belonging to another') may be capable of direct proof, while others ('dishonesty', 'knowing or believing') must be inferred from surrounding circumstances.

14.1.5 WITNESSES ARE DIFFERENT

Although in law the evidence of civilians and of police is of equal weight, in practice they make different kinds of witnesses. Civilians may have given statements to the police some time after the events, and will have rarely made any notes of their own. They may exhibit documents (e.g., receipts) which can be shown to them in the course of their evidence, but they cannot refresh their memory in the witness box from their statement unless it was taken very soon after the actual events. You will want to ask if this was so. Do not expect a civilian witness to repeat, verbatim, in evidence, a conversation which that witness purportedly quotes in his or her statement. The witness will more likely talk of the gist of things rather than the specifics. On the face of it, then, civilians may tend to differ between each other on details. This is not altogether surprising: two people rarely see the same thing in the same way (a common-sense approach which few defence counsel will admit to a jury) and they will have probably given their statements individually to different police officers.

In contrast, police statements ought to resemble one another. It is common and acceptable practice for officers who have witnessed something together to make up their notes together and to pool their recollections, thus producing a single, agreed version of events and of a passage of conversation. At the trial they will tend to stick to what is written in their notebooks as often they will not, months later, have an independent recollection of the events.

It is significant if supposedly corroborating police officers do diverge, and it is always a good idea to check all police statements against each other, word for word. Point out each discrepancy. Many have innocent explanations: mistakes are made in noting dates, names and venues; statements are typed up omitting passages which are in the original notebooks. Police normally do not check the accuracy of their statements against their notebooks before signing them. If something seems to be missing, ask the officers to go back and check their originals.

14.1.6 ADMISSIBILITY

Consider the admissibility in law of all prosecution evidence. It is natural for witnesses to say in their statements everything which they saw, but that may include hearsay, prejudicial comments (including some made by the defendant) and matters which are inadmissible against other defendants. Editing of statements and of interviews is quite normal, and you should point out where this ought to be done, pending agreement with the other side, or, failing agreement, by direction of the trial judge.

The Police and Criminal Evidence Act 1984 and the Codes of Practice are the basis on which most admissibility arguments are founded. There is a wealth of case law on the particularly vexed questions of 'what is an interview?' and 'when, where, how and in whose presence?' may an officer ask a suspect about an alleged offence. You must be wholly up to date and conversant with this aspect of the law, but you cannot assume that the police are. A number remain loyal to their own way of doing things, even after the courts have pronounced otherwise. Counsel must see whether the rules were in fact adhered to, for example, was the suspect cautioned/told of his or her right to free legal advice at the appropriate moment/asked to read and sign the officers' notes, etc.? If there appears to be a breach, then say so. Subject to the receipt of further instructions, you should advise whether a piece of evidence is likely to be admissible or not. If it is not, what effect will that have on the prosecution case? It is worth noting that such advice is subject to the defence asking to exclude some piece of evidence: whether the rules are broken or not, the defence may wish something to go before the jury because it happens to assist their case.

It is now standard practice for the police to supply the CPS with a schedule of unused material. Make sure that you have a copy of it, and ask for a copy of the documents listed, which should include the custody record (a potential mine of information for both sides) and the crime report sheet (which may list witnesses from whom the police have not taken a statement). The information contained in these may be adduced in evidence by agreement, but one should remember that to do so is often in fact hearsay, and it is not fair to expect police officers to know or to surmise why a colleague made a particular entry.

14.1.7   SUBMISSIONS OF LAW

The Criminal Procedure and Investigations Act 1996 requires preliminary hearings to take place before all Crown Court trials. The nature of the hearing differs according to whether the trial is likely to be lengthy or complex. However, in both cases, points of law and arguments relating to the admissibility of evidence should be raised at the preliminary hearing.

Where the case is likely to be complex or lengthy, the judge may order a 'preparatory hearing' to take place. The purpose is to identify the issues in the case, to see how the jury can be assisted to understand those issues, to expedite the trial, and to assist the judge's management of the trial (s. 29).

Under s. 31, the judge can make rulings on the admissibility of evidence or other questions of law likely to arise in the trial. The judge can also order the prosecution to prepare a document setting out the principal facts of the Crown's case, the witnesses who will speak to those facts, and any propositions of law the Crown will rely on. The prosecution can also be ordered to prepare the evidence in a form that is likely to aid comprehension by the jury. Furthermore, the prosecution can be ordered to provide a written notice detailing any documents the truth of which the prosecutor believes the defence should admit. The judge can then order the defence to give written notice of any points of law they will be raising and to state which of the documents referred to in the prosecution notice the defence are prepared to admit; where the defence are not willing to admit the truth of any such documents, they must explain why this is so.

In the case of trials other than those which are likely to be complex or lengthy (in other words, the majority of cases) s. 39 of the 1996 Act enables a pre-trial hearing to take place. This gives statutory effect to the existing system of Plea and Directions Hearings. At this hearing, the defendant is asked to enter a plea. Where the defendant pleads 'not guilty', prosecuting and defence counsel are expected to inform the court of matters such as: the issues in the case; the number of witnesses to be called; any points of law likely to arise (including questions on the admissibility of evidence); and whether any technical equipment (such as video equipment) is likely to be needed. It follows that it is very important that by the time of this hearing, the factual and legal issues in the case should have been identified.

At this hearing, the judge is empowered to make rulings on the admissibility of evidence and on any other questions of law which are relevant to the case. These rulings are binding for the whole of the trial unless there is an application for the ruling to be altered, but such an application can only be made if there has been a material change in circumstances since the ruling was made. This is so whether or not the preliminary hearing and the trial are presided over by the same judge.

14.1.8   PLANS OR PHOTOS

On reading the brief, it may seem that the jury would be assisted by seeing a plan of the area (or of a particular building) or photographs. Sometimes the page from the A–Z will do. Photographs are expensive, however, especially as there should always be enough copies to go round. You should also bear in mind that photographs are not an accurate representation of what things look like, in terms of distances, compared actually to being at the scene. A view is an exceptional procedure and requires a good deal of organisation by the court. If you feel it is essential, then the court should be warned ahead of time and the matter should be canvassed with the judge as early as possible in the trial.

14.1.9 EXPERT EVIDENCE

The defence is required to give the prosecution (and any co-defendants) advance notice of any expert evidence which it is proposed to adduce at trial (Crown Court (Advance Notice of Expert Evidence) Rules 1987 (SI 1987, No. 716)). This has to be in the form of a statement and it should be served on the other party or parties 'as soon as practicable' after committal for trial. The defence is not obliged to serve the statement unless it intends to rely on it. The first step is to ask your instructing solicitor to take a statement from the proposed expert. It is perfectly appropriate for counsel to draft headings or questions to put to the expert. Once the statement has been obtained, the second step is to decide whether in fact it advances your case. It should only be served once you are sure that it does advance your case.

Always have regard to what expertise your witnesses in fact have. For example, in cases of handling stolen goods, it may be that the loser cannot be traced, and that the Crown has to prove the charge relying on the fact that the defendant 'bought' the goods at an obvious undervalue. The person who can give evidence of the value of goods is someone who is in that business. Police officers are not in the video recorder business and you cannot assume that 'we all know' the cost of anything.

At the same time, police can be experts in the street value of drugs or in the way in which particular drugs are packaged and sold or even where they come from. Ensure that there is an appropriate statement from the officer in each drugs case, particularly where the defendant is charged with intent to supply, and that there is a statement complying with the provisions of the Drug Trafficking Offences Act 1986, s. 3.

14.1.10 FURTHER WITNESSES

As is obvious from the above, counsel on both sides may feel that other potential witnesses should be seen by their solicitors. For example, existing witnesses may refer to other people being present. Although the defence is not obliged to prove anything, in practice they must also consider the question of further witnesses. Can someone else corroborate the defendant in some material way? A patently honest defence witness can often persuade a jury that the defendant is telling the truth about other matters as well. In the specimen advice in **14.4**, for example, Leahy's defence counsel might consider whether other people have ever borrowed the Mini or whether it was normally kept locked or whether something about the car made it easy for a thief to start it up.

14.1.11 WITNESSES TO ATTEND COURT

At least 14 days prior to the preliminary hearing the defence should supply the court and the prosecution with a full list of prosecution witnesses they require to attend at the trial. This puts an onus on counsel to advise in relation to a defence brief as soon as it is received. If witness requirements change after the preliminary hearing, the prosecution must be notified at once.

14.1.12 PRE-TRIAL DISCLOSURE

A particularly important aspect of advising on evidence concerns the rules which govern pre-trial disclosure.

If the case is to be tried in the Crown Court, copies of the statements made by the witnesses whom the prosecution intend to call at the trial must be supplied to the defence (if this was not done prior to the mode of trial hearing) before committal proceedings can take place. If the prosecution wish to call a witness whose statement was not used in the committal proceedings, a 'notice of additional evidence' (including a copy of the witness statement) must be served on the defence prior to the trial.

The prosecution are also under a statutory duty to disclose material other than the statements of the people they will be calling as witnesses. Under s. 3 of the Criminal Procedure and Investigations Act 1996, the prosecutor must disclose any prosecution material which, in the prosecutor's opinion, might undermine the case for the prosecution against the accused. This applies to all trials (whether in the Crown Court, the magistrates' court or the Youth Court). Counsel when advising on evidence should be careful to consider whether this duty has been complied with.

Where the case is to be tried in the Crown Court, s. 5 of the Criminal Procedure and Investigations Act 1996 imposes a compulsory duty of disclosure on the defence. The defence must inform the prosecution, in general terms, of the accused's defence and indicate the matters on which the accused takes issue with the prosecution (and why he or she takes issue with the prosecution on those matters). Where the defence case includes an alibi, the accused must give particulars of the alibi to the prosecution (where the defendant says he or she was at the time of the offence and the names and addresses of any witnesses he or she proposes to call in support of the alibi). Counsel for the defence may well be instructed to advise on the drafting of the statement which sets out the defence case.

In the case of summary trial, s. 6 of the 1996 Act enables the defence to make voluntary disclosure of their case.

Section 7 imposes a further duty of disclosure on the prosecution. This additional duty applies to all Crown Court trials, and to summary trials where the accused has made voluntary disclosure under s. 5. Section 7(2) requires the prosecution to disclose to the defence any prosecution material which might reasonably be expected to assist the defence (as revealed in the statement of the defence case served by the defence). This is another matter which prosecuting counsel should be careful to consider when advising on evidence.

Section 9 imposes a continuing duty on the prosecution to keep the question of disclosure under review so that any material which comes to light and which might undermine the prosecution case is disclosed to the accused.

The prosecution may only withhold material under ss. 3, 7 and 9 if the court authorised non-disclosure on the ground of public interest.

Section 11 of the 1996 Act provides that if the defence fail to comply with the compulsory duty of disclosure prior to Crown Court trial, or if the defence case at trial differs from that disclosed to the prosecution (whether the disclosure was compulsory or voluntary), then adverse inferences can be drawn by the jury or magistrates as the case may be.

14.1.13 DEFENCE SOLICITORS CONTACTING THE PROSECUTION

As well as providing a statement of the defence case under the Criminal Procedure and Investigations Act 1996 (see **14.1.12**) and serving any expert evidence on which the defence intend to rely (see **14.1.9**), defence counsel should ask his or her instructing solicitors to deal with other matters which involve contacting the prosecution. The main examples are:

(a) Section 9 statements of certain defence witnesses. Using your judgment, it will be clear that certain matters (e.g., medical) ought to be capable of agreement if possible. Statements of these witnesses should be put in proper section 9 form, rather than on scraps of paper.

(b) Discontinuing proceedings. You may wish to ask the Crown to take a certain view of the matter, for example, in the light of the defendant's mental or physical condition or in light of the fact that he or she has just received a custodial sentence in another matter and is unlikely to be sentenced to a longer term, even if he or she is found guilty of this. Counsel must advise on the merits, and insist that full details be served on the CPS as soon as possible. The prosecution cannot be expected to make snap judgments on the day of the hearing on matters requiring consideration and the taking of instructions from persons not normally working in the court building.

(c) Offer of a plea to a lesser charge. It may appear from instructions that the defendant ought to plead guilty to a lesser charge, whether or not that appears on the indictment. If so, advise accordingly and ask that the offer (should the defendant be willing) be put forward to the Crown.

In addition, the defence are obliged to inform the prosecution whether or not they agree the proposed summary of the taped interview. Defence counsel, having of course first listened to a copy tape (which may have to be requested), must always advise on whether (i) it is agreed; or (ii) an amended summary should be put forward to the Crown; or (iii) the tape itself should be played in court. Judges tend to prefer that the jury simply receives a written summary or transcript, but you may feel that the true flavour of your lay client's case best comes over by listening to the tape. Prosecution counsel should also ask for a copy tape: he or she may also find the police summary to be inadequate.

14.1.14 CONTINUITY

This is a matter frequently omitted by police officers when making their statements. Each exhibit in a case must be given a number at the time it is taken into custody. In the case of a document, it may be necessary merely for the witness to say that he or she produces it, although you should always ask to see a copy. In the case of an object which is passed from one person to another, it is essential that each witness is talking about the same thing. For example, if a suspected stolen object is taken into police custody, the officer must give it a number, AB/1. If it is later identified by someone else, that person must also refer to it as AB/1. It is not good enough — although it is very common — for the loser simply to say, for example, that an unidentified police officer showed her a television set (no exhibit number) which she recognised as her own. That does not prove that it is the same television as AB/1. Further statements may be needed to correct the omission.

In drugs cases, there must be continuity from the moment the exhibit is found. It must be given a number, and the finder must say what he or she did with it, for example, took it back to the police station or handed it to an exhibits officer. The person who sealed it in the drugs bag must say so and give the seal number. The person who transported it or caused its transport to the forensic science laboratory must say so and must refer both to the exhibit number and to the bag number. Otherwise, the object does not tie up with what will eventually be analysed by the scientist.

14.1.15 SUMMARISING

After the body of your advice, summarise in a single paragraph the case against the defendant and give your opinion about its merits. If you want your instructing solicitors to do anything, then recapitulate by listing all of the actions to be taken by them.

14.2 Sample Advice on Evidence for Prosecution

IN THE BARCHESTER CROWN COURT   Case No. P97–1231

BETWEEN

THE QUEEN

v

PETER SMITH

ADVICE ON THE INDICTMENT AND EVIDENCE

I am instructed to prosecute the above-named Defendant, Peter Smith, on two counts, one of theft of a car stereo, between 20th September 1997 and 1st October 1997, the other of handling a mountain bike on 25th March 1998. In my opinion the Indictment is defective for the reasons given at Paragraph 1 below. Furthermore the evidence purportedly in support of the count relating to the theft of the radio from the vehicle is not sufficient to secure a reasonable prospect of conviction upon that count for the reasons set out at paragraph 3 below.

1. The Indictment

The Indictment is defective because it clearly offends against the rule under Rule 9 of the Indictment Rules 1971 in that the two counts, on any view of the matter, cannot be regarded as being either founded on the same facts or as forming part of a series of offences of the same or of a similar character.

The facts on which the theft charge rests are based on the evidence of different prosecution witnesses and there is no nexus between it and the handling matter which is founded on wholly different facts. The fact that the theft count and handling count are similar offences of dishonesty is not sufficient to justify joinder unless they can be said to form a series of offences and for this criterion to be satisfied there must be a sufficient nexus between the offences in both law and fact. On my analysis of the papers there is no such nexus on the facts.

The Crown are advised to attend to the course that I propose at paragraph 2 below within the next five days as it seems that the 56-day time limit, with extension, expires on 24th November 1997.

2. The course proposed

This matter was committed to the Crown Court on 20th September 1998. According to Rule 5 of the Indictment Rules (as amended) if this Indictment has not yet been preferred then the time limit for preferring the Indictment by the officer of the Crown Court can be extended after 28 days by his own volition for a further 28 days without the necessity of an application by the prosecution: see *R* v *Stewart* (1990) 91 Cr App R 301.

However, two Indictments ought to be preferred. The first Indictment will contain the handling count and the second Indictment will contain the theft count. This can be legitimately done as the Defendant was committed on both the Theft and Handling charges: see *R* v *Lombardi* [1989] 1 WLR 73 at p. 76, para. G.

If this defective Indictment has already been preferred then I would advise, that either at the PDH or at the commencement of the trial but before arraignment, the Crown ought to apply for leave to stay this defective Indictment and prefer two Indictments along the lines suggested. I cannot see any difficulty in obtaining the necessary leave provided the Crown gives the Defence appropriate notice of the course that I propose. The course that I suggest was approved in *R* v *Follett* [1989] 2 WLR 512.

3. The lack of evidence in relation to the count of theft from the vehicle

The only evidence that exists in relation to this count is the fingerprints found in the front passenger side of the vehicle on an RAC handbook that was in the glove compartment. When the Defendant was interviewed on tape, he denied being driven in, or driving a Ford XR2 motor car, and could not provide a satisfactory explanation as to the presence of his prints on the RAC book. In my opinion the presence of the prints in the car, although they may be consistent with the Defendant having committed an offence of allowing himself to be carried, cannot alone provide sufficient evidence to found a conviction of theft of the radio from the vehicle. In those circumstances I would suggest that a plea by the Defendant to the handling indictment upon which there is sufficient evidence ought to be accepted. Either no evidence should be offered on the theft Indictment or it should be ordered to lie on the file.

However should the Defendant plead not guilty to both Indictments, then the Defendant should be tried on the 1st Indictment and if convicted the Crown can decide whether to pursue the prosecution of the 2nd Indictment.

Should Instructing Solicitors have any queries in relation to the contents of this advice please do not hesitate to contact the writer.

A. D. PAUL

Eagle Chambers, Bedford Row, London WC1
2nd November 1998

14.3   Sample Advice for Defence

IN THE WEST LONDON COURT

THE QUEEN

v

PETER GRANT

ADVICE ON EVIDENCE

---

1   Introduction

1.1   Mr Grant is a man of good character who is charged with a single count of theft from his employer, alleging that he stole the sum of £60,000 over a two-year period (October 1996 – October 1998). In addition he is charged with six specimen counts of false accounting over the same period. He was committed for trial on 19th March 1998 and the preliminary hearing is fixed for 30th April 1998.

1.2   Mr Grant was employed in the accounts department of this company and it is alleged that he stole £60,000 by drawing money from the company's bank account against bogus invoices prepared by him. It is alleged that he then sought to conceal his activities by altering certain accounting records held on computer.

The prosecution case

1.3   The evidence against him comes from two sources:

    1.3.1   false entries in certain accounts over which he is said to have had sole control; and

    1.3.2   an alleged confession to an internal disciplinary hearing.

The defence case

1.4   Mr Grant denies these offences. His defence (which has already been notified to the prosecution) is as follows:

    1.4.1   he believes another employee, Mrs Eileen Jones, was responsible for the theft;

    1.4.2   in relation to the allegedly false accounting entries, he does not accept that the prosecution's accountant has reached the correct conclusions; and

    1.4.3   he was bullied by his employers into making a confession.

1.5   The lines of defence raised by Mr Grant require further action by the defence and I shall deal with each matter in turn.

2 The person responsible for the theft

2.1 Mr Grant has stated in his proof that he believes that Mrs Jones, a prosecution witness, is responsible for the theft. We know from her statement that she was the managing director's secretary and had been with the firm for 25 years. It is apparent from the statements of other prosecution witnesses that she was very popular with the firm as a whole. It is equally apparent that Mr Grant was unpopular with the management of the firm.

2.2 At present, he has not given any instructions as to the basis for his belief that Mrs Jones was the thief or any instructions as to how she may have stolen the money.

2.3 We would have to be satisfied that Mr Grant's allegations were supported by reasonable grounds before we would be entitled to suggest that Mrs Jones was guilty of these offences.

2.4 Assuming Mr Grant can provide such reasonable grounds, he must be aware that accusing Mrs Jones of theft is a high risk strategy. Unless his suspicions have a substantial evidential basis then such allegations are likely to alienate the jury and rebound on him accordingly. In the event of a conviction, the fact that Mr Grant had sought to blame someone else for the theft would be an aggravating feature in relation to sentence.

2.5 It is necessary for Mr Grant to provide those instructing me with specific instructions on this point. We can then explore it further in conference. Subject to what he says, it may then be necessary to take statements from any potential defence witnesses.

3 The accountancy evidence

3.1 It is apparent from the committal bundle that the evidence in relation to the accounts is complex. The prosecution are relying on the expert evidence of an independent accountant to support their assertions.

3.2 In view of the fact that Mr Grant does not accept her findings, it will be necessary for the defence to instruct an independent accountant to carry out the same exercise. Mr Grant will have to provide detailed instructions on this point in order to assist any accountant instructed by the defence. I advise that it is appropriate to ask the Legal Aid Board to extend Mr Grant's legal aid to cover this essential work.

3.3 Once our accountant has completed his work, we will need to discuss his findings in order to see whether they do in fact advance our case. If we decide that they do advance it, then his findings will need to be put into the form of a statement and served on the prosecution in accordance with the Crown Court (Advance Notice of Expert Evidence) Rules 1987.

4 The confession

4.1 Mr Grant says that once certain alleged discrepancies came to light, he was hauled in front of the managing director and one of the external auditors. He says he was subjected to shouting and other verbal bullying. He was told that if he said he had taken the money, he could save his job by owning up. As a result, he made a false confession. He says that he was not cautioned and no notes were made of any conversations.

4.2 At trial it will be necessary to challenge the admissibility of this confession under the Police and Criminal Evidence Act ('PACE') 1984, ss. 76(2) (a) and (b) and 78.

4.3 Section 67(9) of PACE states that the Codes of Practice apply to 'persons other than police officers who are charged with the duty of investigating offences'. Whether or not persons come within this definition is a question of fact in each case. The Court of Appeal has held that the duty applies to commercial investigators if they are 'charged with the duty of investigating offences' (R v *Twaites and Brown* (1991) 92 Cr App R 106).

4.4   We will argue that the managing director and the external auditor come into this category. The court and the prosecution will be told at the preliminary hearing of our intention to take this point at the trial.

5   Witness orders

The preliminary hearing is fixed for 30th April 1999. In accordance with rule 5 of the Practice Direction we must inform the court and the prosecution of which witnesses we require at trial by 16th April 1999. This can be discussed and finalised when we meet in conference.

6   Unused material

I note that there are references in some of the witness statements to material which has not yet been disclosed to the defence. Mr Grant's main line of defence was made clear in his interviews with the police and the prosecution ought to be asked to disclose any unused material which might assist the defence, pursuant to the Criminal Procedure and Investigations Act 1996.

7   Conclusion

7.1   The following steps need to be taken at once:

> 7.1.1   further instructions on Mr Grant's allegation that Mrs Jones was responsible for the thefts;
>
> 7.1.2   a date for a conference before 16th April 1999; and
>
> 7.1.3   an application for an extension of legal aid to cover expert assistance from an accountant.

CATHERINE PETERS

1 Prince's Buildings
Temple
London EC4

22nd March 1999

14.4   A More Complex Advice on Evidence

THE QUEEN

v

JOHN LEAHY and MARGARET SQUIRES

ADVICE ON EVIDENCE

---

1   The preliminary hearing in this matter has now been fixed for 22nd May, and I am asked to advise on evidence, particularly in the light of the applications which the defence have indicated that they will be making.

2   The defendants appear jointly on the same indictment. Leahy is charged (counts 1 and 2) with possession with intent to supply (alternatively simple possession of)

1,021.2 grammes of cannabis resin, which, according to the statement of DC Trapp dated 27 February 1998, has a street value of £4,080. He is also charged (count 3) with possessing 440 mg of amphetamine sulphate. Mrs Squires is charged (counts 4 and 5) with possession with intent to supply (alternatively simple possession of) 179 grammes of cannabis resin, with a street value of £600.

3   On 2nd May 1998 PCs Williamson and Hooper stopped a white Mini (registration number C841 PLE). The driver decamped before either officer could get a good look at his face. Their descriptions of him are fairly vague.

4   After an unsuccessful search for the driver, four police officers (PCs Williamson and Hooper, now joined by PS Craddock and PC Peel) returned to the Mini. PC Hooper found a plastic carrier-bag in the front driver's well. It contained two slabs of what he took to be cannabis and which indeed was 999 grammes of cannabis resin (DH/1).

5   PS Craddock found, on the floor in front of the passenger's seat, an insurance cover note in the name of Mrs Knightley of 22B Milton Road (MC/1), an envelope bearing the name of John Leahy of 36A Brick Road (MC/2) and five keys on a ring (MC/3). Although the documents are exhibits, there are no copies of them in my brief. I should be grateful if these could be provided. Copies must also be sent to the defence and sufficient made to distribute, in due course, to the jury.

6   PCs Craddock, Williamson and Peel then went to 22B Milton Road, where they hoped to find the driver of the Mini.

7   The door was answered by Mrs Squires. On entering the flat, the three officers went into the lounge. On a coffee table they found a number of bank notes (TW/1) and two cheques (TW/3). PC Williamson refers to a 'sum of money'; the other two officers say £300. I should be grateful if PC Williamson would make a further statement saying what happened to the money throughout and exhibiting it and stating how much was there and in what denominations. Photocopies of the cheques should be provided for the defence and, in due course, for the jury.

8   PC Williamson also found, on the floor behind the door to the junk room, a plastic bag with what appeared to be cannabis resin: TW/2. The bag contained 179 grammes of cannabis resin. As soon as he looked at the bag, PC Williamson (rightly) suspected that it was cannabis, and asked Mrs Squires what it was. He did not caution her and her answer to his question about it is therefore probably inadmissible under Code C (para. C 10.1). She was then arrested and cautioned and everyone went back into the lounge.

9   The officers then asked her a number of questions. It is my opinion that these constituted an interview under the definition in para. C 11.1A ('The questioning of a person regarding his involvement or suspected involvement in a criminal offence or offences which, by virtue of para. C 10.1, is required to be carried out under caution'). As an interview, it took place in breach of para. C 11.1 (it did not take place at a police station), para. C 11.2 (Mrs Squires was not reminded of her entitlement to free legal advice), para. C 11.5(c) (it was not recorded contemporaneously), para. C 11.9 (the reasons for not recording it contemporaneously were not noted), para. C 11.10 (Mrs Squires was not given the opportunity to read the interview record and to sign it as correct although she was in the police station for some time). There was also a breach of para. C 6.6: although she said, 'I want a solicitor', the officers continued to question her. It is highly unlikely that anything said in the flat after the finding of TW/2 will be admissible.

10   In the meantime the Mini had been transported to the police station. There, later on in the evening, PCs Hooper and Craddock searched the vehicle. They found a tobacco tin with cannabis (DH/2 — later sealed in C306510) and two reefer-type cigarettes (DH/3 — C306509). DH/2 was sent to the lab and analysed, and was found to contain 22.2 grammes of cannabis resin. At the lab, it was found also to contain a folded piece of paper with 440 mg of amphetamine sulphate. That was seen by neither

officer, and they naturally never refer to it. This is the entire subject matter of count 3. In the circumstances there is a strong probability that the jury will acquit on count 3. The defence are bound to suggest that the lack of continuity enables the jury to draw the inference that the amphetamine may have been added to the tin, either by the police or by the lab, either by accident or design. In the circumstances it may be difficult for them to be sure about the reliability of other evidence.

11   A computer check revealed that no current owner was shown for the Mini, which means that unless other evidence is forthcoming, the Crown cannot prove that the Mini belonged to Leahy.

12   While in the collator's office, PC Hooper happened to see, amongst several others on the wall, a photograph of a man whom he immediately recognised as the driver — a man he had described as having 'short grey hair, round face'. It is of course important to the prosecution case that this happened quite independently of PC Williamson making the same recognition at the flat with another photograph of Leahy. The defence have indicated that they will oppose the introduction of such evidence under *R* v *Lamb* (1980) 71 Cr App R 198.

13.   In *R* v *Lamb* the witnesses first picked the defendant out from a police photo album of local villains. Lawton LJ said that this was equivalent to the prosecution leading, as part of their case, the fact that the accused had a criminal record. He did however, refer to 'exceptional cases' where producing the photographs can be part of the prosecution case, namely, where the arrested suspect refuses to cooperate in any way and refuses to be put on an identification parade; where 'the prosecution may only be able to get their case going by revealing the fact that the witness was able to pick out the defendant from photographs'.

14   There was no identification parade in the case of Leahy, and the papers do not say why. The argument against producing the collator's photograph is a strong one under *R* v *Lamb*, particularly as PC Hooper had no opportunity to see Leahy's face save during the chase, which took place at night. PC Williamson, however, is in a better position, as he picked out a photograph which was in an ordinary family album, and he in fact went up to the driver in Baker Road. No doubt it can be said, though, that as he went to the flat intending to find Leahy, it is not surprising that he picked out a photograph of Mrs Squires's boyfriend.

15   Leahy was not interviewed until 11th May, when he was interviewed twice, both interviews being taped and in the presence of a solicitor's representative. He admitted that he had lived at 22B Milton Road for about a year with Mrs Squires, and that it is the only place where they had lived together; that he used to live at 36A Baker Road; and that the cheques (TW/3) were his. I would like to listen to these tape recordings.

16.   In short, the evidence against Leahy rests almost entirely on the identification by photographs. True, inside the Mini was an envelope addressed to him at his old address. There is no direct evidence of whose car it was or who had permission to drive it. Whoever was driving the car undoubtedly possessed such a large amount of cannabis that it could only have been intended for supply. Can we prove that that person was Leahy? This is doubtful, having regard to the photograph evidence and the inevitable *Turnbull* direction.

17   Mrs Squires was interviewed as well, but on 3rd May. The admissibility of this will be challenged on the grounds that she was only given half a caution, i.e., 'Firstly I must caution you that you do not have to answer any of my questions unless you wish to but it may harm your defence if you don't'. DC Trapp thus omits the warning that her answers could be used in evidence. Paragraph C 10.4 states that 'minor deviations' do not constitute a breach so long as the sense of the caution is preserved. Mrs Squires is of good character and so had heard the correct caution only once (when she was arrested). Nonetheless, the judge is likely to hold that the most important elements of the caution were administered by DC Trapp and so is likely to admit the evidence of the interview. Again, I need to hear the tape recording.

18   Mrs Squires admitted that the substances found in the flat were hers. She knew what they were worth. She insisted that they were for her sole use. She gave an excuse for having the £300 (to buy a car) although she does not say why it was on the floor or why it was mixed up with cheques made out to Leahy. She said that she buys and sells cars, but they are obviously of small value. She owes Barclays Bank £700, plus rent of £33.75 per fortnight, and obviously has no means by which to buy cannabis of the quantity found. At the same time, no one asked her how much she smokes herself or how she uses it or how she breaks down a block of 179 grammes or whether she had already used any of it or how long she expected it to last.

19.   If the interview is not admitted, then the evidence against her is that £600 worth of cannabis was found in her flat along with £300 loose on the floor and two cheques which did not belong to her. None of the tools of the trade was found: no scales, no small plastic bags, no cling film, no knives with stains, nothing packaged. At best it can be suggested that she was about to go into the drugs business but had not yet bought the necessary kit, or that she was somehow a wholesaler herself. The Crown cannot point to any evidence that she has benefited from the proceeds of drug trafficking: apparently some Abbey National Building Society books were seized in the flat, but the officers do not say so in their statements and I have seen copies of none of them, but in the interview it is said that the total credits amount to some £255.

20   Given the fact that the only evidence against Mrs Squires is what was found in the flat and the only evidence against Leahy relates to whether or not he was the driver of the Mini, a joint trial seems inappropriate. I therefore advise that the indictment be severed.

21   The defence statement served by Mr Leahy simply denies that he was the driver of the Mini stopped by the police and denies possession of any controlled drugs. He says that, at the time when the Mini was stopped by the police, he was in the company of one Michael Phillips. The statement served by Mrs Squires merely repeats what she said to the police in interview. Both statements are very brief, but they appear to comply with the requirements of the Criminal Procedure and Investigations Act 1996.

22   Once the police have interviewed Mr Phillips, and assuming that Mr Phillips supports Mr Leahy's alibi, any record of that interview should be sent to the defence. It seems unlikely that there would be any material in the possession of the prosecution which would assist the case of Mrs Squires as disclosed in her defence statement, but those instructing should ensure that the list of unused material is checked carefully.

23   In the meantime, I should be grateful if the following could be dealt with:

(a)   Sufficient photocopies of a plan or relevant page of the A–Z showing the route of the chase and including Milton Road.

(b)   Sufficient photocopies of the insurance cover note, the envelope, the two cheques, and the Abbey National Building Society books.

(c)   Copies of the custody record must be served. I should also like a copy. The originals must be brought to court.

(d)   All the drugs and the money must be brought to court.

(e)   PC Williamson must make a further statement relating to the money as set out above.

(f)   The alibi witness Michael Phillips should have been interviewed.

(g)   Full transcripts of the tape recorded interviews must be prepared and served on the defence. The transcripts and the tapes themselves must be brought to court.

24   Due to the time factor, it is essential that the CPS ensures that any memo has in fact been received and is being dealt with by the officer in the case.

JOHN BLOGGS

Gray's Inn Place
London WC1

1st May 1999

FIFTEEN

ADVICE ON EVIDENCE AND QUANTUM

15.1 Checklist for Advice on Evidence for Assessment of Damages in a Personal Injury Case

15.1.1 ISSUES

List all issues which are likely to be before the court on the hearing of the assessment of damages to ensure that none are missed.

15.1.2 CASE MANAGEMENT

Which 'track' is the claim in or likely to be allocated to? Have the Pre-Action Protocols for Personal Injury Claims been complied with? Have the Court's Case Management directions and orders been complied with? If not, how can the consequences of non-compliance be mitigated? At each stage below, consider how any further evidence required is to be fitted into the Court's directions or whether further directions can or should be sought. Remember that applications should not be made piecemeal but all necessary directions should be sought at the same hearing, if possible (CPR, r. 1.4(i)).

15.1.3 GENERAL DAMAGES FOR PAIN AND SUFFERING

1 Check medical reports

(a) Is the medical position stable?

If not — are the reports sufficiently up to date?

If not — advise a review.

(b) Have all aspects of claimant's condition been covered? Is a report required from another area of expertise, NB psychiatrist? and the claimant's complaints, if any, of inability to work? (Should it be from a single joint expert (CPR, r. 35.8)?)

(c) Is this a case for provisional damages? Have they been pleaded?

(d) Have reports been disclosed to other side? if not:

(i) Should they now be disclosed?

(ii) Is there non-medical prejudicial material to be edited out?

(e) Have the other side's medical reports been disclosed? If so:

(i) Are there any questions for the experts required for clarification (CPR, r. 35.6)?

(ii)   Can they be agreed?

(iii) Should our expert be asked to comment on them first?

(f)   Have the reports been verified with a statement of truth etc. in accordance with CPR, r. 35.10 and PD 35 (Experts and Assessors), paras 1.2, 1.3 and 1.4?

2   If acting for the claimant

(a)   Does his/her witness statement deal with the medical position? Is it up to date? If not advise an addendum.

(b)   Is it a case where evidence from family and friends will help to establish the extent of the changes in the claimant since the accident? Is there, for example, gross disability or personality change?

(c)   Is a video needed, for example, to demonstrate the extent of the claimant's disability around the home? Or at work?

3   If acting for the defendant

Are there grounds for suspecting the claimant is exaggerating his/her disabilities? If so:

(a)   Have we seen GP notes to check whether any relevant complaints were made before or after the accident?

(b)   Are there proofs from witnesses, e.g. in the neighbourhood or at work, who can say what the true position is?

(c)   Would a video help? Consider cost of enquiry agent against sum at stake.

4   Arrangements for disabled claimant to attend trial

In the case of a grossly disabled claimant, and where acting for claimant, remind solicitors of necessity for making suitable arrangements for the claimant to attend the trial.

5   Photographs

(a)   Is it a scarring case? If the scars are in an embarrassing place (buttocks, breasts, abdomen, etc.) are there up-to-date photographs? Colour is better than black and white. 7″ × 5″ should be the minimum size; 10″ × 8″ is better. Four booklets of photographs (or more if more than one defendant).

(b)   In appropriate cases, are there any pre-accident photographs for comparison purposes?

(c)   Have photographs been disclosed to the other side? If not — should they be?

(d)   Have the other side's photographs (if any) been disclosed? If so — can they be agreed?

15.1.4   DAMAGES FOR FUTURE LOSS AND FUTURE CARE

1   In a case where the claimant has not resumed his/her pre-accident or any employment

(a)   Did the medical reports deal with the claimant's prospects of being able to work again? If not, the omission should be covered.

(b) Is the evidence of future loss sufficiently full? Does it deal with the prospects of the claimant's promotion? Is evidence required from his/her former immediate superior as to his/her pre-accident abilities? If the claimant had only been in the pre-accident job for a short time, would evidence from a former employer help?

(c) In what financial state was/is the previous employer? Would the claimant have been made redundant?

2 In a case where the claimant has not resumed his/her pre-accident employment but has obtained less well-paid job

(a) Is there adequate evidence of the comparative earning rates?

(b) Is there adequate evidence of the claimant's abilities and promotional prospects in his/her present employment?

3 Claimant fit to resume work

If it is a case where the claimant is fit to resume work, his/her pre-accident job is not available but he/she is claiming that he/she has been unable to obtain alternative employment — is there documentary evidence of job seeking? Has it been disclosed? Can it be agreed?

4 Is there evidence of claimant attending a rehabilitation or retraining assessment course?

5 In a case where the claimant has resumed his/her pre-accident employment

(a) Is he/she likely to be at a disadvantage on the labour market, e.g. because of future disability (e.g. osteoarthritis) or present disability which does not prevent present work if he/she were to lose job?

(b) If so, is there evidence (1) as to the claimant's experience and qualifications and (2) of how secure his/her present job is likely to be?

6 Has the claimant lost pension rights?

If so:

(a) Have they been valued? (NB *Auty* v *National Coal Board* [1985] 1 WLR 784; and is accountancy help required?)

(b) Have/can the calculations be agreed?

7 In a case of gross disability

(a) Will there be a need for long-term care? If so, has it been properly costed? There should be an expert's report, if so can it be disclosed/agreed? If not, should there be a joint expert?

(b) Is this a case where a member of the claimant's family is providing the care? If so, is there a proof from the provider? Does it deal with his/her loss of earnings? This is to be taken into account when quantifying the value of his/her services (*Donnelly* v *Joyce* [1974] QB 454 but note that the court may award only a gratuity rather than a 'wage': see *Housecroft* v *Burnett* [1986] 1 All ER 332 (CA) and *Hunt* v *Severs* [1994] 2 WLR 602). Does the medical expert confirm the need for such care?

8 Is the loss of earnings supported by documentary evidence?

If not, it should be. If so, has it been disclosed? Can it be agreed?

9 Is further surgery likely?

If so, will it be performed privately? If so, has it been costed?

15.1.5 SPECIAL DAMAGES

1 Loss of earnings

Is this properly documented? Can the figures be agreed?

2 Additional benefits from employer

(a) Are these properly documented?

(b) Can the figures be agreed?

3 Other items

These can range from prescription charges and bus fares to specially adapted cars and even specially adapted accommodation. In the case of each major item:

(a) Does it require expert evidence to justify the expense? If so has a report been obtained/disclosed?

(b) Is item supported by documentary evidence? If so has it been disclosed?

If acting for the claimant

Has a schedule of past and future losses and expenses been prepared and served on the other parties in accordance with CPR, Part 16, PD 16, para. 4.2? If not, advise solicitors that they should prepare the schedule or give instructions for counsel to do so.

Note that the following items need to be dealt with (where applicable):

(1) Loss of future earnings.

(2) Loss of future earning capacity.

(3) Medical or other expenses relating to or including the cost of care, attention, accommodation and appliances in the future.

(4) Loss of pension rights.

If acting for the defendant

(a) Have the items of special damages been agreed?

(b) If not, can they be?

(c) If not, can the documentary evidence supporting any item be agreed?

(d) Do the witness statements adequately cover the evidence which you intend to adduce in relation to special damages? If necessary advise solicitor to prepare supplementary witness statements.

15.1.6 ADMISSIONS AND HEARSAY EVIDENCE

Is there any of your evidence that can be made the subject of a notice to admit facts or a notice to admit hearsay evidence under the Civil Evidence Act? If so, advise accordingly.

It may be advisable to ring solicitors and ask whether the solicitor wants you to draft the notice in question.

15.1.7 WITNESSES

List:

(a) The witnesses whose attendance you will or *may* require at the trial in any event.

(b) The other witnesses who will have to attend if facts, documents or statements are not admitted by the other side.

(c) Have statements been taken from all relevant witnesses, and in a form suitable for disclosure? Consider each witness statement to see whether it contains embarrassing or contradictory material. Advise solicitor as appropriate, and check whether solicitor wishes you to prepare amendments.

15.1.8 TIME ESTIMATE

A time estimate should be given, especially where acting for the claimant.

15.1.9 PART 36 OFFERS, PAYMENT INTO COURT AND INTEREST

If acting for the claimant: Have you made any Part 36 offer to settle? If not, should one be made and if so, how much?

If acting for the defendant:

(a) There should have been a payment into court (because the trial is of quantum alone). Is it enough? Should it be increased?

(b) Have you remembered to take interest into account?

15.1.10 SKELETON ARGUMENT

Prepare a skeleton argument for lodging with the court (and exchange with opponent) under the provisions of the *Practice Direction (Civil Litigation: Case Management)* [1995] 1 WLR 262 and any case management directions.

15.2 Sample Advice on Evidence on Quantum

MARCUS ALLEN

v

SAMUEL WOOLF

ADVICE ON EVIDENCE

---

1   On 1st September 1997 the Claimant was travelling in his Vauxhall Astra motor car registration number A837 BJA in the direction of Macclesfield on the A34 in Cheshire. The Defendant was driving a Jaguar XJS registration number ACE 1 on the opposite carriageway in the direction of Wilmslow. The Jaguar car veered out of control across the carriageway colliding with the Claimant's motor car. The Claimant sustained serious injuries as a result of the collision. He was taken to Macclesfield Royal Infirmary where examination revealed bruising to the head, fractures to the right wrist and ankle, and a soft tissue injury to the neck. In response to the recent 'Letter of Claim' sent pursuant to the Pre-Action Protocol for Personal Injury Claims, liability has

been admitted by the Defendant's insurers. I am asked on behalf of the Claimant to advise on the evidence required for the assessment of damages.

2   The Claimant complains of a wide range of symptoms which are set out in some detail in the reports of Mr Kenneth Brand FRCS dated 2nd October 1997 and 5th June 1998. In summary the Claimant continues to suffer from severe headaches which occur some two or three times a week, reduction in cognitive ability with poor short-term memory, pain and restricted movement in the neck, loss of grip and mobility in the right wrist, and extreme difficulty in walking as a result of the failure of the right ankle fracture to heal properly. The Claimant also complains of psychological trauma consequent on the accident and its aftermath. He is depressed and irritable and this is imposing a severe strain on his marriage. He and his wife have no children.

3   Mr Brand is an orthopaedic surgeon and, as he explains in his letter of 5th June 1998 which accompanied the report of that date, he cannot express confident opinions as to the Claimant's neurological or psychological condition. He is however, a very experienced surgeon and forensic doctor, and his concern that the Claimant's symptoms may go somewhat further than the physiological evidence would substantiate have to be taken seriously. The financial consequences of the accident have been grave. The Claimant was born on 3rd July 1973 and at 24 years of age at the date of the accident had a promising and well paid career as a North Sea diver with Dodd-Comex Limited. He has now been dismissed, and cannot find any suitable alternative employment.

4   In addition to his claim for general damages for pain suffering and loss of amenity, and for loss of employment prospects, the following heads of claim may be advanced on behalf of the Claimant:

(1)   loss of earnings and pension;

(2)   loss of earnings for Mrs Allen;

(3)   the excess on the Claimant's motor insurance policy;

(4)   the value of personal effects damaged in the accident;

(5)   the cost of adaptation to house and car;

(6)   the cost of carrying out the maintenance, decorating and gardening tasks which the Claimant undertook before the accident;

(7)   travel for treatment, cost of medication, and miscellaneous expenses.

Medical evidence

5   It is essential that the Claimant's medical condition is properly investigated. Mr Brand refers to the findings of the Neurological Registrar at Macclesfield Royal Infirmary, but these are not sufficient for forensic purposes. Would my Instructing Solicitor please instruct both a consultant neurologist and a consultant psychiatrist to examine and report on the Claimant's present condition and prognosis. Additionally the Claimant's cognitive and memory abilities should be assessed by a clinical psychologist. The consultant experts should be asked to consider expressly how the Claimant's complaints compare with the clinical findings and, if appropriate, the consultant psychiatrist should comment on the genuineness of the Claimant's complaints so far as they go beyond what would ordinarily be anticipated on the basis of the clinical findings. The Defendant's Solicitors should be invited to agree to the instruction of joint experts in accordance with CPR, r. 35.8 and the procedure set out in paras 3.14–3.20 of the Pre-Action Protocol.

6   In addition to this expert evidence my Instructing Solicitor should please take statements from Mrs Allen, and if possible one or two friends and the Claimant's former

colleagues at work, explaining the type of person the Claimant was before the accident and how they have found him since.

Claimant's loss of earnings

7   A number of important issues arise in relation to this head of claim:

(a)   the Claimant's ability as a diver and his future prospects at Dodd-Comex Limited;

(b)   the Claimant's prospects of employment when his career as a diver ended;

(c)   the Claimant's ability to find alternative employment following his injuries;

(d)   the appropriate multiplier;

(e)   loss of pension calculation.

8   (a) *Ability and future prospects*
In addition to the Claimant's own evidence I hope that it will be possible to obtain a statement from a director or senior manager of Dodd-Comex Limited covering the Claimant's ability as a diver, his prospects with the company or in the industry generally and the pay and other benefits which the Claimant could reasonably expect to earn. I understand that there was some ill feeling between himself and his employers on the termination of the Claimant's employment. If Dodd-Comex Limited will not cooperate the necessary evidence as to the Claimant's abilities and prospects can be given by Mr Phillips, the Claimant's diving instructor who appears to hold him in high regard, and the former colleague Mr Charles Jones to whom the Claimant refers in his recent letter.

(b)   *Prospects of employment after end of diving career*
As I understand the position few deep sea divers work as such after reaching the age of 40. However, there are considerable opportunities both in the UK and abroad for experienced deep sea divers as consultants or instructors. The Claimant needs to be in a position to adduce evidence both as to his prospects of further employment in the diving industry after he reached 40, and as to the remuneration which may be anticipated with that employment. Mr Phillips, and if they will assist a Dodd-Comex Limited witness, should be able to give the required evidence. Would my Instructing Solicitor please take draft proofs of evidence, and if appropriate ask Mr Phillips to introduce a further witness with the necessary experience to cover this part of the case.

(c)   *The Claimant's ability to obtain alternative employment*
The Claimant's witness statement should cover his academic record and comment upon the areas of work in which, despite his injuries, he might obtain employment. I appreciate that the Claimant's sole ambition in life was to be a diver and that his academic record was poor. But while his opportunities following his accident may be limited the Claimant still has an obligation to seek alternative work. This is a suitable case for instructing an expert employment consultant to consider what, if any, work at what remuneration is available to the Claimant given his medical condition. If it is possible to find an employment consultant with experience of the diving industry he could also assist the Claimant with evidence under point (b) above. Again, a joint expert should be instructed if possible.

(d)   *Appropriate multiplier*
Following the House of Lords decision in *Wells* v *Wells* [1998] 3 All ER 481, and subject to the Lord Chancellor's power under s. 1 of the Damages Act 1996 to prescribe a rate of return to be assumed by the court (which can still be departed from in appropriate cases) the multiplier should be selected based on a discount rate of 3% using the Ogden Tables.

(e)   *Loss of pension*
The Claimant's employment was pensionable. A jointly instructed forensic accountant should be asked also to calculate the loss of pension (on *Auty* v *National Coal Board*

principles) and provide the necessary tax and national insurance calculations for the remuneration figures under (*b*) and (*c*) above.

Mrs Allen's loss of earnings

9   Mrs Allen took time off work as a secretary and personal assistant at IEA plc to look after her husband after the accident. Her statement should cover this matter and explain what earnings she lost as a result. A statement should also be obtained from the Personnel Department of the company confirming the dates on which Mrs Allen was off work and the pay she lost as a result.

Excess on insurance policy, loss of personal effects

10   The Claimant must disclose his insurance documents which will show the relevant excess and set out a list of the personal effects damaged in the accident and their costs in his witness statement. Disclosure must be given of any receipts or vouchers of which the Claimant retains possession. The figures under these heads of claim should be capable of agreement with the Defendant's insurers. If any item is disputed and the relevant claim cannot be compromised, the Claimant will have to give evidence of the purchase of the item and its current replacement cost.

Cost of adaptations of car and home

11   My Instructions indicate the Claimant wishes to carry out a fair range of alterations to his present house in order to accommodate his difficulties in walking and moving his neck. He also wishes to have a specially adapted car. A joint report should be commissioned from a rehabilitation expert as to the alterations that may be appropriate and their capital and annual maintenance cost. I suggest that although the expert should be instructed now he or she should be asked not to finalise the report until the further medical evidence I have requested above is to hand.

Maintenance, decorating and gardening costs

12   The courts do regularly award damages for 'DIY claims' assessed on multiplicands of £500 and upwards. It is necessary however that the Claimant and Mrs Allen cover in their statements what it was that the Claimant did in fact do about the house before his accident which he has been unable to do since, and comment on any expenditure they have in fact incurred on such items since the accident. The rehabilitation expert should be able to give evidence of the cost of assistance in the Claimant's locality, but it would also be advisable for my Instructing Solicitor to obtain letters from local decorators and gardeners as to the amounts they charge for their work. These letters should be forwarded to the Defendant's solicitors for their agreement and if and only if they cannot be agreed should witness statements be taken from the relevant witnesses.

Travel, medicines and miscellaneous costs

13   A list of these items should be prepared on the Claimant's instructions and agreed with the Defendant's solicitors.

Summary

14   In accordance with proper case management, we should aim to be virtually ready for trial by the time we issue proceedings if the claim cannot be settled. Witness statements and experts' reports are to be obtained from the following witnesses.

Factual Witnesses

    (1)   The Claimant
    (2)   Mrs Allen
    (3)   One or two friends/colleagues (see paragraph 6 above)

(4)   Dodd-Comex Limited's witness
(5)   Mr Phillips
(6)   Mr C Jones
(7)   Local decorator/gardener (see paragraph 12 above)

Expert Reports

(1)   Mr Kenneth Brand FRCS
(2)   Consultant Neurologist
(3)   Consultant Psychiatrist
(4)   Clinical Psychologist
(5)   Employment Consultant
(6)   Forensic Accountant
(7)   Rehabilitation Expert

15   I would be grateful for an opportunity to consider the witness statements and experts' reports before exchange. Once the above information is to hand we should be in a position to settle the Schedule of Damages which we are required to send to the Defendant 'as soon as practicable' pursuant to para. 3.13 of the Pre-Action Protocol. I shall be happy to settle the Schedule if so instructed. At the same time I will advise if required on the contents of the trial bundle. I leave it to my Instructing Solicitor to consider whether the Claimant should be warned that the Defendant's insurers may well instruct a firm of private investigators to carry out video surveillance of him.

JOHN DOE

1 Wilberforce Chambers
Temple
London EC4

14th June 1999

SIXTEEN

ASSESSMENT CRITERIA

16.1 Assessment of Opinion Writing Skills

All assessments in opinion writing skills will require you to write a full opinion. The content of the opinion may be any of the following, or a combination of them:

(1) Opinion on the merits.

(2) Opinion on liability.

(3) Advice on quantum.

(4) Advice on evidence.

(5) Advice on practical steps to be taken.

(6) Advice on specific issues.

(7) Advice on appeal.

The content of the opinion may be within a civil or a criminal case, at any stage from before commencement of proceedings until the hearing of an appeal. You may be asked to advise any party to the proceedings or matter in dispute.

16.2 The Use of Assessment Criteria

Whenever you are assessed in opinion writing you will be assessed on criteria drawn as appropriate from the following list. These criteria may be used in combinations to make composite criteria. They are not wholly distinct from each other. They frequently overlap.

You can also use these criteria for self-assessment, and assessment of your fellow students. Select appropriate criteria for the opinion under consideration and decide whether they have been fulfilled.

Make a careful study of these criteria. It will help you to understand and learn what is required to write a good opinion.

16.3 List of Assessment Criteria

In order to be graded competent or above, you must show your ability to write an opinion which:

(1) Is written in correct grammatical English.

(2) Is written in clear, plain language.

(3)   Contains no spelling mistakes.

(4)   Is fluent.

(5)   Is written in language and in a style appropriate to an opinion.

(6)   Is properly headed, laid out and signed.

(7)   Makes sensible use of subheadings where appropriate.

(8)   Is neat on the page.

(9)   Is appropriately punctuated.

(10)   Accurately identifies all the material facts, the relevant law and the real issues.

(11)   Shows a thorough grasp of the material facts, evidence and issues.

(12)   Shows a sound understanding and application of the relevant law.

(13)   Distinguishes one issue from another.

(14)   Shows a practical analysis of the facts, the law, the evidence and the issues.

(15)   Shows a good understanding of relevant rules of procedure.

(16)   Shows an understanding of the appropriate use of procedural rules.

(17)   Has a clear and appropriate structure.

(18)   Is divided into an appropriate number of paragraphs.

(19)   Is of a suitable length.

(20)   Deals with each issue in a logical order.

(21)   Deals with one issue at a time.

(22)   Gives each issue its due weight and significance.

(23)   Is concise in that:

   (a)   it is succinct and to the point,

   (b)   it contains no irrelevancies,

   (c)   it deals with the heart of the matter,

   (d)   it is no longer than reasonably necessary.

(24)   Is complete in that:

   (a)   it covers everything that needs to be covered,

   (b)   it is fully reasoned,

   (c)   it gives a whole answer to every question,

   (d)   it gives full advice,

   (e)   it is not unfinished.

(25)   Answers all the questions raised expressly or implicitly in the instructions.

(26) Expresses sound and justifiable conclusions.

(27) Expresses a definite conclusion where appropriate; or

(28) Explains why there can be no definite conclusion.

(29) Explains any legal and factual alternatives.

(30) Sets the conclusions out clearly and prominently.

(31) Identifies any gaps in the instructions.

(32) Asks for relevant further information.

(33) Does not ask for irrelevant further information.

(34) Explains why the further information is needed.

(35) Adopts a practical approach to the case.

(36) Identifies and addresses the needs and objectives of the client.

(37) Gives advice which is:

  (a) clear,

  (b) sound,

  (c) full,

  (d) practical,

  (e) identifiable.

(38) Gives reasons for the advice given.

(39) Follows a clear line of reasoning.

(40) Gives advice on the matters identified in the instructions.

(41) Gives advice on the matters implicit in the instructions.

(42) Advises on any practical and procedural steps to be taken.

(43) Advises on the strengths and weaknesses of the case.

(44) Advises on the weight of the evidence.

(45) Advises on the admissibility of the evidence.

(46) Indicates what further evidence is required.

(47) Is consistent with professional standards and the Code of Conduct.

16.4   Example of Assessment Criteria

The criteria for an opinion writing assessment might be drafted as follows:

In order to be graded competent or above, you must show your ability to write an opinion which:

A (i)   Is written in clear, grammatical English, correctly spelt and appropriately punctuated.

     (ii)   Is written in language and in a style appropriate to an opinion.

(10%)

B (i)   Identifies and addresses the material facts and issues.

     (ii)   Does not address immaterial facts and issues.

     (iii) Is based on a sound understanding and application of the relevant law.

(20%)

C Has a clear and appropriate structure in that:

     (i)   it is properly and neatly laid out;

     (ii)   it is divided into an appropriate number of paragraphs;

     (iii) it makes appropriate use of subheadings;

     (iv) it deals with each issue in a logical order;

     (v)   it gives each issue its due weight and significance;

     (vi) it is of a suitable length overall.

(20%)

D (i)   Expresses sound and justifiable conclusions.

     (ii)   Expresses a definite conclusion where appropriate, but not where inappropriate.

     (iii) Sets your conclusions out clearly and prominently.

(20%)

E Gives advice which:

     (i)   is based on a sound and practical analysis of the law, facts and issues;

     (ii)   is justified by sound reasoning;

     (iii) answers all the questions expressly or implicitly asked in the instructions;

     (iv) explains where appropriate why you cannot express a definite conclusion;

     (v)   identifies and asks for relevant further information;

     (vi) indicates any practical and procedural steps to be taken;

     (vii) addresses the needs and objectives of the client.

(30%) (Liability 20%; Quantum 10%)

16.5   Application of Assessment Criteria

You will see that the criteria in **16.4** expressly or impliedly incorporate all the criteria listed in **16.3**. They would be applied as follows.

Criterion A covers criteria (1), (2), (3), (4), (5), (9). As well as the obvious matters, you would be penalised for illegibility, archaic or pompous expressions, being impolite, excessive informality, using note form etc.

Criterion B covers criteria (10), (11), (12), (13), (14). As well as the obvious matters, you would be penalised for irrelevance, muddled thinking, an academic approach to the law, leaving out important issues etc.

Criterion C covers criteria (6), (7), (8), (17), (18), (19), (20), (21), (22), (23), (24), (39). As well as the obvious matters, you would be penalised for a poor introductory paragraph, excessively long or short paragraphs, writing too much, untidiness on the page, jumping from one issue to another, going off at a tangent, being difficult to follow, failing to finish, leaving things out etc.

Criterion D covers criteria (26), (27), (30). As well as the obvious matters, you would be penalised for getting the answer wrong, being too definite or too uncertain in your conclusions, contradictory conclusions etc.

Criterion E covers criteria (10), (11), (12), (13), (14), (15), (16), (24), (25), (26), (27), (28), (29), (31), (32), (33), (34), (35), (36), (37), (38), (39), (40), (41), (42), (43), (44), (45), (46), (47). As well as the obvious matters, you would be penalised for lack of awareness of practical realities, an unprofessional attitude, leaving out important matters, failing to give reasons for your conclusions, adopting a sketchy or superficial approach, giving bad advice, failing to consider the strength of the case or the evidence, asking for irrelevant information, leaving the solicitor or client unsure what to do next, etc.

16.6 Assessment Criteria for an Advice on Evidence (Criminal)

16.6.1 CRITERIA

In order to be graded competent or above, you must show your ability to write a advice which:

A (i) Is written in clear, grammatical English, correctly spelt and appropriately punctuated.

(ii) Is written in language and in a style appropriate to an advice.

(10%)

B (i) Deals with material matters.

(ii) Does not deal with immaterial matters.

(iii) Is based on a sound understanding of the relevant law.

(iv) Shows a good understanding of the relevant rules of criminal procedure.

(20%)

C Has a clear and appropriate structure in that:

(i) it is properly and neatly laid out;

(ii) it is divided into an appropriate number of paragraphs;

(iii) it makes sensible use of subheadings;

(iv) it deals with each matter in a logical order;

(v) it gives each matter its due weight and significance;

(vi) it is of a suitable length overall.

(20%)

D Gives clear advice on the drafting of the indictment which:

(i) is based on a correct application of the law;

(ii) is based on a sound and practical analysis of the evidence;

(iii) is justified by sound reasoning;

(iv) deals with all the points raised in the instructions;

(v) explains any amendments that should be made to the draft indictment.
(20%)

E Gives clear advice on evidence which:

(i) is based on a sound and practical analysis of the evidence and the issues;

(ii) is justified by sound reasoning;

(iii) deals with all the points raised in the instructions;

(iv) advises on the strength of the prosecution case;

(v) advises on the admissibility of the evidence;

(vi) indicates any further evidence that may be required;

(vii) indicates any practical and procedural steps to be taken.
(30%)

16.6.2 APPLICATION OF ASSESSMENT CRITERIA

You will see that the criteria in **16.6.1** expressly or impliedly incorporate nearly all the criteria listed in **16.3**. They would be applied as follows.

Criterion A covers criteria (1), (2), (3), (4), (5), (9). As well as the obvious matters you would be penalised for illegibility, incorrect terminology, inappropriate jargon, being impolite, using note form etc.

Criterion B covers criteria (10), (11), (12), (13), (14), (15), (35). As well as the obvious matters you would be penalised for muddled thinking, addressing the wrong issues, an academic approach to the law, not knowing the elements of an offence, relating evidence to the wrong element, poor understanding of evidential effect, misunderstanding the correct procedure etc.

Criterion C covers criteria (6), (7), (8), (17), (18), (19), (20), (21), (22), (23), (24), (39). As well as the obvious matters you would be penalised for excessively long paragraphs, over-elaborate detail, untidiness on the page, making points in a disorganised way, failing to finish, leaving things out etc.

Criterion D covers criteria (10), (11), (12), (14), (24), (25), (26), (29), (30), (35), (36), (37), (38), (39), (40), (41), (47). As well as the obvious matters you would be penalised for leaving out important matters, giving advice that would lead to the wrong verdict, misunderstanding the law, breach of professional guidelines etc.

Criterion E covers criteria (10), (11), (12), (13), (14), (15), (16), (24), (25), (26), (29), (35), (36), (37), (38), (39), (40), (41), (42), (43), (44), (45), (46), (47). As well as the obvious matters you would be penalised for lack of awareness of practical realities, an unprofessional attitude, leaving out important matters, giving bad advice, failing to recognise weaknesses in the evidence etc.

16.7 Assessment Criteria for an Advice on Evidence (Civil)

16.7.1 CRITERIA

In order to be graded competent or above you must show your ability to write an advice which:

(1) (i) Is written in clear, grammatical English, correctly spelt and appropriately punctuated.

    (ii) Is written in language and in a style appropriate to an advice.

    (10%)

(2) (i) Deals with material matters.

    (ii) Does not deal with immaterial matters.

    (iii) Is based on a sound understanding of the relevant law.

    (iv) Shows a good understanding of the relevant rules of civil procedure.

    (20%)

(3) Has a clear and appropriate structure in that:

    (i) it is properly and neatly laid out;

    (ii) it is divided into an appropriate number of paragraphs;

    (iii) it makes sensible use of subheadings;

    (iv) it deals with each matter in a logical order;

    (v) it gives each matter its due weight and significance;

    (vi) it is of a suitable length overall.

    (20%)

(4) (i) Deals with all the matters and issues that need to be dealt with at this stage.

    (ii) Does not deal with matters and issues that are not relevant at this stage.

    (20%)

(5) Gives clear advice on evidence which:

    (i) is based on a sound and practical analysis of the evidence and the issues;

    (ii) is justified by sound reasoning;

    (iii) deals with all the points raised in the instructions;

    (iv) advises on the strength of the case;

    (v) advises on the admissibility of the evidence;

    (vi) indicates any further evidence that may be required;

    (vii) indicates any practical and procedural steps to be taken.

    (30%)

16.7.2 APPLICATION OF ASSESSMENT CRITERIA

You will see that the criteria in **16.7.1** expressly or impliedly incorporate nearly all the criteria listed in **16.3**. They would be applied as follows.

Criterion A covers criteria (1), (2), (3), (4), (5), (9). As well as the obvious matters you would be penalised for illegibility, incorrect terminology, inappropriate jargon, being impolite, using note form etc.

Criterion B covers criteria (10), (11), (12), (13), (14), (15), (16), (35). As well as the obvious matters you would be penalised for muddled thinking, an academic approach to the law, poor understanding of evidential effect, misunderstanding the correct procedure, poor tactical awareness etc.

Criterion C covers criteria (6), (7), (8), (17), (18), (19), (20), (21), (22), (23), (24), (39). As well as the obvious matters you would be penalised for excessively long paragraphs, over-elaborate detail, untidiness on the page, making points in a disorganised way, failing to finish, leaving things out etc.

Criterion D covers criteria (10), (23), (24), (25). This criterion requires you to recognise what needs to be covered at this stage and what does not, and then to deal with the right matters.

Criterion E covers criteria (10), (11), (12), (13), (14), (15), (16), (24), (25), (26), (29), (35), (36), (37), (38), (39), (40), (41), (42), (43), (44), (45), (46), (47). As well as the obvious matters you would be penalised for lack of awareness of practical realities, an unprofessional attitude, leaving out important matters, giving bad advice, failing to recognise weaknesses in the evidence etc.

SEVENTEEN

EXERCISES

17.1 Exercise 1

Consider these instructions and the opinion which follows. Identify the faults in the opinion. How could these be put right? What omissions are there in the opinion? Discuss.

17.1.1 INSTRUCTIONS

Re: SUSANNA AND EMMA WILLIAMS DECEASED

Counsel has herewith:

(a)   Statement of Michael Morley.

(b)   Letter dated 20th July 1999 from Clifford Thwaite.

Counsel is instructed by Gatwicks on behalf of Mr Michael Morley, the executor of the estate of his late cohabitee, Susanna Williams, who died on 6th February last in the circumstances explained in Mr Morley's statement. Probate of Miss Williams's estate was granted to Mr Morley out of the Brighton District Probate Registry on 29th July 1999. Your instructing solicitor has sent letters before action to both Mr Thwaite, the owner of 24 Eastside, and Benedict Brutus, the estate agents. Mr Thwaite's reply is enclosed with these instructions. Benedict Brutus have responded only by telephone asserting that they can have no responsibility for this accident.

Counsel is requested to advise whether a claim may be brought in respect of this tragic accident and, if so, against whom, and whether it would be worthwhile bringing a claim in respect of Emma Williams's death. Counsel's advice on quantum is not required at this stage.

Would counsel therefore please advise on liability.

MICHAEL MORLEY of 18 Carlton Terrace, London SW1 will say:

I was born on 21st November 1969 and have since 1993 been living with Susanna Williams at the above address. We considered ourselves to have a stable relationship, but we never married. We had two children, Mark, who was born on 3rd March 1992, and Emma who was born on 12th October 1998. I am presently unemployed, having been dismissed from my job as an investment analyst at the Biological Bank on 1st November 1998. Susanna Williams was born on 14th October 1969 and worked as a commodity broker.

On 6th February 1999 Susanna and I went to inspect 24 Eastside, Clapham Common with a view to purchasing it. This was a fine Victorian six-storey property overlooking the Common and was offered for sale at £650,000. It had an ornate wrought iron balcony on the fourth floor. We went with our children and met Miss Jackie Welland of Benedict Brutus, the estate agents, at about 10.00 a.m. at the property. She opened up and showed us round. She was very enthusiastic about the property's potential not least, perhaps, because she could not enthuse about the existing state of the property which was dilapidated. She did indeed warn us to take care as we went about the property in case, as she laughingly put it, we fell through the floor. In the event her joking turned very sour. When we reached the fourth floor front room Susanna asked if she could go out on to the balcony from which there were fine views of the Common. Miss Welland produced a key and opened the door. Susanna went out on to the balcony holding Emma in her arms. I turned to say something to Mark and as I did so heard a crash and a scream. A large section of the balcony was rotten and it had given way under Susanna's weight. She and Emma fell to the paved patio area below and both were killed in the fall.

Messrs Gatwicks
42 Cheapside
London EC

42 Burley Street
York

20th July 1999

Dear Sirs

Re: Susanna and Emma Williams Decd

I was sorry to learn of the death of your clients while inspecting my property at 24 Eastside, Clapham earlier this year. As requested I have passed your letter on to my insurers. However, I would like to point out that since inheriting the property from my aunt last year I only visited it on one occasion, sometime in January 1999. I instructed Benedict Brutus to sell the property for me and I went with Miss Busby of that firm to look it over. It was evident that the property was not in good repair and she suggested that I had it done up before sale. I was not too keen on this idea, but agreed that Benedict Brutus should draw up a specification of work and obtain tenders, while at the same time putting the property on the market at a good price.

On 11th February 1999 I received a specification from Mr Johnson of Benedict Brutus following his inspection on 4th February, which showed amongst other matters that the balcony was in urgent need of substantial repair. I do not feel that I am to blame for this tragic accident.

Yours faithfully

Clifford Thwaite

17.1.2   OPINION

Re: MICHAEL MORLEY
COUNSEL'S ADVICE

The facts

Mr Clifford Thwaite inherited a house at 24 Eastside, Clapham Common, from his aunt in 1998. He only visited it once, in January 1999, when he instructed Estate Agents, Benedict Brutus, to sell it for him. They advised him to have it done up before sale. He was not keen, but agreed that Benedict Brutus should draw up a specification of work and obtain tenders, while at the same time putting the property on the market at a good price.

On 6th February 1999 Susanna Williams and Michael Morley, who had been living together in a stable unmarried relationship since 1993, went to inspect 24 Eastside, Clapham Common with a view to purchasing it for £650,000. It was a fine Victorian six-storey property overlooking the Common with (inter alia) an ornate wrought iron balcony on the fourth floor. They went with their children, Mark, aged 6, and Emma, aged 4 months. They were shown around by Miss Jackie Welland of Benedict Brutus. She was very enthusiastic about the property's potential and warned them to take care as they went about the property in case, as she laughingly put it, they fell through the floor.

In the event, this joke turned very sour, for when they reached the fourth floor front room, Susanna asked if she could go out on the balcony from where there were fine views of the Common. Miss Welland produced a key and opened the door. Susanna went out on to the balcony holding Emma in her arms. Mr Morley turned to say something to Mark and as he did so he heard a crash and a scream. A large section of the balcony was rotten and it had given way, causing both Susanna and Emma to fall and be killed on the paved patio beneath.

A week later, Mr Thwaite received a specification from Benedict Brutus, which showed amongst other matters that the balcony was in urgent need of substantial repair.

Mr Morley obtained probate of Susanna Williams's estate on 29th July 1999, and Instructing Solicitors have written letters of claim to Mr Thwaite and Benedict Brutus, both of whom have denied liability, Mr Thwaite by a letter dated 20th July 1999 and Benedict Brutus by telephone.

Counsel is asked to advise whether a claim may be brought in respect of this tragic accident and, if so, against whom, and whether it would be worth bringing a claim in respect of Emma's death.

Conclusion

In my opinion Benedict Brutus are liable but Clifford Thwaite may not be. Instructing Solicitors should therefore sue Benedict Brutus and recover substantial damages (although I am not asked to advise on quantum at this stage). In my opinion the claim will be brought under the Fatal Accidents Act 1976.

By s. 1(1) of this Act, if death is caused by any wrongful act, neglect or default which is such as would (if death had not ensued) have entitled the person injured to maintain an action and recover damages in respect thereof, the person who would have been liable if death had not ensued shall be liable to an action for damages, notwithstanding the death of the person injured. By s. 1(2) the action shall be for the benefit of the dependants of the deceased. By s. 1(3) both Mr Morley and Mark are dependants. By s. 2 Mr Morley can therefore bring a successful action against whoever is liable in law.

The law

The relevant law in this case is set out in the Occupiers' Liability Acts 1957 and 1984. The 1957 Act deals with liability if the claimant was a lawful visitor of the occupier, while the 1984 Act applies if he was a trespasser or other non-visitor. Under the 1957 Act, an occupier owes a common duty of care to all his visitors to take such care as in all the circumstances of the case is reasonable to see that the visitor will be reasonably safe in using the premises for the purposes for which he is invited or permitted to be there. On the other hand, the duty under the 1984 Act is a lesser one, which only arises in limited circumstances. However, in my opinion, since Susanna Williams was being shown around the house by Benedict Brutus with Mr Thwaite's permission, there can be no doubt that she was a lawful visitor and so there is no need to consider the Occupiers' Liability Act 1984 any further.

We must therefore consider who was the occupier of the house at the material time and whether they were negligent. If so, they will be liable to Mr Morley.

Who was the occupier

The occupier is the person who has a sufficient degree of control over the premises to impose upon him a duty of care to those who enter the premises. Mr Thwaite is the owner, but he was not in actual occupation of the premises at the time. He may or may not therefore be the occupier (*Harris v Birkenhead Corporation* [1976] 1 WLR 279). He would not be if he had effectively given control over to Benedict Brutus. I would ask Instructing Solicitors for further information on how much control he had over the premises, and for a copy of any contract he may have made with the Estate Agents.

However I submit that Benedict Brutus are occupiers at the same time (*Wheat v Lacon & Co. Ltd* [1966] AC 552), because they actually opened up the premises on the fateful day.

Negligence

It seems that Benedict Brutus were aware that the balcony was unsafe on the 4th (of February, not floor!), because Mr Johnson made an inspection on that date as a result of which he reported the need for repair. They therefore should not have been showing clients around on the 6th, even if the appointment was made before the 4th (will Instructing Solicitors please ascertain how, when and where the appointment was made). It follows that Benedict Brutus have been negligent.

In the case of Mr Thwaite his negligence is less clear. He was aware that the property was not in good repair and he had been advised that he ought to have the property done up before selling it. Therefore it may well have been reasonably foreseeable that parts of the property were in a dangerous condition, but he nevertheless allowed Benedict Brutus to show prospective purchasers around. It is certainly a possibility that this was in breach of his duty of care as an occupier, because it is arguable that the reasonable occupier would not allow visitors to enter until he was satisfied that all necessary repairs had taken place. If this can be established, then in my submission, Mr Thwaite would also be liable.

Alternatively, and this is a much stronger cause of action, Mr Thwaite is liable for employing negligent agents. I have already advised that Benedict Brutus were negligent, and in these circumstances a reasonable owner would not have employed them. They are by definition his agents and as such he must be vicariously liable for their actions. In my opinion therefore both Benedict Brutus and Mr Thwaite are likely to be found liable in this claim.

Contributory negligence

There remains the question of whether there is any contributory negligence on the part of Susanna, Emma or Mr Morley. In the case of Emma, since she was only 4 months old at the time of her death, I think that it is most unlikely that the court would find her to have been contributorily negligent. But in the case of Mr Morley and Susanna, I foresee that the defendants may argue that they should have taken greater care for their own safety, and that Susanna should not have gone onto the balcony following Miss Welland's express warning, and that Mr Morley should have tried to prevent her doing so. Instructing Solicitors should be prepared for this possibility, and I would like more information on this issue.

Further information required

Will Instructing Solicitors please provide me with the following:

(a) A copy of the grant of probate.

(b) A copy of Mr Johnson's report and specification.

Boswell Chambers   JOHN DOE
Temple EC4

17.2 Exercise 2

Consider the following instructions. Draw up a skeleton plan for your opinion, identifying the issues and stating your conclusions.

Re: SOUTHERN FRUIT GROWERS LTD

Instructing solicitors act for Southern Fruit Growers Ltd (the 'Company') which owns extensive orchards in Kent. Fruit is usually picked in September or October of each year, stored in refrigerated storage chambers over the winter and marketed in the following spring to take advantage of the more favourable prices prevailing then. The Company insures with the Greenwich Insurance Co. Ltd (the Insurers) against loss, including loss of profit on premature sale of fruit stored, caused by mechanical failure of the refrigeration plant. The policy of insurance dated 18 April 1997 is subject to certain special conditions, set out in enclosure 1 herewith. The Company employs (see enclosure 2 herewith) Refrigeration Systems (the Engineers) to carry out the inspection, do the work and provide the certificate required by special conditions 1 and 2 of the insurance policy.

In accordance with clause 1 of the maintenance contract the Company paid the Engineers £800 on 1 July 1998. In accordance with clause 2 of the contract, the Company notified the Engineers by letter (see enclosure 3) of its intention to start loading the storage chambers on 29 September 1998. The Engineers acknowledged receipt of that letter but despite frequent reminders by telephone and letter failed to inspect the plant. By 1 October, the storage chambers had been loaded with pears to their full capacity (50 tonnes). The refrigeration plant was then operating normally. On 21 October, however, a valve stuck in the heat exchanger causing a complete breakdown of the refrigeration plant. This took two weeks to repair. No notification of the breakdown was given to the Insurers until the plant had been completely repaired. Due to the sudden rise in temperature in the storage chambers, the pears had to be sold. The Company's labour force which at that time was engaged on picking 'Bramley drops' (apples) had to be redeployed on grading and packing pears. The 'Bramley drops' deteriorated and became completely unsaleable.

The pears were sold for £100,000. If they had been kept until the following spring, the figure would have been in the region of £150,000. The 'Bramley drops' would have realised around £21,000. The Company submitted a claim to its Insurers for the loss it had suffered as a result of the breakdown. The Insurers, however, repudiated liability on the grounds that there had been a breach of special conditions 2 and 3 of the insurance policy.

Counsel is asked:

(a)   to advise the Company whether it can recover its loss from the Engineers; and

(b)   to advise on quantum.

ENCLOSURE 1: SPECIAL CONDITIONS

1   The Company shall before the commencement of each storage season engage a firm of competent refrigeration engineers to inspect the refrigeration plant, put the same into good operating condition and provide a certificate that the plant is in such condition.

2   Insurance cover shall be suspended during any storage season in respect of which no such certificate has been obtained.

3   The Company shall notify the Insurers of any breakdown at the time it occurs. Such notification shall be a condition precedent to the liability of the Insurers for any loss ensuing.

ENCLOSURE 2: MAINTENANCE CONTRACT

Dated: 1 July 1997

Between: Refrigeration Systems (the Engineers) and Southern Fruit Growers Ltd (the Company).

1   The Company agrees to pay to the Engineers £800 a year on 1 July in each year during the continuance of this contract.

2   The Engineers agree on receiving from the Company at least three weeks' notification in writing of intention to load to inspect the Company's refrigeration plant and put the same into good operating condition and provide a certificate that the plant is in such condition within three weeks of receiving such notification.

3   This contract may be terminated on 1 July in any year by three months' previous notice in writing.

ENCLOSURE 3: LETTER

1 September 1997

Dear Sirs,

We hereby give you notice in accordance with clause 2 of the maintenance contract that we intend to start loading on 29 September 1998.

Yours faithfully,

Southern Fruit Growers Ltd

The following Exercises 3–17 are 'mini-opinion' exercises, designed to enable you to practise some of the sub-skills that are part of the skill of opinion writing. In each case try to advise clearly and fully, with reasons, in a concise way: a few short paragraphs will do. There is no need to set out what you are asked to advise about or to summarise the facts (as you would in a full opinion).

17.3   Exercise 3

At 11.00 a.m. on 1st March 1999 Mr Robbie Nutt was riding his motor cycle along Sandy Road in Westbury at about 55 m.p.h. when he struck a ramp, or 'sleeping policeman' and was thrown from his motor cycle and injured.

Sandy Road is on land owned by the Duke of Westland and leased for the past five years to the Westbury District Council. There are six ramps on Sandy Road, which were put there by the Duke of Westland more than five years ago. They were painted with yellow stripes at the time of the lease, but the paint has long since worn off. The ramps were not marked in any other way. There was, however, a small sign placed by the District Council at the entrance to Sandy Road which said 'Westland Estate. Private Road to Sandy Beach. No right of way. Public enter at their own risk. Caution: Ramps: Max. speed 20 m.p.h.'. Mr Nutt, who was on his way to the beach, saw neither the sign nor the ramp.

Advise Mr Nutt whether the Duke of Westland and/or Westbury District Council is liable to him for his injuries.

17.4   Exercise 4

On 2 January 1998 at about 8.15 a.m., a cold and icy morning, Mr John Dedham was driving at about 45 m.p.h. along Castle Street in Faverstock, up a moderately steep hill, when a car driven by Mr Stephen Tribe came over the brow of the hill, also travelling at about 45 m.p.h., started down the hill, skidded on a patch of black ice, veered on to the wrong side of the road, and struck Mr Dedham's car on the driver's door. Castle Street is subject to a 30 m.p.h. speed restriction. The road becomes derestricted at the top of the hill.

Advise Mr Dedham, who was injured in the accident, whether Mr Tribe is liable to him and whether there was any contributory negligence on his part, and if so how much.

17.5 Exercise 5

On 1 May 1998 at about 9.00 p.m., Mr Underwood was driving along Offchurch Lane. It was dusk but not yet fully dark. It was not raining but the road was wet from an earlier downpour. He had his headlights on. He stopped at the junction with the A45, intending to turn right. The road seemed clear, so he moved forward about 4 or 5 feet but saw a car approaching from his right and stopped again. This car was driven by Mr Willis, and was travelling at about 60 m.p.h. with its sidelights but not headlights on. As Mr Willis's car approached, a third car driven by Mr Gatting struck the rear of Mr Underwood's car and pushed it forward into the path of Mr Willis's car causing a collision.

Mr Willis and Mr Underwood were injured. Mr Willis's car had damage to the front end, and Mr Underwood's car had damage to its rear end and its front end. It is not clear whether Mr Underwood's injuries were caused by the collision between his car and Mr Gatting's, or his car and Mr Willis's, or both.

Mr Willis has brought a claim against Mr Underwood, who has counterclaimed against Mr Willis and made a Part 20 claim against Mr Gatting claiming contribution or indemnity in respect of Mr Willis's claim and damages in respect of his own injury and loss.

Advise Mr Underwood how liability will be apportioned in respect of Mr Willis's claim and his own claim and counterclaim.

17.6 Exercise 6

Mr James Salmon suffered an injury to his leg as a result of the negligence of his employer, Teviot Decorations Ltd. Six months later, while crossing the road on the way to visit the hospital for physiotherapy treatment to his injured leg, he was struck by a lorry and suffered a further injury to his leg, as a result of which it was amputated. The driver of the lorry was not prosecuted.

Advise Mr Salmon whether his employer is liable for his loss on a continuing basis, whether it is liable for the increased loss caused by the amputation, or whether its liability is limited to the six months prior to the second accident.

17.7 Exercise 7

On 28th April 1999 Mrs Jenkins was chopping onions in the kitchen of her house when Mr Wates negligently drove his car into the front wall of the house. This so frightened Mrs Jenkins's dog that it ran between her legs, causing her to fall and injure herself with the chopping knife. Advise Mrs Jenkins whether Mr Wates is liable for her injury.

17.8 Exercise 8

Mr and Mrs Roberts have a large house, with a self-contained attic flat, which they let to tenants. They engaged Mr Cork, a painter and decorator, to redecorate it prior to letting it in two weeks' time to Mrs Heller on a six-month lease. Mr Cork agreed to do the redecoration within two weeks at a price of £600. At the end of two weeks he had finished the work, but he had done it so badly that Mrs Heller refused to accept the flat and went elsewhere. Mr and Mrs Roberts had to get the entire flat redecorated at a cost of £500 and find a new tenant. They instructed an agent to find a new tenant, but it was five months before a new tenant was found and moved in.

Advise Mr and Mrs Roberts whether Mr Cork is liable to them and if so to what extent.

17.9 Exercise 9

Dreamy Travel Ltd is a package holiday operator, whose managing director is Mr Dream. Greed Hotels Ltd owns and operates holiday hotels. According to Mr Dream in December 1998 Mr Greed, the managing director of Greed Hotels Ltd, had a private business lunch with Mr Dream and told him that Greed Hotels Ltd had just completed a new luxury hotel in Brighton, which would be available in the 1999 summer season. He described the facilities in great detail and provided Mr Dream with photographs, including one of what Mr Dream took to be the swimming-pool.

Acting in reliance on these representations, Dreamy Travel booked accommodation at the new hotel and sold holidays to its customers at the hotel. In fact it turned out that the hotel was unfinished. The swimming-pool was not ready and the photograph was obviously not of the swimming-pool at that hotel. Dreamy Travel had to compensate its customers and suffered heavy losses.

Advise Dreamy Travel Ltd whether it would be appropriate to allege fraud on the part of Greed Hotels Ltd.

17.10 Exercise 10

Captain Brassbound was employed as sales director, at a salary of £96,000 p.a. by Undershaft Ltd, which is an arms manufacturer, on a ten-year contract commencing 1 November 1995. The contract contained the following clauses:

> 4 The employee agrees that during the period of five years following the determination of this contract he will not solicit any of the customers of Undershaft Ltd.

> 5 The employee agrees that during a period of one year following the determination of this contract he will not accept employment with any firm or body that manufactures or sells armaments.

Captain Brassbound has recently handed in his notice, and intends to become employed by Wonderweapons Ltd, another arms manufacturer, and a direct competitor of Undershaft Ltd.

Advise Undershaft Ltd whether clauses 4 and 5 are enforceable against Captain Brassbound.

17.11 Exercise 11

Captain Brassbound was employed as sales director at a salary of £96,000 p.a. by Undershaft Ltd, on a ten-year contract commencing 1 November 1995, without any provision for early determination. The contract contained the following clauses:

> 2 The employer agrees to reimburse the employee for any legitimate expense incurred by the employee in the performance of his duties.

> 3 The employee agrees to perform all duties which are assigned to him by the board of directors.

6   The employer and employee agree that in the event of any breach of any term, whether express or implied, of this agreement, the party at fault will pay to the other party as liquidated damages a sum equivalent to one month's salary of the employee.

Undershaft Ltd recently repudiated the contract without cause and with six and a quarter years still to run. Advise Captain Brassbound whether his damages will be limited to one month's salary under clause 6.

17.12   Exercise 12

Daphne decided to attend a 'gourmet weekend' at a 4-star hotel. She took her favourite diamond necklace (value £20,000) with her. On arriving at the hotel Daphne asked the receptionist if it would be possible to leave her necklace in the hotel's safe when she was not wearing it. The receptionist replied that it was all part of the service and then gave Daphne a form to sign. Daphne did not bother to read the form but signed it and gave it back to the receptionist along with the diamond necklace.

During the weekend the necklace was stolen after the safe door was left open by the receptionist who had been distracted by one of the thieves.

When Daphne claimed against the hotel for the loss of the necklace the hotel's manager drew her attention to an exclusion clause on the form, which she had signed, which disclaimed all liability for thefts from the hotel other than those committed by the hotel's employees.

The exclusion clause is printed clearly and visibly. Advise Daphne whether the hotel can rely upon it.

17.13   Exercise 13

Tactile Ltd, a company of roofing contractors, entered into a contract with Lord Blunder for the re-roofing of his ancestral home in Buckinghamshire (which is his private residence). One of the terms in the contract provided as follows:

Tactile Ltd's liability for any damage, howsoever caused, whether by reason of the negligence of Tactile Ltd its servants or agents or otherwise, occurring to the premises or to movable property (including *all* furnishings and valuables) during the period of the contract to be limited to £1,000.

During a storm one of the temporary canopies covering the roof was displaced and rain caused £3,000 worth of damage to the plasterwork in the room below and also caused approximately £2,000 worth of damage to an antique four-poster bed and carpets worth £10,000 were ruined.

Advise Tactile Ltd whether it may be liable for the full extent of the damage. The company concedes that the canopy was not properly fixed to the roof.

17.14   Exercise 14

Mrs Albert left her green Mini parked outside her house on 28 June 1999. When she returned home she found it had been seriously damaged, apparently by another car. Flakes of red paint were found on her car, which forensic examination shows to be a paint used by Ford on Escorts and Mondeos. There are twice as many Escorts as Mondeos in this country painted in this colour.

Mrs Albert's neighbour, Mr George, owns a Ford Mondeo painted this colour. It was undamaged on 27 June, but on 28 June, when Mrs Albert found her car damaged, it had damage to its front nearside wing, consistent with having struck Mrs Albert's car.

However, there was no sign of green paint on Mr George's car. Mr George denies having damaged Mrs Albert's car, and alleges his car was also damaged while parked outside his house on 28 June.

Another neighbour, Miss Fry, says that she heard a bang at about 3.00 p.m. on 28 June and looked outside, where she saw a red Ford Escort with a damaged front nearside wing speeding away. She then saw Mrs Albert's car had been damaged, but Mr George's car was not outside his house.

Advise Mrs Albert as to her chances of establishing that her car was damaged by Mr George.

17.15 Exercise 15

On 7 June 1999 Thomas Boulder knocked on the door of Mr Charles Muffett's house and told Mr Muffett that his name was John Tulip, that he was an experienced roofer and that Mr Muffet's roof needed mending. He said he could mend the roof for £5,000. Mr Muffett wrote out a cheque, payable to John Tulip, in the sum of £5,000 and gave it to him. Boulder said that he would start the work within two weeks.

The next day Boulder opened a bank account in the name of John Tulip, depositing Mr Muffet's cheque into the new account. A week later he wrote out a cheque for £4,999 drawn on the John Tulip account and payable to Thomas Boulder. He paid this cheque into another account in his own name.

On 22 June he withdrew £4,999 in cash from the Boulder account. The cashier says he was suspicious, but since Boulder was able to establish his identity and since there were sufficient funds in the account, he had no option but to pay the cash.

A week later Boulder was arrested and confessed that he had no intention of repairing the roof.

Advise the prosecution with what offence or offences Boulder should be charged.

17.16 Exercise 16

Simbad Jones was stopped by the police driving a Ford Orion car which had been reported stolen. He attempted to run away when challenged, and was found to be in possession of a stolen cheque book belonging to Elsie Evans and personalised in her name which had been stolen two weeks earlier. Two days after the cheque book was stolen, a cheque from the book was used to purchase the Orion car from James White, a car dealer. The person who wrote out the cheque, which bounced, was described by Mr White and the description matches the appearance of Simbad Jones; however Mr White failed to pick Jones out at an identification parade. Jones says that he bought the car from a man in a pub car park and found the cheque book in the glove compartment. The car is still registered at DVLA in the name of James White.

Jones made no answer when asked why the car was not registered in his name.

Advise the prosecution whether the evidence is sufficiently strong for a jury to convict Jones of stealing or receiving the cheque book and obtaining the car by deception.

17.17 Exercise 17

Advise as to the likely sentence in each of the following cases:

(a) *Manslaughter* In an argument with X, aged 62, whom D had met by chance, D struck X in the eye, causing him to fall, hit his head and sustain injuries from which he died three months later. D was initially charged with common assault, which was increased to manslaughter when X died.

(b) *Rape*   Victim, who had known D for one year, came to D's house looking for her friend, D's cousin. D made sexual advances, which were rejected, and then raped her. D had previous convictions for indecent assault on a boy of five and indecent assault and incest.

(c) *Theft*   D was a hospital porter who stole $1,000 from a tourist injured in a road traffic accident whom D was wheeling. Currently under a three-month suspended sentence for theft from a customer at a restaurant where he had worked, D had many previous convictions and custodial sentences.

INDEX